THE ROSE

*An Encyclopedia of North American Roses,
Rosarians,
and Rose Lore*

Sean McCann

STACKPOLE
BOOKS

Published by
STACKPOLE BOOKS
5067 Ritter Road
Mechanicsburg, PA 17055

Printed in the United States of America

First Edition

10 9 8 7 6 5 4 3 2 1

Illustrations by Rosemary Wise

Library of Congress Cataloging-in-Publication Data

McCann, Sean.
    The rose: an encyclopedia of American roses,
  rosarians, and rose lore/Sean McCann.
      p.   cm.
    ISBN 0-8117-1490-X
    1. Roses—Encyclopedias. 2. Rose
  culture—Encyclopedias. 3. Roses—United
  States—Encyclopedias. 4. Rose culture—United
  States—Encyclopedias. 5. Rose breeders—United
  States—Biography.
  I. Title.
  SB410.95.M38   1993
  635.9′33372—dc20
                                          93-9589
                                            CIP

CONTENTS

PREFACE

MY GREAT ENTHUSIASM IS ROSES. I WANT to know them all—to grow them, to breed them—and to know the great growers and the gardens of the present and the past. This enthusiasm led me to write this book. I decided to tell the story of the North American rose and to present the lives of those who had roughed out the path for us. I wanted to collect this information while those who know it best are yet with us, and to get it all down on paper before the details turn to legend.

My interest in the history of the United States and Canada began even before I found my love for the rose. As a boy I knew more about Red Cloud than I did about the heroes of my own native land of Ireland. I shuddered with a sort of second sight when I stood beside the great statue in Portland, Oregon, in which an Indian points out over the Oregon Trail and the inscription reads, "The white man comes . . ." I read Zane Grey, O. Henry, and Bret Harte long before I read James Joyce—and probably enjoyed them more.

Then came my association with roses, an association that has brought me to every state and to every leading city to give talks on roses. And then came my work on this book; I never thought I would have so much learning still to do, and so much fun doing it.

I immersed myself in the project, following roses from Captain George Waymouth's voyage in 1605 (when, on the first landing "northward of Virginia," he found "wild Pease, Strawberries, Gouseberries and Rose bushes") through California with Father Junipero Serra (when the remote past became yesterday as I read his comments on the Rose of Castile).

I became engrossed in the history of American roses. Once, when I was told that someone had gone to the "celestial rose garden," no thought of death or heaven came to mind; I immediately got out my notebook and wanted to know where the Celestial Rose Garden was.

In creating this book, I have made many wonderful friends who suffered my constant questioning, and I have received magnificent help. I hope that what I present here is a book that will give you enjoyment and new insight into some aspects of the wonderful story of the American rose.

I hope this book becomes an unassuming friend that will carry you into the rose gardens of your mind. It is for those who love the rose and want to love her more.

Come with me, then, into a wonderful garden where "roses grow and angels play their morning tunes . . ." □

—Sean McCann

ACKNOWLEDGMENTS

APART FROM THOSE MENTIONED IN THE text, the following gave me unstinted help in researching photographs, personalities, and events.

Royal National Rose Society; Kay and Pete Taylor; R.J. Hutton (Conard-Pyle); Robert W. Van Diest (Jackson and Perkins); Mrs. Ruby Buck; Martin J. Martin; Dorothy Michelis; Rose Gilardi; Ann Hooper; Laurabelle Larson; Montine Herring; David C. Bonnett; Colonial National Historical Park Library; United States Department of the Interior; Mr. and Mrs. John Fleek; Robert Pearles; Lois C. Stack; Stack; Mrs. Ann Cook Nitsch; Albert H. Ford; Marilyn Wellan; Don Reiu; Rebecca Ann Fitchko; Scott C. Stuhl; Barbara F. Cyrus; Lawrence Smith; Lynn Sohafer; Jane Baber White; Richard Schulof (Arnold Aboretum); Kathy Brazelton Brown (Park Ranger); Joe and Larry Burks; Sister Jane Hays; Ellen Salter Leloy; Donna Fuss; Helen Bale and the Auburn Journal; Mr. and Mrs. P. Hunter; Robert E. Ehm; Barbara Berry; Oline M. Reynolds; Jodie Forrest; David Kenny; Jennifer S. Gaines; Bob and Joyce Fleming; Floyd (Stretch) Johnson; Don Gers; Thomas A. Brown; John and Judy Schroeder; John C. Barna.

I offer my sincere thanks to each one of them. □

THE AMERICAN ROSE

THE EVOLUTION OF THE ROSE ON THE American continent is very special, and yet in the numerous written histories on the beginnings of the rose it often seems that America hardly existed. Greek, Roman, and Asian roses fill literature as if they were the only classical beauties in the world. The United States had no Cleopatra whose wealth clothed her palace with rose petals as she greeted her lover, no Sappho to sing the praise of the American rose, no poet like the rose-loving Herrick to advise citizens of the new nation that they should

> Gather ye rose-buds while ye may
> Old Time is still a-flying.

Canada, likewise, had no Empress Josephine or Madame du Barry, no great house like Malmaison, no Shakespeare. But native species once bloomed from northern Canada to the swamps of Florida and across to the Pacific Coast, all with as much grace, fragrance and beauty as any rose anywhere in the world.

Researchers put an age of about 30 million years on rose fossils found early this century in Colorado, Montana, and Oregon. These fossils clearly show rose foliage, in one case complete with the shell of a small snail, and even an unopened rose bud. We don't know how many different sorts of native roses there might have been. But a small nucleus survives to show that America certainly had roses found nowhere else on earth—roses that would eventually become garden specimens.

Native roses survived the opening of frontiers, the tilling of the soil, the clearcutting, the building of towns, and the race of the railroads.

As settlers were moving west, some American roses were traveling east to English and French gardens. Many of these were grown direct from seeds. Thomas Jefferson in 1803 sent half a bushel of seeds of wild roses "of every kind" to a friend in France. One of the earliest recorded shipments is that of *Rosa virginiana,* which was sent to England in 1724. This native American rose was already known in England and was listed by John Parkinson in his *Theatrum Botanicum* in 1640. It wasn't too long after the settling of the nation that dealing in roses became a two-way trade. Within a year of a new rose's introduction in France, it would be for sale in the New World.

Seeds and cuttings of Old World roses became part of the precious cargo in covered wagons heading to open up new lands. Many a family history includes the story of a rose cutting or slip being carried lovingly across the Atlantic and then over the Great Plains. That great trek was difficult and wagons often had to be lightened. Valuable items were unceremoniously dumped by the trail side: stoves, anvils, furniture, even food and plants. There among the rotting, once-treasured mementos of another life, roses rooted and bloomed. But many seeds, cuttings, and even entire rose bushes survived to their destinations.

As the wagon trains moved west, rose cultivation was already under way along the Pacific Coast. In 1767 Father Junipero Serra headed religious missions as part of the Spanish expansion commanded by Juan Gaspar de Portola; he brought roses along. Other visitors to the shores of California brought roses, too. The yellow-white *Rosa banksiae* arrived on board a visiting galleon and was in cultivation long before the pioneers brought their roses from the gardens and nurseries of the east.

California was set to become the Eden of the rose, where roses bloomed and bloomed in the perfect environment.

The rich heritage of the rose in the New World extends through the Puritans, Thomas Jefferson, and George Washington to today's American rosarians. On North American soil English, French, German, Spanish, Dutch, Irish, and Scottish immigrants and descendants all became involved in the business of roses, as producers, writers, or just very enthusiastic gardeners. They have brought the limitless beauty of the rose within everyone's grasp. □

AFFLECK, THOMAS (1812–1868)

Born in Scotland, Thomas Affleck made his mark in the United States in rose growing, agricultural writing, and innovative farming.

THOMAS AFFLECK ONCE BOASTED THAT IF A European rose breeder produced a new variety one year, he would have it on sale in his nursery the next. This sort of goal would be hard enough to meet in the 1990s, never mind in 1851. But the Scottish-born immigrant always took a positive stand and in that year cataloged 162 types of roses, many of them new.

For his female customers, Affleck often recommended a range of varieties that he considered suitable among the more graceful, highly perfumed, easy-to-grow French varieties. For the men, mostly farmers and ranchers, he suggested the tall, thorny, robust Cherokee Rose (see entry), to be planted instead of erecting walls and fences around their boundaries. That this advice was taken could be seen in the number of rose hedges in Texas in the early part of this century.

From the time he arrived in the United States at the age of 20, Affleck was involved with farming. His first venture, truck farming in Cincinnati, was a failure. Despite this, his interests always stayed close to the land and soon he was writing with "charm and lucidity" for the magazine *The Western Farmer and Gardener*, doing so well that he became its editor.

Misfortune struck when his wife and child died. Another attempt at farming, a crop of mulberries, failed. Things turned better when he met a widow at a fair in Mississippi and married her in 1842. Affleck set up a highly successful nursery in Natchez, Mississippi, where he first showed an interest in roses. As the Civil War began to threaten, business slackened—so much so that by the mid-1850s he was close to bankruptcy. His name and reputation were good enough, however, to get a loan for him to buy land in Texas at Gay Hill, close to the thriving nursery center of Brenham in Washington County.

Affleck built Glenblythe Plantation House, a grand home of distinction on 3,400 acres, where fruits and flowers were plentiful. Into the house he built a cellar that would eventually hold the wine he would make from the native Texas Mustang grape. In his 1860 catalog he recommended the wine as "a pleasant and wholesome table drink, and a Tonic for patients recovering from prostrating fevers, and for females who may have been in delicate health, it is unequalled." Roses remained high on his list of priorities. He maintained a long and up-to-date list and wrote numerous articles about roses.

Always a pioneer, Affleck came up with many schemes that he hoped would create a new South at the end of the Civil War. He tried to introduce Scottish workers to replace the former slaves at his plantation and nursery; he sought to bring the apple to Texas and once ordered as many as 70,000 seedlings; he promoted carbolic acid as a sheep dip. All failed. He continued to write and was held in high esteem for his gardening advice. Affleck died at Glenblythe in 1868 at the age of 56 (he had been caught in a storm and contracted pneumonia), leaving behind memories of a man who was innovative and well intentioned. □

ALASKA

It takes dedication to grow roses in the frigid North.

A SMALL GROUP OF ROSE FANCIERS PERSE-veres in Alaska. Indeed, in Anchorage there was even a society affiliated with the American Rose Society, but it is now defunct. In one of the coldest parts of America, it takes dedication to plant roses.

The way to treat roses in Alaska is like annuals. Enjoy them while they flower and replace them next year. People who bury their roses to beat the frost have to go down very deep; others take the easier path and uproot the bushes when the cold begins, taking them indoors to go dormant until spring.

The Anchorage rose garden, the most northerly in the world, was started in 1967 to commemorate the hundredth anniversary of the purchase of Alaska from Russia. Some 250 rose bushes are planted each spring in the garden maintained by the city's parks and recreation department. Growing there is the Sitka Rose, which is believed to have been brought from Russia many years ago and grafted onto a local wild rose. It comes in most colors from light pink to dark red. It grows up to eight feet high and resists cold, heat, drought, and poor soil—in other words, it's the perfect rose for Alaska. □

ALL-AMERICA ROSE SELECTIONS

A select few roses pass rigorous testing to win this honor as best new roses of the year.

M ORE THAN 140 ROSES OF ALL SHAPES, sizes, colors, and nationalities have been deemed worthy of holding the title of All-America Rose Selection winner since the award was introduced in 1940. Although winners were considered the outstanding roses available to American gardeners in any particular year, many have disappeared from nursery catalogs. There is just no way you could get together a full collection of these winners from commercial sources—or even from searching private gardens throughout the world.

The All-America Rose Selection came about through an association of commercial growers dedicated to the testing and selection of new roses. In 1939 four commercial nurserymen met to discuss the future of the rose. They were Harry Marks, president of Germain Seed and Plant Company of Los Angeles; Fred Howard, a rose breeder (among his roses was the first 'Los Angeles', now superseded by another rose carrying the same name) and president of Howard and Smith of Montebello, California; Awdry Armstrong of Armstrong Nurseries in Ontario, California; and Herb Swim, then a young and promising hybridizer with Armstrong Nurseries. They decided that American gardeners needed some guidance on new roses, but not before the roses were thoroughly tested and evaluated.

The idea appealed to other members of the rose trade and it was decided to hold tests at centers throughout the United States. Tests are conducted at gardens at growers' premises, universities, and public parks. Varieties entered for trial are evaluated as poor, fair, good, very good, or excellent in a series of categories: novelty value, bud form, flower form, color opening, color finishing, substance, fragrance, stem/cluster, habit, vigor/renewal, foliage, disease resistance, flowering effect, and overall value. Judges are not left entirely to their own devices and a guidebook is provided for their use. In the category for novelty value, the judge is asked to look at the rose and then to consider, "Does it make your heart throb, or does it put you to sleep? Do you remember it in your garden, or do you have to take another look to see what was there?" The final crunch question comes in the section for overall value, where judges are asked: "Now taking all factors into consideration, would you plant this rose in your own garden, or recommend it to your best friend?"

No one is infallible and even the top rose judges have failed fairly frequently. The result is that many winning varieties have drifted out of commerce for various reasons, and even some of the winners from the 1970s are no longer available.

Why do some roses fail? It has been suggested that the existence of so many test gardens in California, where conditions are easy for roses, makes it tough on winning roses when they are moved to less ideal locations. Other winning roses were unlucky by appearing the same year as a particularly outstanding variety that got most of the publicity. Sometimes a rose is simply out of sync with the roses of the time; this happened in the case of 'Rose Parade', a pink, low-growing variety from J. Benjamin Williams of Maryland and one of the three winners for 1975. His rose

was different (he called it by the trademarked name of mini-flora) and was years ahead of its time. Nurserymen did not really know what to do with a rose variety with medium-size blooms on a bush that was very low; thus 'Rose Parade' failed to reach the mark it should have attained. But for all the failures, few roses have made a mark in America without coming successfully through the All-America Rose Selection system.

The first award winners, named in 1940, were as follows:

- 'Dickson's Red' from Ireland, considered one of the top red roses of its time. It also won the British Clay Cup for fragrance and a Portland Gold Medal in 1941. It was a great cutting variety, but didn't have quite enough petals to hold out in hot summers.
- 'Flash', a climbing hybrid tea from grower R. Marion Hatton of Harrisburg, Pennsylvania, and introduced by Conard-Pyle. It also won a gold medal in Rome in 1939. The up side of this rose was its eye-catching color of velvet scarlet-red with yellow reverse; the down side was that it wasn't always sure to bloom more than once in a season.
- 'The Chief' from Walter Lammerts (see entry), a coral and copper hybrid tea but not a very strong grower.
- 'World's Fair', as rich a red as you could find. From Kordes of Germany (where it is known as 'Minna Kordes'), it had been introduced at the New York World's Fair in 1938. It was a hybrid polyantha then, low and fragrant, but is now classified as a floribunda.

The four were great roses in their day, but fame doesn't always last. There is no known commercial source for any of them today.

Here is the full list of All-America Rose Selection winners:

YEAR	WINNERS	COLOR	CLASS	ORIGINATOR
1994	Secret	pink–white blend	hybrid tea	E. G. Hill
	Midas Touch	deep yellow	hybrid tea	Jack Christensen
	Caribbean	orange	grandiflora	Kordes
1993	Rio Samba	yellow-orange blend	hybrid tea	William Warriner
	Child's Play	white-edged pink	miniature	Harmon Saville
	Solitude	orange; yellow reverse	grandiflora	Pernille Poulsen Oelsen and Mogens Oelsen
	Sweet Inspiration	soft pink	floribunda	William Warriner
1992	All That Jazz	sunset salmon pink	shrub	Jerry Twomey
	Pride 'n Joy	orange and yellow	mini	William Warriner
	Brigadoon	coral and white	hybrid tea	William Warriner
1991	Shining Hour	yellow	grandiflora	William Warriner
	Sheer Elegance	pink with dark edge	hybrid tea	Jerry Twomey
	Perfect Moment	yellow-orange-red	hybrid tea	Reimer Kordes
	Carefree Wonder	pink	shrub	Meilland
1990	Pleasure	pink	floribunda	William Warriner
1989	Class Act	white	floribunda	William Warriner
	Debut	red blend	miniature	Jacques Mouchotte
	New Beginning	orange, red, yellow blend	miniature	Harmon Saville
	Tournament of Roses	coral pink–pale pink	grandiflora	William Warriner
1988	Amber Queen	amber yellow	floribunda	Jack Harkness
	Mikado	scarlet-yellow blend	hybrid tea	Seizo Suzuki
	Prima Donna	deep pink	grandiflora	Takeshi Shirakawa

YEAR	WINNERS	COLOR	CLASS	ORIGINATOR
1987	Bonica	light pink	shrub	Alain Meilland
	New Year	apricot	grandiflora	Sam McGredy
	Sheer Bliss	near white	hybrid tea	William Warriner
1986	Broadway	reddish pink–yellow	hybrid tea	Anthony Perry
	Touch of Class	pink with coral and cream	hybrid tea	Michel Kriloff
	Voodoo	yellow-peach-orange	hybrid tea	Jack Christensen
1985	Showbiz	brilliant scarlet	floribunda	Mathias Tantau
1984	Impatient	orange-red	floribunda	William Warriner
	Intrigue	deep plum	floribunda	William Warriner
	Olympiad	clear crimson	hybrid tea	Sam McGredy
1983	Sun Flare	bright yellow	floribunda	William Warriner
	Sweet Surrender	silvery pink	hybrid tea	O. L. Weeks
1982	Brandy	golden apricot	hybrid tea	Herb Swim
	French Lace	ivory	floribunda	William Warriner
	Mon Cheri	red blend	hybrid tea	Jack Christensen
	Shreveport	orange blend	grandiflora	Reimer Kordes
1981	Bing Crosby	orange	hybrid tea	O. L. Weeks
	Marina	coral-orange	floribunda	Reimer Kordes
1980	Love	red with white reverse	grandiflora	William Warriner
	Honor	white	hybrid tea	William Warriner
	Cherish	shell pink	floribunda	William Warriner
1979	Friendship	pink	hybrid tea	Robert Lindquist, Sr.

YEAR	WINNERS	COLOR	CLASS	ORIGINATOR
1979 cont.	Paradise	lavender and pink	hybrid tea	O. L. Weeks
	Sundowner	orange	grandiflora	Sam McGredy
1978	Charisma	multicolor red with yellow	floribunda	Robert Jelly
	Color Magic	coral blend	hybrid tea	William Warriner
1977	Double Delight	red and white bicolor	hybrid tea	Herb Swim
	First Edition	coral	floribunda	Georges Delbard
	Prominent	hot orange	grandiflora	Reimer Kordes
1976	America	salmon	climber	William Warriner
	Cathedral	golden apricot	floribunda	Sam McGredy
	Seashell	peach and salmon	hybrid tea	Reimer Kordes
	Yankee Doodle	sherbet orange	hybrid tea	Reimer Kordes
1975	Arizona	bronze-copper	grandiflora	O. L. Weeks
	Oregold	pure yellow	hybrid tea	Mathias Tantau
	Rose Parade	pink	floribunda	J. Benjamin Williams
1974	Bahia	orange-pink	floribunda	Walter E. Lammerts
	Bonbon	pink and white bicolor	floribunda	William Warriner
	Perfume Delight	clear pink	hybrid tea	O. L. Weeks
1973	Electron	rose-pink	hybrid tea	Sam McGredy
	Gypsy	orange-red	hybrid tea	O. L. Weeks
	Medallion	apricot-pink	hybrid tea	William Warriner
1972	Apollo	sunrise yellow	hybrid tea	David L. Armstrong
	Portrait	pink	hybrid tea	Carl Meyer

YEAR	WINNERS	COLOR	CLASS	ORIGINATOR
1971	Aquarius	pink blend	grandiflora	David L. Armstrong
	Command Performance	orange-red	hybrid tea	Bob Lindquist
	Redgold	red edge on yellow	floribunda	Pat Dickson
1970	First Prize	rose-red	hybrid tea	Gene Boerner
1969	Angel Face	lavender	floribunda	Herb Swim & O. L. Weeks
	Comanche	scarlet-orange	grandiflora	Herb Swim & O. L. Weeks
	Gene Boerner	pink	floribunda	Gene Boerner
	Pascali	white	hybrid tea	Louis Lens
1968	Europeana	red	floribunda	George deRuiter
	Miss All-American Beauty	pink	hybrid tea	Alain Meilland
	Scarlet Knight	scarlet red	grandiflora	Alain Meilland
1967	Bewitched	clear phlox pink	hybrid tea	Walter E. Lammerts
	Gay Princess	shell pink	floribunda	Gene Boerner
	Lucky Lady	creamy shrimp pink	grandiflora	David L. Armstrong
	Roman Holiday	orange-red	floribunda	Bob Lindquist
1966	American Heritage	ivory tinged carmine	hybrid tea	Walter E. Lammerts
	Apricot Nectar	apricot	floribunda	Gene Boerner
	Matterhorn	white	hybrid tea	David L. Armstrong
1965	Camelot	shrimp pink	grandiflora	Swim and Weeks
	Mister Lincoln	deep red	hybrid tea	Swim and Weeks

YEAR	WINNERS	COLOR	CLASS	ORIGINATOR
1964	Granada	scarlet, nasturtium yellow	hybrid tea	Bob Lindquist
	Saratoga	white	floribunda	Gene Boerner
1963	Royal Highness	clear pink	hybrid tea	Swim and Weeks
	Tropicana	orange-red	hybrid tea	Mathias Tantau
1962	Christian Dior	crimson-scarlet	hybrid tea	Francis Meilland
	Golden Slippers	orange-gold	floribunda	Gordon J. Von Abrams
	John S. Armstrong	deep red	grandiflora	Herb Swim
	King's Ransom	chrome yellow	hybrid tea	Dennison Morey
1961	Duet	salmon pink and orange-red	hybrid tea	Herb Swim
	Pink Parfait	dawn pink	grandiflora	Herb Swim
1960	Fire King	vermillion	floribunda	Francis Meilland
	Garden Party	white	hybrid tea	Herb Swim
	Sarabande	scarlet-orange	floribunda	Francis Meilland
1959	Ivory Fashion	ivory	floribunda	Gene Boerner
	Starfire	cherry red	grandiflora	Walter E. Lammerts
1958	Fusilier	orange-red	floribunda	Dennison Morey
	Gold Cup	golden yellow	floribunda	Gene Boerner
	White Knight	white	hybrid tea	Francis Meilland
1957	Golden Showers	daffodil yellow	climber	Walter E. Lammerts
	White Bouquet	white	floribunda	Gene Boerner
1956	Circus	multicolor	floribunda	Herb Swim

YEAR	WINNERS	COLOR	CLASS	ORIGINATOR
1955	Jiminy Cricket	coral-orange	floribunda	Gene Boerner
	Queen Elizabeth	clear pink	grandiflora	Walter E. Lammerts
	Tiffany	orchid pink	hybrid tea	Bob Lindquist
1954	Lilibet	dawn pink	floribunda	Bob Lindquist
	Mojave	apricot orange	hybrid tea	Herb Swim
1953	Chrysler Imperial	crimson red	hybrid tea	Walter E. Lammerts
	Ma Perkins	coral–shell pink	floribunda	Gene Boerner
1952	Fred Howard	yellow penciled pink	hybrid tea	Fred H. Howard
	Helen Traubel	apricot pink	hybrid tea	Herb Swim
	Vogue	cherry coral	floribunda	Gene Boerner
1951	None			
1950	Capistrano	pink	hybrid tea	Theodore Morris
	Fashion	coral pink	floribunda	Gene Boerner
	Mission Bells	salmon	hybrid tea	Theodore Morris
	Sutter's Gold	golden yellow	hybrid tea	Herb Swim
1949	Forty-Niner	red and yellow	hybrid tea	Herb Swim
	Tallyho	two-tone pink	hybrid tea	Herb Swim
1948	Diamond Jubilee	buff	hybrid tea	Gene Boerner
	+ High Noon	yellow	climbing hybrid tea	Walter E. Lammerts
	Nocturne	dark red	hybrid tea	Herb Swim
	Pinkie	light rose pink	floribunda	Herb Swim
	San Fernando	currant red	hybrid tea	Theodore Morris
	Taffeta	carmine	hybrid tea	Walter E. Lammerts

YEAR	WINNERS	COLOR	CLASS	ORIGINATOR
1947	Rubaiyat	cerise red	hybrid tea	Sam McGredy
1946	Peace	pale gold	hybrid tea	Francis Meilland
1945	Floradora	salmon rose	floribunda	Mathias Tantau
	Horace McFarland	buff pink	hybrid tea	Charles Mallerin
	Mirandy	crimson red	hybrid tea	Walter E. Lammerts
1944	+ Fred Edmunds	apricot	hybrid tea	Francis Meilland
	Katherine T. Marshall	deep pink	hybrid tea	Gene Boerner
	Lowell Thomas	butter yellow	hybrid tea	Charles Mallerin
1943	Grande Duchesse Charlotte	wine red	hybrid tea	Ketten Brothers
	Mary Margaret McBride	rose pink	hybrid tea	Jean H. Nicolas
1942	Heart's Desire	deep rose pink	hybrid tea	Fred H. Howard
1941	Apricot Queen	apricot	hybrid tea	Fred H. Howard
	California	golden yellow	hybrid tea	Fred H. Howard
	Charlotte Armstrong	cerise red	hybrid tea	Walter E. Lammerts
1940	Dickson's Red	scarlet red	hybrid tea	Alex Dickson
	Flash	oriental red	climbing hybrid tea	R. Marion Hatton
	The Chief	salmon red	hybrid tea	Walter E. Lammerts
	World's Fair	deep red	floribunda	Minna Kordes

+ Sectional recommendation.

ALLEN, RAYMOND C. (1907–1993)

Beginning with a childhood garden, Raymond C. Allen became director of a major arboretum, a leader in the American Rose Society, and a best-selling rose writer.

ONE OF AMERICA'S LEADING ROSE WRITERS and administrators, Ray Allen's love of the rose began when he was growing up in Barre, Massachusetts, where he had his own garden. He earned his Ph.D. in plant physiology, genetics, and ornamental horticulture at Cornell University and then stayed on to teach and conduct rose research for twelve years. Allen was director of the Kingwood Center in Mansfield, Ohio, rated among the top ten botanical gardens and arboretums in the United States.

Allen held all executive offices of the American Rose Society (see entry), starting as executive secretary when the Society moved from Harrisburg, Pennsylvania, to Columbus, Ohio. He became president of the Society in 1974 after giving many years of guidance in the planning, planting, and administrative aspects of the organization. During this time he was awarded just about every horticultural honor in the United States for his unselfish service to the rose. He was honored repeatedly by the Men's Garden Club of America and by most state rose societies. He won the Distinguished Service medal of the American Iris Society and held the title of Master Gardener. He was first president of the World Federation of Rose Societies and treasurer and vice president of the American Horticultural Society.

A cultured writer, he was particularly interested in the history of the American Rose Society and was the author of a series of articles on the subject published in the *American Rose* magazine in 1991. He also wrote *Roses for Every Garden,* an outstanding success with more than 60,000 copies sold, and prepared material on roses for the *Encyclopaedia Britannica* and *World Book Encyclopedia.* He wrote forewords to books by J. Horace McFarland (see entry) and edited *What Every Rose Grower Should Know.* □

'AMERICAN BEAUTY'

The "million-dollar rose" is the most distinguished and costly social rose in the history of American floriculture.

IN THE 1920s AND 1930s, NO DINNER, BALL, banquet, wedding, or society reception was complete without garlands, bowls, and vases of 'American Beauty'. "Immense domes of palatial halls are solidly roofed overhead with thousands upon thousands of them," wrote Georgia Torrey Drennan in 1912, "while snowflakes are falling and ice glittering in the light of winter nights." Drennan's story of the 'American Beauty' phenomenon, in her book *Everblooming Roses,* went on to describe "dozens upon dozens at prices beyond belief used for social amenities at Christmas and New Year; quantity adorning public and private social functions in every city and community where tastes are cultivated and where wealth panders to taste."

How did this rose so captivate American society? Probably it was its name. After all, who could doubt that such a name would bring success? Certainly it was more appropriate than its French name, 'Mme Ferdinand Jamain'. Was it a French rose? Rose writer Drennan believed that it was all-American. But the rose was in fact bred in France and introduced to America by George Bancroft and the Field brothers in 1886. E. Gurney Hill (see entry) wrote in 1914 that "the Hon George Bancroft, the historian, was a great lover of the Rose, and after his demise a beautiful variety, without a label to disclose its identity, was found growing in his garden. Mr. George Field discovered the value of this Rose for forcing, and the provisional name of 'American Beauty' was given to it, a name which has clung to it ever since, and now it would be impossible to change it."

The rose amazed people with its beauty and its everblooming qualities. Hill, a leading grower of indoor roses, said that 'American Beauty' was grown by the hundreds of thousands. "Some places," he wrote, "are given over entirely to this one variety. It brings the highest price of any cut Rose, and is eagerly sought on account of its fragrance, its long stiff stem, its grandly beautiful leafage, as well as the loveliness of the bloom."

Stems were said to be a yard long, with prices to match. Right from its launch in 1886 the price per stem was at least two dollars, which meant that it was a rose for the rich. Amateurs were told not to bother growing it; 'American Beauty' needed controlled conditions and the professional touch. Special houses were built in which the rose could be grown with temperatures maintained at about sixty degrees Fahrenheit and with water regularly sprayed over the plants to ensure best results.

Fortunes could be made with a good crop of evenly balanced, long stems. "A good rose grower, one that can show results and please the public, receives as much pay as a college professor," a florist commented. For over a quarter of a century, 'American Beauty' commanded the top prices. No wonder they called it the million-dollar rose. It may even have cost financier and high-society flyer "Diamond" Jim Brady that sort of money at the turn of the century when he sent 'American Beauty' roses by the roomful to express his love for vivacious singer and actress Lillian Russell, who was known as the American Beauty.

The color of the rose is difficult to describe, probably because of the varying temperatures and conditions under which it was grown. It has been described as light red and pink. The official color is crimson, carmine-shaded rose. "It has over it," went Georgia Torrey Drennan's description, "a soft violet tinge as if a film of blush smoke hovered over the red velvety petals." The color was copied in dyes and called — what else — American Beauty Red. The rose was very fragrant. The flower had impact; it was showy and way ahead of the rather weak-necked tea roses that it replaced (it is classified as a hybrid perpetual). But it wasn't hardy enough to grow in a garden. It was purely a cossetted greenhouse rose.

The name has remained tops in the language of American florists for over a century, but when people today ask for (and they still do) 'American Beauty' roses, it won't be the original they will be given. Roses age, lose their beauty, and are overtaken by newer varieties. The original 'American Beauty' exists today only in garden museums, although one or two nurseries make an effort to grow it for the real enthusiast. A sport of 'American Beauty' found in 1897 in one of the glasshouses of the Floral Exchange Company of Edgley, Pennsylvania, was pure pink; it was eventually named 'Pink American Beauty'. 'White American Beauty' was one of the names given to 'Frau Karl Druschki', and it is still regarded as one of the world's great white roses. Its former name, 'Snow Queen', made it possible to sell this German-bred rose in the 1930s when anything German was increasingly unpopular. □

'AMERICAN PILLAR'

Almost rejected at first, 'American Pillar' became one of the world's most widely planted climbers.

HYBRIDIZED IN 1902 BY DR. WALTER VAN Fleet (see entry), who was king of the climbing rose breeders of that day, 'American Pillar' was the result of a cross between the Japanese *Rosa wichuraiana* (see entry) and a native American rose, *Rosa setigera* (see entry). Van Fleet offered the rose to the Conard-Jones Company (later Conard-Pyle) for propagation, but the firm wasn't interested in single roses. "Another wild rose" was the attitude. Antoine Wintzer, head propagator of the firm, argued: "It's an American rose. Call it 'American Pillar'. It will fight its battles and win everywhere." It did, and is one of the most used climbers in the world today. This hardy rose, with its giant clusters of carmine-pink blooms, white at the center, grows as an almost impenetrable hedge that is both practical and beautiful. □

AMERICAN ROSE SOCIETY (FOUNDED 1892)

Commercial growers led the stylish early years of the American Rose Society. Amateur growers now lead the society in its campaigns for excellence of the American rose.

FORMATION OF A ROSE SOCIETY BY THOSE who wished "to widen and deepen an interest in the culture and production of the rose" had been discussed as early as the 1880s. It wasn't until 1892, however, that a number of commercial growers formed the American Rose Society. The original group was very much a commercial enterprise, with no amateurs involved. By 1900 the society had published its first bulletin (unfortunately no copies are extant), held its first rose show, and had a membership of 204.

Early members set a standard for doing things in style, holding their 1901 rose show in New York's Waldorf-Astoria hotel. The grand ballroom became a living garden, with formal hedges, clipped trees, rhododendrons, lilacs, tulips, lilies, potted plants, and orchids, with bougainvillea massed around the balconies. And there were roses. There to pay homage were the top socialites of the city, including W. W. Astor. Clearly the rose was at the top of the social ladder.

In March 1907 Washington, D.C., rolled out the red carpet for a rose convention, show, and social. All the roses were indoor varieties, and voted the best in the show was the omnipresent 'American Beauty', with fifty blooms in a bowl winning the top award. Thousands of people came to see the roses and listen to the light orchestral music. President Theodore

Roosevelt welcomed American Rose Society delegates to the White House, and the society sent along a bowl of fifty blooms of 'Richmond', a new rich red hybrid tea that was then in the public eye. The man who hybridized it, E. Gurney Hill (see entry) from Richmond, Indiana, was there to meet the president.

In 1916 the society elected an amateur rose grower to its governing committee for the first time. He was Admiral Aaron Ward of Long Island. Eight years later the society for the first time elected an amateur grower as president. This was Dr. Edmund M. Mills, a Methodist preacher from Syracuse. By the middle of the 1930s, the amateur membership of the society was well established and commercial growers formed their own group, All-America Rose Selections (see entry).

The American Rose Society has grown rapidly and now has 385 associate rose societies with a total membership of more than 22,000. The history of the society has not been without its problems, the most disastrous of these coming in 1990 when legal actions caused by the dismissal of senior commercial staff brought society finances down to rock bottom. This meant a number of changes, including economizing in production of the famous annual, which was first published in 1916. The annual, once hardcover, is now in magazine style. But the society has never lost sight of its early motto: "A rose for every home and a bush for every garden."

The American Rose Society originally had headquarters at Harrisburg, Pennsylvania, because it was the home of the editor, J. Horace McFarland (see entry). The society later relocated to Columbus, Ohio, and in 1974 moved to Shreveport, Louisiana, in a forest of 118 acres, 42 of which are devoted to rose gardens with a total of about 20,000 bushes. The society organizes two national conventions and shows each year at changing venues in the United States. The society's specially selected Consulting Rosarians provide expert advice to rose growers in every area of the country, and its magazine, *The American Rose,* is edited for the rose enthusiast; both hobbyist and professional. □

ANATOMY OF A ROSE

A simple, specialized vocabulary is used to discuss the parts of a rose.

THE SPECIAL VOCABULARY OF THE ROSE IS not hard to learn. *Specimen* is the name given to the combined flower and foliage. *Corolla* is the technical name for the bloom or flower. *Sepals* are the components of the green outer covering of the bloom that open and fold downward as the flower opens. *Peduncle* (or the neck) is the area of the stalk from beneath the bloom to the first set of leaflets. The *stem* is the whole stalk that supports foliage and flower. The leaf *axil* is the point where leaf and stem meet and the bud eye grows. When a stem is cut above one of these eyes, growth will begin for a new flower to be born. Strictly speaking, roses don't have thorns. Botanically, thorns are stiff, pointed, leafless branches. A rose's "thorns" are properly termed *prickles.* □

ANGLO-AMERICAN EXPOSITION LONDON, 1914

THE ROSE CONFERENCE AT THE 1914 Anglo-American Exposition in London

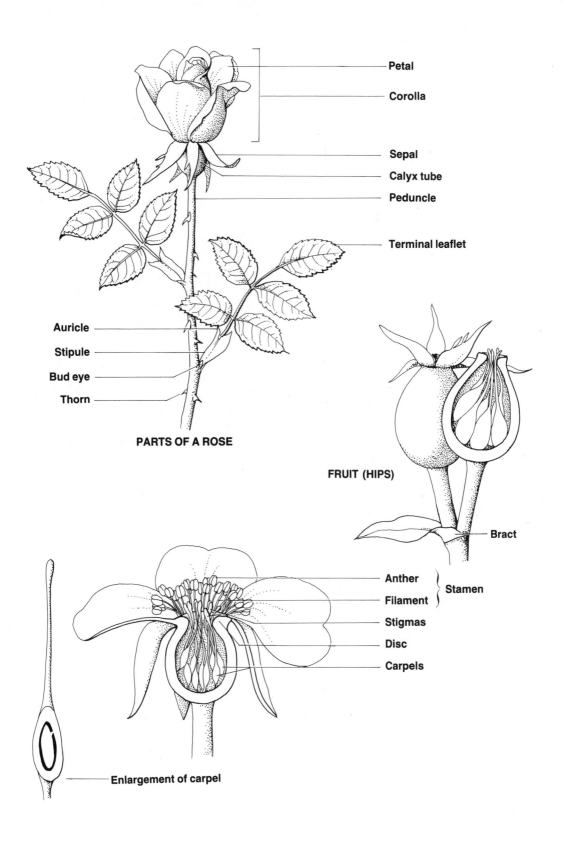

Petal

Corolla

Sepal

Calyx tube

Peduncle

Terminal leaflet

Auricle

Stipule

Bud eye

Thorn

PARTS OF A ROSE

FRUIT (HIPS)

Bract

Anther

Filament

Stamen

Stigmas

Disc

Carpels

Enlargement of carpel

helped celebrate one hundred years of peace between Great Britain and the United States and a century in the development of the rose. In 1815 only 250 roses were known; by 1828 the number had increased ten times. By the time of the 1914 conference, 12,000 were known. A call was made for some of the roses to be eliminated. "There are," said one British speaker, "far too many names in the catalog." But new roses are still being named and introduced, and by the year 2000 the number of named roses will easily top 25,000. □

ARMSTRONG, JOHN S. (1866–1965)

Tuberculosis didn't stop John S. Armstrong from creating a pioneering Southern California nursery.

WHEN DOCTORS TOLD 23-YEAR-OLD JOHN S. Armstrong in 1889 that his life was doomed by the disease of tuberculosis, he decided to make the best of the time left to him. He left his home in Ontario, Canada, with six dollars in his pocket and traveled until he found a town where the oranges were golden on the trees, the air was light, and the sun was always (well, almost always) shining. It was also called Ontario—Ontario, California.

Armstrong worked as a porter in the Ontario Hotel. One day he saw a "boy wanted" sign outside a nursery and he got the job. Here now was work that caught his imagination. Within a couple of years he decided that he too would propagate plants and sell them. He started his own nursery at the house he had bought for his widowed mother and his six younger brothers. He called it Ontario Nursery. In an odd twist, his former employers then put up a sign with the same name, Ontario Nursery, over their doors. The situation was settled when Armstrong agreed to accept fifteen dollars to let the other operation keep the name. He would just call his nursery Armstrong's.

Armstrong's tuberculosis was clearing up in the California sunshine as he started the business that brought to America some of its greatest stories of horticultural success. Armstrong eventually sold millions of grapevines, fruit trees, shade trees, camellias, and roses. His first catalog, published in 1902, listed only sixty-four rose varieties, mostly European and none from California. He made up for this omission by bringing to the firm famous hybridizers like Walter E. Lammerts and Herb Swim (see entries), who produced magnificent roses like 'The Chief', 'Mirandy', 'Sutter's Gold', 'Helen Traubel', 'Mojave', 'Circus', 'Garden Party', 'Pink Parfait', and many others.

His most successful rose was Lammert's hybrid tea 'Charlotte Armstrong' (named for John S. Armstrong's wife). It is still considered among the top roses of our time, selling millions of bushes since its introduction in 1940 and being in the background of many top roses. Yet the rose is very low on fragrance.

When John S. Armstrong retired, the company passed to his son John Awdrey Armstrong, who brought the same enthusiasm to the business. John Awdrey's three children then took their part in the business, with one of them, David L. Armstrong, handling plant breeding and winning many All-America Rose Selection awards for his roses. In the 1980s, when Armstrong's was the seventh largest wholesale nursery in the nation, it was gobbled up in a number of takeovers. None of these proved successful, but finally, ninety-four years after its beginnings, the company was swallowed up in the giant Jackson & Perkins enterprise (see entry). □

ARMSTRONG, LOUIS (1900–1971)

THE GREAT JAZZ MUSICIAN WAS ADMIRED by world-famous rose breeder Sam Mc-Gredy, who created two roses in his honor. The first was 'Satchmo', a bright orange-red floribunda that stands out memorably in European gardens such as Mainau in Germany. The second was 'Trumpeter' (bred from 'Satchmo'), one of the best red floribundas. People who have roses named for them usually request many plants for their homes, their family, and their friends, but when McGredy asked Louis Armstrong how many bushes of 'Satchmo' he would like, the answer was: "Just one, for my yard in Hoboken." □

ARNOLD ARBORETUM OF HARVARD UNIVERSITY

The arboretum has one of the great collections of international trees and shrubs, including a significant selection of species roses.

THREE ACRES OF THE ARNOLD ARBORETUM is given over to roses in the Bradley Collection of Rosaceous Plants. Organized by subfamily, the garden focuses on shrub species and contains a fairly diverse collection of roses. The place of the arboretum in the world of roses is based on its collection of species roses.

Built at Jamaica Plains just outside Boston, on lands left to Harvard College by James Arnold (1781–1863), the arboretum became one of the great collection places for international shrubs and trees. The main credit for its success goes to Charles Sprague Sargent (1841–1927), who was its director for fifty-four years. From a wealthy Boston family, Sargent was the son of a banker and was noted for being "gruff, withdrawn, tenacious, methodical . . . though with wit and occasional charm," according to S. B. Sutton of the Arnold Arboretum (1971). Charles Sargent showed little interest in the academic life, although he graduated from Harvard College (eighty-eighth in a class of ninety) before taking on management of the family estate to learn more about horticulture.

Sargent succeeded so well that he became professor of horticulture at Harvard College. Under his leadership, it was said that every tree and shrub that could be found anywhere that might prove hardy in the New England climate was brought to the Arnold Arboretum.

Roses do not figure prominently in the overall story of Arnold Arboretum, but nevertheless plants brought there have proved significant in the development of roses in the United States. One of them, *Rosa wichuraiana* (see entry), became part of the collection of species roses for which the arboretum is justly famous. Another rose that entered America through efforts of the arboretum staff was the Golden Rose of China, Father Hugo's Rose or *Rosa hugonis*.

The man who played such a vital part in the work of the arboretum is remembered with 'Sargent', a semiclimbing hybrid *wichuraiana* with a three-inch open semidouble bloom in pale pink and noted for its huge clusters of blossoms (up to sixty flowers in one truss).

There is also a rose called 'Arnold', a glowing scarlet single-flower bred in 1893 and introduced in 1914. It was a cross of *Rosa rugosa* and 'General Jacqueminot' (see entry) and can still be found in the arboretum's Bradley Collection.

Another principal individual in the history of the Arnold Arboretum was Jackson Dawson, who successfully propagated the plants received at the arboretum from all over the world. Dawson was also a hybridizer and was responsible for creating 'Sargent' and 'Arnold'. Dawson may also have been the hybridizer of a rose called 'Lady Duncan', which could have been the forerunner of our ground-cover roses of today (see entry on ground cover).

In the book *The Arnold Arboretum* by S. B. Sutton (1971), there is a wonderfully evocative picture of Jackson Dawson the gardener in hard hat and open waistcoat with watch chain and a pipe in his smiling mouth. Here was a man of the soil who showed that he loved it. He is remembered in the rose named 'Dawson'. □

BEAUVOIR PLANTATION HOME
BILOXI, MISSISSIPPI

Roses are a central motif of the Jefferson Davis home.

LEGEND SAYS THAT AT THE MOMENT JEFFERson Davis was told he had been elected president of the Confederate States of America, he and his wife, Varina Howell Davis, were in their rose garden at Davis Island, cutting a bloom from a bush of 'Gloire de France'. Roses certainly were important in the life of the Davises, and Beauvoir is a living testament to their love of the flower. The Louisiana-style plantation home to which the family retired when Davis was stripped of his citizenship at the end of the Civil War sits on the beachfront in Biloxi. Roses have always adorned its grounds; at first a full acre was given over to them. Varina Davis regularly sent blooms via railway to her daughter Margaret Hayes Davis in Memphis.

Inside the house, now maintained by the Mississippi Division of the Sons of Confederate Veterans, is a wealth of rose-related material. Needlepoint of the most delicate type is everywhere, always with roses as the central theme. The work was done mainly by Varina Davis and her daughter Winnie. Roses adorn the piano, sofa, vases, and parlor chairs, and hanging in one room is a painting by Winnie of lavender roses.

The garden was badly tended in the early part of this century, and what remained of it was swept away when Hurricane Camille roared through in 1969. The gardens were remodeled in 1985. The Rose Friends of Beauvoir now raise funds to maintain and improve the garden and to plant as many of the roses as possible from the time of Jefferson Davis, who died in 1889. □

BENARDELLA, FRANK (BORN 1932)

Frank Benardella's rose successes range from an almost-black miniature to the first striped hybrid tea.

FRANK BENARDELLA, FORMER PRESIDENT (1977–79) of the American Rose Society, is an exhibitor and hybridizer who has produced a range of successful varieties. 'Black Jade' was his first award-winning miniature, earning a Big 'E' award (see entry) in 1985 as one of the top miniatures in the United States.

There's a little personal story behind 'Black Jade'. One day as I was visiting Frank's home in Old Tappan, New Jersey, I noticed an almost-black miniature in his greenhouse. Frank was not going to do anything with it; he felt the blooms were too large for a miniature and too small for a floribunda. I saw it as a completely new rose. My enthusiasm was so great that he went ahead and introduced it as a miniature. And no one has ever complained that the flower is too big.

Since then Benardella has had similar success with many miniatures and large roses, including 'Jennifer', 'Figurine', 'Old Glory', 'Jim Dandy', 'Lavender Jade', and 'Pele'. He introduced the first striped hybrid tea obtained through modern hybridization methods with 'Tinseltown' in 1992. □

BENNETT, DEE
(1923–1988)

One of the few female rose breeders in the world, Dee Bennett was a top breeder of miniature roses.

DEE BENNETT WAS BORN IN AUSTRALIA but settled in Chula Vista, California. She set up an extensive miniature rose retailing business in Chula Vista in 1973. Among the fine miniatures she hybridized are 'Jean Kenneally', 'My Sunshine', 'Pucker Up', 'Rosy Dawn', 'Herbie' (for her husband), and 'Always a Lady'.

The nursery she established in California, Tiny Petals, continues in operation under the guidance of her daughter Sue and son-in-law Pat O'Brien. A rose variety now carries the name of Dee Bennett—a tribute from hybridizer Harmon Saville, surely the highest praise from a man who was once a competitor. □

BENNETT, HENRY
(1823–1890)

Englishman Henry Bennett's hybrid perpetuals earned a great deal of attention in the United States.

WHEN ENGLISH CATTLE BREEDER HENRY Bennett turned his attention to hybridizing roses, he produced many varieties of hybrid perpetuals that were sturdier and stronger in many ways than the tea roses they preceded. He announced ten new varieties in 1879, calling them "pedigree hybrids" (obviously a name that was a throwback to the cattle business).

Interest in England was lukewarm, but his roses were snapped up in America for what he called "a small fortune." One of his roses—'Her Majesty', a large pink hybrid perpetual—won the Gold Medal of the National Rose Society in Britain the first time it was offered. He sold the complete stock to an American firm, but the variety never became popular. The following year, 1886, Bennett sold a red hybrid tea to a cut-flower grower in Philadelphia for the then incredible sum of $5,000. □

BIG 'E' AWARD

This award of excellence is presented by the American Rose Society for the top miniature of the year.

TEST GARDENS TRY OUT MINIATURE ROSES AT Shreveport, Louisiana; Rose Hills, Whittier, California; Crosby Gardens, Toledo; International Trial Garden, Portland, Oregon; and the Denver Botanical Garden. Roses are judged each month for garden effect, color, form, plant habit, health, and general value in bloom production. The award was instituted in 1975, when, to catch up with the backlog of new varieties, eleven awards were made—ten of them to varieties raised by Ralph Moore (see entry). No award was granted in 1982; Harmon Saville's yellow, 'Center Gold', was selected for honor but not awarded because the rose was being used for promotion. □

YEAR	WINNERS	COLOR	ORIGINATOR
1993	Billie Teas	scarlet	John Hooper
	Boomerang	red blend	Ray Spooner
	Child's Play	white, edged pink	Harmon Saville
	Kristin	red blend	Frank Benardella
	Palmetto Sunrise	orange-red blend	Michael C. Williams
1992	Cal Poly	medium yellow	Ralph Moore
	Figurine	light pink	Frank Benardella
	Sincerely Yours	medium red	Ralph Moore
	Debidue	deep pink	M. C. Williams
1991	Golden Halo	medium yellow	Harmon Saville
	Good Morning America	medium yellow	Harmon Saville
	Just For You	deep pink	Ralph Moore
	Suzy	medium pink	Dennis and Suzy Bridges
1990	Regine	pink blend	John Hefner
1989	Dee Bennett	orange blend	Harmon Saville
	Tipper	medium pink	M. Jolly
	Nighthawk	medium red	Donald L. Hardgrove
	Jim Dandy	red blend	Frank Benardella
1988	Old Glory	orange-red	Frank Benardella
	Heavenly Days	apricot blend	Harmon Saville
1987	Ring of Fire	yellow blend	Ralph Moore
	Sequoia Gold	medium yellow	Ralph Moore
1986	Jean Kenneally	apricot blend	Dee Bennett
	Rainbow's End	yellow blend	Harmon Saville

YEAR	WINNERS	COLOR	ORIGINATOR
1985	Black Jade	dark red	Frank Benardella
	Centerpiece	red	Harmon Saville
	Jennifer	pink blend	Frank Benardella
	Loving Touch	apricot blend	Niels Jolly
	Winsome	mauve	Harmon Saville
1984	Baby Eclipse	light yellow	Ralph Moore
	Hot Shot	orange-red	Dee Bennett
	Julie Ann	orange blend	Harmon Saville
	Little Jackie	orange blend	Harmon Saville
1983	Cornsilk	light yellow	Harmon Saville
	Cupcake	pink	Mark Spies
	Hombre	pink-orange blend	Niels Jolly
	Snow Bride	white	Betty Jolly
	Valerie Jeanne	mauve pink	Harmon Saville
1981	Pacesetter	white	Ernest Schwartz
	Party Girl	apricot blend	Harmon Saville
1980	Holy Toledo	orange blend	Jack Christensen
	Pink Petticoat	pink blend	Leslie Strawn
1979	Puppy Love	orange blend	Ernest Schwartz
	Cuddles	orange-pink	Ernest Schwartz
	Zinger	medium pink	Ernest Schwartz
	Red Flush	medium red	Ernest Schwartz
1978	Rise 'n' Shine	yellow	Ralph Moore
	Gloriglo	orange blend	Ernest Williams

YEAR	WINNERS	COLOR	ORIGINATOR
1978 cont.	Humdinger	orange-pink	Ernest Schwartz
	Avandel	yellow blend	Ralph Moore
1977	Peaches 'n' Cream	pink blend	Edward Woolcock
	Jeanne Lajoie	pink	E. P. Sima
1976	Red Cascade	red	Ralph Moore
	Hula Girl	orange blend	Ernest Williams
	Peachy White	white	Ralph Moore
1975	Beauty Secret	red	Ralph Moore
	Judy Fischer	pink	Ralph Moore
	Lavender Lace	mauve	Ralph Moore
	Magic Carrousel	red blend	Ralph Moore
	Mary Marshall	orange blend	Ralph Moore
	Over the Rainbow	red blend	Ralph Moore
	Sheri Anne	orange-red	Ralph Moore
	Starglo	white	Ernest Williams
	Toy Clown	red blend	Ralph Moore
	White Angel	white	Ralph Moore

BILTMORE ESTATE ASHEVILLE, NORTH CAROLINA

The walled garden at the opulent Biltmore estate boasts a collection of some 3,000 rose bushes.

PATTERNED ON A CHATEAU IN THE LOIRE Valley in France, the huge house was begun in 1890 and took five years to complete. The halls and galleries of the 250-room house are filled with priceless antiques, books, and works of art. When George Washington Vanderbilt established the house, he planned an elaborate arboretum and nursery. The arboretum was never completed, and in 1916 a flood destroyed the nursery. The extraordinary gardens include an Italian garden of a sixteenth-century design, a famous collection of azaleas, and a shrub garden with many unusual plantings.

The walled garden is the eye-opener. Here grow some 3,000 roses of all sorts, from old garden roses to miniatures. This garden, originally the house kitchen garden and vegetable plot, has been replanted and reworked extensively in recent years, with roses being replaced at the rate of one hundred a year. Among the roses that have held court here are 'Aloha' (covering an impressive archway), the white 'Evening Star', the ever-changing 'Masquerade', the stately 'Queen Elizabeth', and the trio of 'Love', 'Honor', and 'Cherish'. □

BLUE ROSE

The rumors and the controversy continue in the search for the world's first true blue rose.

EVERY FEW YEARS THE RUMORS BEGIN ANEW: a blue rose is just about to be marketed. Yet it seems we are as far away as ever from this momentous arrival.

Blue is the fugitive in matters of rose color; the vital pigment delphinidin is missing from its makeup. Roses have come close to blue — but only as close as allowed by the pigment cynadin, which is responsible for shades of lavender.

Tales originating in books, family stories, and rose hybridizing houses suggest that blue roses have appeared in breeding lines but were immediately thrown out as being totally wrong — sacrilege, a violation of the whole idea of the rose. In Ireland in the 1920s, Sam McGredy II argued that any such blue rose should be burned because "such a color would corrupt the tastes of the public."

Jean Henri Nicolas (see entry) in his book *A Rose Odyssey* writes that Father George M. A. Schoener (see entry) of Santa Barbara, California, once told him that he had a "heavenly blue" but that it didn't grow. Numerous roses

over the years have been called Blue Something-or-other, but they were all shades of lilac, magenta, and lavender. And these weren't very well received. The lavender-gray climber, rugged and tough, called 'Veilchenblau' drew the scorn of J. Horace McFarland (see entry), who called it "the worst color that could be imagined." So much for one man's taste; certainly I like the rose, and its coloring is always a surprise.

Different tones of blue can be found in the aging blooms of modern red roses. This blueing is looked upon as a fault by rose breeders, who seldom market such a rose and have spent years trying to eliminate the so-called defect. Strangely enough, the blueing is found most frequently in very fragrant red varieties such as 'Fragrant Cloud' and 'Crimson Glory'. Some rose authorities suggest that if breeders had taken the opposite path and tried to increase the blueing of blooms, the azure blue rose would have been with us a long time ago.

In the past decade the bluest rose was from Griffith Buck (see entry) in Iowa, but the color was impossible to catch correctly and lighting changed the tones. He told me that when he applied for a patent, he had to have the color copied by an artist because no camera could catch it correctly. Called 'Blue Skies', it still doesn't catch the blueness that some want in a rose. Other "near blues" include 'Silver Spoon' (Weeks) and 'Silverado' (Christensen). The current rumor is that a blue rose will be on sale very soon. The Japanese Suntory Corporation and the Australian Calgene Company say they have spliced a blue gene from a petunia into the rose. Geneticists say it is possible. Keith Zary, head of research for the Jackson & Perkins rose company (see entry), says that with enough effort and money, the blue rose will certainly arrive from the chemists in the next few years. □

BOBBINK, LAMBERTUS C. (1866–1950)

This Netherlands-born hybridizer introduced Americans to the antique roses of Europe and founded a pioneering nursery operation.

DUTCHMAN LAMBERTUS C. BOBBINK ARrived by steamer in Hoboken, New Jersey, in 1895. He had been a salesman for a nursery in Holland; he was an expert plantsman by vocation and a rose lover by avocation.

Bobbink was fascinated with antique roses, and he believed there was a great market for them in America. He traveled to Europe, purchased a large collection of the oldest roses, and brought them to the United States. Soon after these roses were sold, the big problem facing American nurserymen became apparent: there was no easy way to propagate roses on the available understock. Solving this problem became a high priority for him. He was joined by F. L. Atkins in 1899 to form the Bobbink and Atkins Company, and one of their first decisions was to experiment with the Japanese species *Rosa multiflora*. It was an immediate success—the new roses were easily propagated on the understock—and the company produced what was described as the most complete list of field-budded hybrid teas in America, as well as pioneered widespread field budding of roses on *Rosa multiflora*.

Bobbink brought a new dimension to rose descriptions, leading the way for catalog writers of today by describing many roses in terms like "strange" and "haunting." The firm will also be remembered for many of the great roses it introduced from American breeders—roses like 'Bloomfield Daisy' from Captain George Thomas and 'Chevy Chase' (regarded as an improvement on 'Crimson Rambler') from nearby New Jersey breeder Martin R. Jacobus—as well as roses from international sources.

Bobbink was awarded the Gold Medal of the American Rose Society in 1945, the Johnny Appleseed Award in 1946, the Thomas Rowland Medal from the Massachusetts Horticultural Society in 1946, and a citation from the state of New Jersey for bettering agriculture in that state. Bobbink's daughter, Dorothy White, started a memorial garden to her father in Rutherford, New Jersey, and transferred it to Lincroft, New Jersey, in 1977, where it now comes under direction of the Monmouth County Park System. □

BOERNER, GENE (1893–1966)

Known as the father of the floribunda, Gene Boerner is credited with an instrumental role in the popularity and profusion of floribunda roses.

GENE BOERNER WAS BORN IN CEDARBURG, Wisconsin, in 1893, but he didn't begin work in roses until after service as a pilot in World War I. He began working for the Jackson & Perkins rose company (see entry) in 1920 and spent his entire rose-breeding career with the company. In 1927, when he purchased a share of the business, Boerner was involved only with marketing. On the death of Jean Henri Nicolas (see entry) in 1937, he

took charge of research and hybridizing at J&P.

Boerner introduced more than 180 roses into commerce, many of them floribundas, which display large clusters of flowers instead of just one bloom per stem. Fourteen of Boerner's roses became All-America Rose Selection winners. Two of his most famous floribundas were 'Fashion' and 'Vogue'—roses with a little story of their own. Boerner found four seeds in a hip he harvested from a cross he made between 'Pinocchio' and the marvelous 'Crimson Glory'. He sowed them separately—unusual, as seeds are normally placed in greenhouse rows an inch apart. When the four seeds came to life, two were in striking new colors that the J&P people called cherry coral and

coral pink. The two roses were selected for further trials. One day as Boerner was looking at them in his glasshouse, a fashion consultant from Nieman Marcus in Dallas came in, was immediately attracted by the colors, and went away to plan a fashion show around the two roses. This incident gave Boerner the idea for the names 'Fashion' and 'Vogue'.

J&P put some $60,000 into promotion and readied 300,000 bushes of 'Fashion' for the market. "Three hundred thousand," Charlie Perkins, one of the J&P bosses, would say in future years. "What a fire we would have had if it didn't make it!" But it did make it, selling about half a million bushes every year for quite some time. 'Fashion' brought in almost a quarter of a million dollars in royalties and won gold medals all over the world. And its twin, 'Vogue'? It didn't do too badly, either. It also became an All-America Rose Selection and won its share of gold medals.

Other great roses from Boerner included 'Ma Perkins', 'Ivory Fashion', 'Goldilocks', 'Apricot Nectar', 'Jiminy Cricket', 'Saratoga', and the marvelous and well-named 'Masquerade' that changes, as the flower ages, from yellow to deep red. Boerner didn't introduce only floribundas. He also produced many hybrid teas, including the beautiful 'Diamond Jubilee', the white 'John F. Kennedy', 'Polynesian Sunset', 'Hawaii', and 'First Prize', one of the top exhibition roses in the United States for many years.

A jovial, gregarious man, Boerner was famous for entertaining at his Penn Yan, New York, home. His name is honored in the rose called 'Gene Boerner', introduced by J&P two years after his death. It was an All-America Rose Selection winner. □

BOOKS ABOUT ROSES

From 1844 to the present day, important books help tell the story of the American rose.

AMERICAN ROSE PUBLICATIONS DID NOT really begin until 1844, with *The Rose Manual* by Scottish-born Robert Buist (see entry). Already author of *American Flower Garden Directory,* his book on roses was highly popular, presenting an up-to-date picture of French roses and growers. For the modern reader it presents a useful record of roses grown in the Delaware Valley a century and a half ago.

Buist's book got a three-year head start on the first publication from one of the most notable early rose writers, Samuel B. Parsons, who made a European tour in 1845 and two years later published *Parsons on the Rose.* In it he, too, praised French growers such as Vibert, Laffay, and Hardy for their improvements to the rose and their "charming manners." He found the English "cold," but praised them for their ability to grow great roses (although they were not so good at breeding them).

Not to be outdone, Parsons's nurseryman rival William Robert Prince, the fourth generation of the Prince Nursery firm founded in 1737, published Prince's *Manual of Roses.* Since then many notable books on roses have been published in the United States. In the 1970s, Earl Coleman reproduced a series of famous old books either long out of print or too expensive for the general garden-lover. The titles included the books by Buist, Parsons, and Prince.

Many of these reprints appeared with forewords by Léonie Bell, already an author and illustrator, who knew her subjects and conveyed her knowledge with enthusiasm. She described the careers of people like Ethelyn Emery Keays, Samuel Parsons, Thomas Rivers, and William Robert Prince. The introductions to the other Coleman reprints were provided by such leading figures in the world of Heritage roses as Lily Shohan, Edith C. Schurr, Richard Thomson, Beverly R. Dobson (see entry), and Helen L. Blake.

The reprinting of these books, most of them now themselves out of print and only available through specialist book collectors, began in quite an extraordinary way. Lily Shohan had been staging a display of old roses at the Dutchess County, New York, fair when she got into conversation with a neighbor who asked if there were any old books on roses she would like to see reproduced. Lily reeled off eight names and to her astonishment the reply came: "I'm a publisher—I'll do them."

He introduced himself as Earl Coleman, who had been involved in facsimile reproduction of books since the mid-1960s. As Leonie Bell wrote in retelling the story in *The Heritage Rose* letter: "Lily and I shared our incredulity. Was this actually happening? What should we ask him to take on? What books did old-rosers need most?" They quickly settled on the first six titles and later on more. Today they form an indispensable part of every rose enthusiast's library.

Among other rose books of historical and horticultural interest published in recent years are the following:

All the World's Roses (1974), by Sean McCann
Antique Roses of the South (1990), by William C. Welch

Anyone Can Grow Roses (1952), by Cynthia Westcott (see entry)

The Book of Old Roses (1966) and *Roses of Yesterday* (1967), both by Dorothy Stemler (see entry)

The Book of Roses (1866), by Francis Parkman

Climbing Roses (1933), by G. A. Stevens

The Complete Book of Miniature Roses (1977), by Charles Marden Fitch

Growing Good Roses (1988), by Rayford Clayton Reddell

Hennessy on Roses (1942), by Roy Hennessy

The History of the Rose (1961), by Roy E. Shepherd (see entry)

How to Grow Roses (1923), by Robert Pyle

Immortal Roses and *Pageant of the Rose* (1953), both by Jean Gordon

In Search of Lost Roses (1989), by Thomas Christopher

Landscaping with Antique Roses (1992), by Liz Druitt and G. Michael Shoup

Miniature Roses for Home and Garden (1985), by Sean McCann

Miniature Roses: Their Care and Cultivation (1991), by Sean McCann

My Friend the Rose (1942), by Francis E. Lester

Old Roses (1935), by Ethelyn Emery Keays (see entry)

Parsons on the Rose (1847), by Samuel B. Parsons

Rockwell's Complete Book of Roses (1966), by Frederick Frye Rockwell

The Rose (1882), by Henry B. Ellwanger (see entry)

The Rose Question and Answer Book (1962), by John Milton

Roses (Time-Life Series, 1974), by James Underwood Crockett

Roses (1988), by Roger Phillips and Martyn Rix

Roses for Canadian Gardens (1959), by Rosecoe A. Fillmore

Roses for Every Garden (1948), by Raymond C. Allen

Roses of America (1990), by Stephen Scaniello and Tania Bayard

Southern California Gardens (1961), by Victoria Padilla

A Year in the Rose Garden (1936), *A Rose Odyssey* (1937), and *The Rose Manual* (1939), by Jean Henri Nicolas (see entry)

A series of historically important rose books were written by J. Horace McFarland, who edited the *American Rose Annuals* and *Modern Roses* for many years. His use of color prints was a pioneering step in book and catalog publishing. Among his books are *The Rose in America* (1923), *Roses of the World in Color* (1936), and *Memories of a Rose Man* (1949).

The Earl Coleman reprints of American rose books beginning in 1979 were *The Rose Manual* (1844), by Robert Buist; *Manual of Roses* (1846), by William Robert Prince; *Parsons on the Rose* (1888), by Samuel Parsons; *The Rose* (1882), by Henry Ellwanger; *Old Roses* (1935), by Ethelyn Keays; and *The History of the Rose* (1954), by Roy E. Shepherd. ☐

BREEZE HILL HARRISBURG, PENNSYLVANIA

Hundreds of rose varieties were on public display over the years in the great garden at the home of J. Horace McFarland.

THE 2.4 ACRES OF BREEZE HILL, ONCE PART of an old vineyard, were set in a developing suburban area of Harrisburg called Bellevue Park and in 1909 became the site of the home of J. Horace McFarland (see entry). His Breeze Hill garden became a rose center, taking in new varieties from all over the world and putting them on trial. Roses grew in large beds and, because it was a time of innovative rose breeding, many climbers and ramblers cascaded around hedges, trees, and pergolas.

Eventually there were a great many roses, and McFarland began replacing them so often, he wrote, that "it was never necessary to buy wood for open fires in those years." At one time the garden boasted more than 300 varieties of climbers alone. McFarland reckoned that he grew some 3,000 plants in more than 700 varieties in the garden, which drew thousands of visitors every year.

The year 1926 saw the introduction of a rose named 'Breeze Hill', an enormous, vigorous plant with large double-flowered blossoms of flesh-tinted orange-apricot-buff. The rose might have been named for McFarland, but the U.S. Department of Agriculture didn't quite approve of him because he had been a thorn in the department's side for a long time, criticizing aspects of USDA rose breeding and the department's attitude toward roses in general. Ordinarily, the USDA has no authority over the naming of roses, but this rose was bred in their experimental station by Van Fleet (see entry).

The house and gardens are now gone, and even the 'Breeze Hill' rose is not, to my knowledge, available in the United States. □

BROOKLYN BOTANIC GARDENS

The botanic gardens in New York form one of America's foremost institutions for horticultural learning, teaching, and growing.

WITHIN THE ARBORETUM AT BROOKLYN Botanic Gardens is the impressive Cranford Rose Garden, which opened in June 1928, just a year and a half after Walter V. Cranford, head of a construction engineering firm, gave $15,000. Four days after the check was received, construction started. By the fall of 1927, a thousand rose bushes had been planted; by the end of 1928, another 650 plants had been added. Eight years later the garden was expanded with a gift from Mrs. Cranford on the death of her husband.

On the 1.5 acres devoted to the rose at the 52-acre Brooklyn Botanic Gardens, well-kept lawns and trees surround the roses, which are kept in their own wonderful world by white wooden trellises and a white-latticework pavilion. The garden includes some 6,000 bushes and climbers in 1,000 varieties, many of which were among the first roses planted here. Every type of rose has a place, from the most modern hybrid teas to old garden roses. A great group of roses planted closely together down the center of the garden in a wide, long bed with varieties mixed together should illustrate how not to grow roses, but it works out well. One might expect a scene of disaster as small bushes become enveloped by more vigorous ones and scramblers take over space needed by more compact ones, but it doesn't happen that way. Good pruning and good care combine to produce a well-balanced but electrifying myriad of colors.

The style of the garden has changed over the years as some varieties proved they were not winter-hardy and others proved unsuitable because of their invasive vigor. Roses that survive here today have a good chance of surviving anywhere, as weather ranges from hot and humid in summer to freezing and harsh in winter. Garden rosarian Stephen Scaniello, who is a writer, lecturer, judge, and consulting rosarian of the American Rose Society, handles the rose garden with the help of a group of dedicated volunteers. He is author, with Tania Bayard, of *Roses of America,* published by the Brooklyn Botanic Gardens. □

BROWNELL, JOSEPHINE AND WALTER

The husband and wife team of Walter and Josephine Brownell researched hardy roses in their Rhode Island nursery and produced roses that were vigorous, disease resistant, fragrant, and hardy.

BEGINNING WORK IN THE EARLY PART OF the twentieth century, the Brownells decided that "longevity seemed to us to hang on survival through environmental conditions, which could be controlled by definite resistance to subzero temperatures and immunity from certain fungus infections." In half a century of hybridizing, they produced at least fifty varieties that made a significant move toward bushes that would survive extreme cold.

Working mainly with *Rosa wichuraiana* and its hybrids, they produced climbers with fragrant hybrid tea-type blooms, especially in the yellow flower range. One of the most notable of these was 'Mrs. Arthur Curtiss James', said

to be of great richness and beauty. Others included 'Golden Glow'—a glowing yellow used a lot by Ralph Moore in his breeding of miniatures—and 'Carpet of Gold', which, although classified as a climber, was better known for its ground-covering ability.

Stephen Scaniello and Tania Bayard point out, in their book *Roses of America* (1990), that numerous Brownell roses still grow in Cranford Rose Gardens at the Brooklyn Botanic Gardens. They write in glowing terms of varieties like 'Curly Pink', which makes a fragrant hedge and is "always in bloom"; 'Break o' Day', very vigorous, fragrant, and a great producer of flowers; thorny 'Country Doctor', with its large, silvery pink, fragrant flowers; 'Maria Stern', having large, cupped orange blooms with a spicy fragrance, and a disease-resistant rose; 'Golden Arctic', a yellow, very fragrant, vigorous, and disease-resistant climber; and 'White Cap', which reaches up to ten feet of carefree and hardy growth.

Not many Brownell roses are still in commerce, but both 'Maria Stern' and 'Curly Pink' have devotees among a few nurseries. □

BUCK, GRIFFITH (1915–1991)

Griffith Buck spent thirty-six years as head of the horticulture department of Iowa University at Ames, where he produced many top roses.

GRIFFITH BUCK SET OUT WITH ONE IDEA when he began breeding roses—he wanted to produce varieties that were hardy, disease resistant, constant blooming, and better for landscaping than those already on the market. Iowa University was a good place to

pursue this ideal: its legacy of rose breeding reached back to 1870, and earlier university researchers had even imported roses from Siberia in their search for hardiness.

Buck developed some eighty-five new roses during his time at the University—all of them meeting his criteria. He let nature do its own sorting by planting all seedlings in field conditions. The plants that did not stand up to the outdoor conditions or fell to disease were immediately dropped from the program.

Many of his roses were still largely untested at his death, but 'Carefree Beauty' is a rose that truly lived up to its name. Although it was passed over when entered in the All-America Rose Selection trials, some judges encouraged Buck to persevere with it. He did, and

Conard-Pyle saw its potential as a no-care rose; they introduced it commercially, and it became an international success. One description of 'Carefree Beauty' in *Organic Gardening* said: "Remarkably disease resistant over a broad range, overwinters without protection under subzero conditions, boasts gorgeous pink flowers all season, and can be planted as a hedge or stand alone as a specimen plant."

One of Buck's great breakthroughs came quite by chance. He decided he would make some crosses involving a Spanish-bred silver-gray rose—'Sour de Automne'—but because only one of the expected parent roses was in bloom, he had to use his own variety, 'Distant Drums', which had some tan and lavender in its parentage. One of the resulting seedlings had a lavender flower with a blue cast. Some people saw it as the closest a rose breeder had come to a blue rose. Buck himself was uncertain about its color: "One day it's blue and the next day it isn't," he said. But it was a commercial success when named 'Blue Skies' and marketed by Cooperative Rose Growers in Tyler, Texas.

Buck produced wonderful names for his roses. Since he was striving for hardiness, he started with "prairie" names; of these, 'Prairie Princess' and 'Prairie Breeze' picked up a big following among rose fanciers. Soon afterward he dropped the "prairie" tag, probably because Canadian breeders, also searching for hardiness, were using it for their roses. Among his roll of named roses you will find 'Mountain Music', 'Earth Song', 'Music Maker', 'Distant Drums', 'Country Music', 'Pearlie Mae' (for Pearl Bailey), 'Rural Rhythm', 'Incredible', and 'Gee Whiz'.

When asked which variety he liked best, he

gave that instinctive reply that all rose lovers give: "Whichever I'm looking at. Like one's children, it is better not to have favorites."

After his retirement in 1985 most of his work at the university was destroyed. Fortunately for rose breeders of the future, who will benefit from the crosses he made, a great number of the bushes had been planted in his own garden. His wife, Ruby, and daughter, Mary, however, are still trying to put together a complete collection of his roses. □

BUIST, ROBERT
(1805–1880)

This Scottish nurseryman, who set up shop in Philadelphia, boasted that he grew the largest collection of roses in the country in the mid-1800s.

BUIST BROUGHT TO PHILADELPHIA THE LATest European introductions. He put the first Chinese rose, probably 'Old Blush', into commerce in Philadelphia and bought 'Madame Hardy', the lovely French white rose from Monsieur Hardy himself, in 1832.

He acknowledged that the French were the leaders in everything connected with the rose at that time but delighted to be in Philadelphia, which he called "a hotbed of roses."

He wrote the first book in America solely devoted to the rose, *The Rose Manual*. He was noted for his persistence in encouraging women to grow roses, especially varieties that could be grown indoors in containers. □

BURBANK, LUTHER
(1849–1926)

The California horticulturalist Luther Burbank was "the most self-deceived rose man in America," according to J. Horace McFarland.

LUTHER BURBANK HYBRIDIZED AND SOLD roses by mail order. Despite his success in the business, he did not win much respect from professional colleagues.

J. Horace McFarland (see entry) said that he was "soured" on Burbank when he saw a catalog offering, all on one page, four roses that were described as the best roses ever. "Not one of them," wrote McFarland, "has since proved worthwhile."

According to Raymond C. Allen (see entry), "the reason that a lot of people did not take Luther Burbank seriously was because he did practically no real scientific hybridizing. His method was to produce seed and grow huge populations of seedlings, and by the process of selection he succeeded in obtaining some improvements."

For all that, some of the Burbank roses were considered fine varieties by other rose people, and today there is a revered spot in Santa Rosa, where the Luther Burbank home is maintained. He was buried under a tree on the grounds of the home, but the tree was later removed. Today no one can identify the site of the grave. □

CABBAGE ROSE

THE WORDS "CABBAGE ROSE" CONJURE IMages of Granny's garden, heavy blossoms, and pink heads hanging heavy with perfume. And yet there is no individual cabbage rose. It is in fact a class (botanically *Rosa x centifolia*). The long canes are excellent for working over low fences or pegged down on a slight hill or formed into an arching shrub. By pegging down the long arching stems, instead of just leaving them to wave about in the air, you can produce many more flowers. Some of the varieties within this class do not measure up to the pictures in our minds. The rose in the class that brings us closest to the "cabbage" ideal is 'Bullata' (look for it in some catalogs as *Rosa x centifolia bullata*). It is large and fragrant—and likeliest to revive memories. □

CAIRNS, THOMAS (BORN 1940)

Rose grower, exhibitor, and editor.

ROSE GROWERS IN THE UNITED STATES HAVE long been indebted to the work of Scottish-born, California-based Tommy Cairns, a senior research chemist with the United States Food and Drug Administration. Roses for him are an all-embracing hobby: he grows them, exhibits them, and writes about them. He won the Ralph Moore Trophy for miniature roses at three levels—local, national, and international—in a single year. In 1991 and 1992 he took some 500 miniature blooms from his Southern California garden to shows in England, where he carried off the show championship both times. He edited the mammoth *Modern Roses 10*, (1993) the stud book of the roses hybridized throughout the world. A large exhibition-type hybrid tea, 'Editor Tommy Cairns', is named in his honor. □

CALIFORNIA ROSE GROWERS

The rose growers of Old California kept up to date on the newest varieties from Europe.

THE YEAR WAS 1849. GOLD-RUSH TIME. AND as the wagons headed west, some travelers had their eyes set on their own sort of gold: roses. Among them was William C. Walker, who set up the Golden Gate Nursery on three acres near South Park in San Francisco and produced his first catalog in 1858. A copy is extant at the California Historical Society in San Francisco. Walker's catalog describes many roses that were still new in France, where they were produced. How they got so quickly to California is not recorded.

Research in the 1980s by landscape architect Thomas A. Brown of Petaluma, California, showed that in the period up to 1900, more than 400 nurseries operated in the state. From a large number of old catalogs and price lists, he found that no fewer than 1,200 different types of roses had been introduced three or four years after their introductions in Europe.

There are many tales of perseverance among California's rose pioneers. Col. James Lloyd Lafayette Warren packed up a large part of his Nonantum Vale Nursery near Boston, printed his California Nursery Catalog, and arrived in the state in 1853. He settled in Sacramento but suffered the fate of a number of entrepreneurs of the time when he was flooded out by storms. He rescued what he could, sold it off, and moved on to San Francisco, where he became editor of the *California Farmer.* Sacramento nurseryman A. P. Smith suffered a similar tragedy by flood. Smith purchased fifty acres from Captain Sutter and established a nursery on the south bank of the American River, but the storms of 1861 and 1862 sent the river over its banks and buried the nursery under three to six feet of silt.

The heritage left by the nurserymen of early-day California can still be found. Searchers for old roses say that the California gold country produces more "lost" varieties of roses than almost anywhere else, and they say that many old settlements and churchyards have yet to be fully searched. □

CALIFORNIA'S ROSE

See Rosa californica.

THE CANADIAN ROSE SOCIETY

THE CANADIAN ROSE SOCIETY BEGAN OPERA-ting under the name of the Rose Society of Ontario in 1913 and, apart from the years 1943–1945, has been active since then. It publishes a Rose Annual, and the secretary is Anne Graber, 10 Fairfax Crescent, Scarborough, Ontario, Canada. □

CARRUTH, TOM (BORN 1952)

Research director and hybridizer.

PART OF THE NEW GENERATION OF AMERICAN rose breeders, Tom Carruth is hybridizer and director of research for Weeks Roses, following work at both Jackson & Perkins (see entry) and Armstrong Roses. Always on the lookout for new varieties with enhanced growth and beautiful flowers, Carruth was responsible, with Jack Christensen, for importation of the glowing coral 'Touch of Class', one of the most widely praised roses in America for many years. At Armstrong they were also responsible for hybridizing 'Origami', a pink-coral floribunda with flowers of a perfect formation; 'Crystalline', a leading exhibition rose; and 'Fire 'n' Ice' for the cut-flower trade. Carruth's initial roses for Weeks have mostly been miniatures, including 'Peach Fuzz', 'Heartbreaker', and 'Little Paradise'. These are being followed by larger roses, such as the 1992 introduction 'Columbus', an old-rose pink floribunda with large, shapely flowers. □

CEMETERIES

*American rosarians have a great fondness for ceme-
teries as places to find old roses, the lost treasures of a
great past.*

TAKE AN ENTHUSIASTIC ROSE GROWER TO AN
old town, and the first inquiry will be,
"Which way to the cemetery?" The attraction
is in old, untamed cemeteries where forgotten
roses grow. The older the cemetery and the
more abandoned it looks, the greater the challenge — and the potential rewards.

The rose was more often than not the
chosen plant with which to remember a loved
one, often a tiny stick of 'Harison's Yellow' that
burgeoned into bloom and dropped its golden
flowers on the grave, or 'Old Blush' with its
large pink petals. Walking into one of these
old, silent places, the rosarian looks around,
searching for a nodding bloom or a wild
scramble of prickly stems; anything that may
tell of a rose.

Cemeteries have long been noted for their
roses. In 1849 Andrew Jackson Downing
wrote of the cemetery at Laurel Hill near
Philadelphia as being a wilderness of roses,
fine trees, and monuments. Famous writers
and rose searchers like Georgia Torrey Drennan and Francis Lester encouraged rose lovers
to go out and find the old forgotten roses in
out-of-the-way graveyards. The result is that
graveyards have returned to commerce hundreds of old roses that would otherwise have
been lost.

Maureen Reed Detweiler wrote in *New Orleans Plants and Gardens,* in 1989, of her pride
in discovering a 'Louis Philippe', from 1834,
near her mother's family tomb. "The rose's

canes had grown so large and so heavy that a
couple were resting on a marble slab between
two tombs and had taken root in the dust," she
wrote. Now, "whenever I visit our tomb to
care for our roses, I water and feed it, too."

That cemetery story can be repeated from all
parts of America. In 1989 at the Evergreen
Cemetery in Victoria, Texas, searchers (they
call themselves rose rustlers) found roses like
'Old Blush', 'Marie Pavie', 'Cramoisie Supe-
rieur', 'Tip Top', and an unidentified red China
rose. The cemeteries of the South are treasure
houses of old roses because even the tender
ones have been able to survive.

The Huntington Botanical Gardens (see entry) near Los Angeles has a long tradition of
plant-collecting expeditions, and it has found
that pioneer cemeteries are a great source of
otherwise forgotten roses. Curator Clair Martin has written many times about his successes.
Martin tells of a visit to the cemetery at Volcano, California, once a booming gold-rush
town, which revealed an interesting rose at the
site of the grave of three infant boys who died
in the 1850s. The rose — with very dark green
leathery foliage, and flowers in clusters with
red buds that open to pink and fade white —
remains unidentified. And the bush still grows
on the grave, for rose searchers never harm a
bush. Cuttings are merely taken, which often
leaves the bush stronger than it might otherwise have been.

The longtime connection between cemeteries and old roses has led to a remarkable floral
display in Lynchburg, Virginia, where the Old
City Cemetery has been replanted in old roses.
The replanting came about as a result of a Virginia tradition that goes back to 1866, when
local groups were set up to ensure perpetual

care for grave sites. More than a hundred years later, in 1981, some young women in Lynchburg who had inherited this responsibility from older relatives set out to do their task in a very ambitious way. They turned to Carl Cato of Lynchburg, a nationally known old-rose enthusiast, for advice on restoring the beauty of the cemetery's roses.

Cato gave them some bad news. Everything would have to be restarted from scratch because the old roses were beyond saving. The decision was made to replant the famous Old Brick Wall on the southeast side of the cemetery with old roses. Some sixty varieties were selected as representative of rose history to the twentieth century. Plants were selected from all parts of the country, and the largest single donor was Pickering Nurseries of Ontario, Canada. Among the American-bred old roses are 'Champneys', 'Pink Cluster', 'Gardenia', and 'Baltimore Belle'.

The graveyard planting has given Lynchburg a place in the history of old roses, and the planting has continued elsewhere in the area. In the corner of the cemetery is a medical museum that is being softened by the random plantings of old roses. The home of poet Anne Spencer (see entry) is part of another project. And to finally make Lynchburg almost a national repository for old roses, members of the Blue Ridge Rose Society worked to rejuvenate another garden, known simply as Mr. Elder's Garden and containing all old heritage roses. □

CHAMPNEYS, JOHN (1743–1820)

Without John Champneys, the world would never have had those magnificent roses called Noisettes.

JOHN CHAMPNEYS, A RICE PLANTER, IS CREDited with being the first person to hybridize a rose in the United States. In 1802 he lived in a large house, with extensive gardens, in Charleston, South Carolina. His hobby was rose growing. Champneys produced a new rose as a result of crossing two famous old roses—one of them certainly being 'Old Blush' (see entry), the other probably being a musk or damask, both of them immigrant roses.

Among the seedlings of the new rose, he found one rose that looked like 'Old Blush' but had the ability to bloom on and on, right through summer and fall. Called 'Champneys' Pink Cluster', it was an instant success, and the seeds were sown everywhere. But being a hybrid, the rose's seeds produced many variations on the original. The only way to propagate a hybrid is to take cuttings and either root them or have them budded or grafted onto another stock. Even today in old cemeteries and homes around the South, roses can be found that are slight variations on Champneys's original as a result of the seed being sown or scattered by nature.

That cross made by John Champneys was to produce a whole range of new roses called Noisettes. They got their name from two nurserymen brothers, Philippe and Louis Noisette. Philippe, who lived in Charleston, sent a seedling and some seeds from 'Champneys' Pink Cluster' to Louis in France. The first of these seedlings was a slightly more compact and better-growing variety than Champneys's rose, with huge clusters of blush-white blooms, and Louis introduced it in France as 'Blush Noisette'. Later he introduced more of the seedlings that came from his brother in Charleston, and they became known as 'Rosier de Philippe Noisette'. The roses were an immediate success in France, and soon the class name was shortened to Noisette. The French took over the new class and expanded it widely. Vigorous, fragrant, colorful, and graceful well describe these aristocratic plants that established a new dynasty in the rose world, thanks to a rice planter in South Carolina.

Many people wish that Noisettes had been called Champneys. Henry B. Ellwanger, in his book *The Rose* (1883), charged the Noisette brothers with not giving credit to Champneys "as the originator of the class which has ever since borne the wrong title of Noisette Rose." South Carolina paid its own handsome tribute to the originator when, in 1986, they designated 'Champneys' Pink Cluster' as the Charleston rose. The city has also given credit to Philippe Noisette, whose land within the city limits is still known as the Rose Garden. In 1976 the Noisette Rose Garden was planted in recognition of his work. So both honors have been satisfied. ◻

CHARTWOOD ROSE GARDEN CHARTWOOD, NORTH CAROLINA

THERE IS A HIDDEN ROSE PARADISE IN Chartwood, a place now home for old roses. Albas, damasks, bourbons, and moss roses spread through the garden at Chartwood

because Helen Watkins loved them. She moved to the house at the site of the garden in the 1950s with her then husband Charles Blake, an ornithologist, and they founded the Hillsborough Historical Society. Helen Watkins began cataloging old gardens, formed a group of the Heritage Rose Society, and dedicated herself to saving old roses. The Chartwood garden is now on the National Register of Historic Places. Roses dating to the fifteenth century grow there in the protection of the white clapboard house in a little town off the main highway between Durham and Greensboro. The garden remains an essential extension of Old World beauty. ◻

CHEROKEE ROSE
(Rosa laevigata)

With its Indian name and all its legends, surely here is a native rose. But not so.

THE CHEROKEE ROSE ORIGINATED IN CHINA. It is spread so widely through the United States, however, that it may have been imported even before trade with China was opened up via Europe. It could have been brought by early Spanish explorers and then become widely naturalized in the South and taken as their own by the Cherokee Indians.

Rose writer Leonie Bell, in the Heritage Rose Letter (February 1989), pointed out the long-held supposition that the rose had arrived in America from China as a plant. "Nothing is said about the possibility of arrival by seed," she wrote. "Instead it very likely came as stowaway in a bag of rice, just as did 'our' daisies, dandelions and clover with hardier grains. Along with these, I am afraid, the beautiful Cherokee is—a weed." Noting that Charleston, South Carolina, was an early importer of rice (rose pioneer John Champneys was in the rice business in Charleston), Bell speculated that the seed could have arrived there in a rice shipment. "The seed must have germinated easily in the warm alluvial soils near Charleston, later to be carried far away by birds," she wrote.

To many, the rose was nothing more than a weed in China and wherever else it grew. But there were some who loved it. A century ago Francis Parkman wrote of its rampant growth, buds of unsurpassed beauty, and flowers of the purest waxen white. He didn't even mention its lovely perfume. It became the emblem of the state of Georgia and was a rose ordered by Thomas Jefferson from the Prince nursery.

There are numerous Indian legends about the rose. One tells of braves carrying blooms when they went courting. The Cherokees also used it for something more practical: they planted a trail with the rose as a marker to take them from East Texas to Northern Arkansas. The trail became known as the Cherokee Trace, and a historical marker on the grounds of the Upshur County Courthouse in Gilmer, Texas, tells the story:

> Near this site the Cherokee Indians blazed an early Texas trail. They wanted a road from their settlements near Nacogdoches to their home reservation on the White River in Arkansas.
>
> About 1821 the Cherokees selected a man for his uncanny sense of direction. Mounting a horse and dragging buffalo skins

behind him, he set a northward course. A group of Indians followed, blazing the trees to mark the trail. Another group cleared away the heavy underbrush and trees. A third group established camping grounds by springs and planted Cherokee roses which still mark the route today.

The route also became a trail for settlers from Arkansas, Kentucky, and Tennessee. Surely then the Cherokee Rose deserves the title of being the first rose immigrant, even if it is impossible to put a date on when it might have been brought by seed or plant from the Orient. □

CHILDBIRTH

Roses come to the aid of two expectant mothers.

ROSES HAVE ALWAYS BEEN KNOWN TO HAVE a calming influence on people in sickness and in health. Barbara Stander, a hospital worker in Pensacola, Florida, and president of her local rose society, recalled one interesting incident in an issue of their bulletin in August 1990:

> This week a Labor and Delivery nurse in the hospital where I work called me, requesting two roses, as she knew it was my habit to bring them to share with my coworkers. But she quickly added: "They must be mostly open."
>
> She chose two 'Princess of

Monaco' blooms as she explained her unusual request. She had two prospective mothers who were not progressing well in their labor and might require C-sections. She recounted an old midwifery technique of helping the patient conjure up a mental image of a beautiful flower transforming from a tightly closed bud to a bloom and finally to a fully blown specimen. Although she could talk her patients through the unfolding process, how much more realistically and beautifully so if the mothers-to-be could focus on a real rose.

The technique worked. Both mothers gave birth that day, aided by focusing on a rose. □

CHRISTENSEN, JACK (BORN 1948)

Hybridizer and researcher.

JACK CHRISTENSEN WAS THIRTY-FOUR WHEN his rose 'Mon Cheri' made him the youngest hybridizer ever to win the prestigious All-America Rose Selection award. 'Mon Cheri' is a very good hybrid tea and probably stands up well to the prose that described it: "These vivid red and pink beauties create a romantic combination that will lure and seduce even the most critical rose fanciers to whisper, 'My dear.'"

That same year, Christensen worked with Herb Swim to produce 'First Lady Nancy' (graceful and stately), 'Brandy' (as "heartwarming as its namesake"), and 'Jennifer Hart' (luxuriant with long-stemmed large blooms). Christensen was in charge of the research unit at Armstrong Roses (after Swim retired from the company in 1973), and was personally responsible for such fine roses as 'Brandy', 'Cricket', 'Foxy Lady', 'Heidi', 'Holy Toledo', 'Honest Abe', 'Hopscotch', 'Katherine Loker', 'Sunspray', 'White Lightnin', and many others. He began free-lance hybridizing when Armstrong Roses was closed. □

CLASSIFICATIONS OF ROSES

Roses are categorized into a variety of principal types.

THE CLASSIFICATION OF ROSES IS A SUBJECT for a lifetime's discussion and one that starts many an argument. Enthusiasts have tried for many years to agree on a classification for roses of different types. We should perhaps heed the words of J. Horace McFarland (see entry), who said that "general agreement upon classifications in this much-mixed genus is apparently an impossible dream." Different countries go different ways, and even within countries there are variations. The American Rose Society opts for fifty-six variations; the British Association of Rose Breeders reduced this to thirty. The World Federation of Rose Societies argues every three years about its suggested thirty-seven classifications. What follows is a generalization of the classifications of the most popular and most widely grown roses.

Hybrid teas are large-flowered roses with generally one bloom to a stem. Bushes grow anywhere from three to six feet high, depending on location and soil, and produce an excellent supply of blooms for cutting. Hybrid teas were the result of a marriage between hybrid perpetuals and tea roses. The resulting plants were smaller than hybrid perpetuals, less vigorous, and, in some cases, less hardy. But they did bloom continuously and carried the high-pointed flowers that we now call the classical shape in roses. 'La France'—silvery pink, large, double, full, and very fragrant—was introduced in 1867 and is considered the first hy-

brid tea. Not until 1893 did Great Britain's National Rose Society (now the Royal National Rose Society) formally recognize the new class. A Baltimore rose from John Cook (see entry), 'Souvenir of Wooton' (1888), rich velvety red and also very fragrant, is generally regarded as the first American-bred hybrid tea. Since then, the group has been improved immeasurably in bloom size and color and in bush sturdiness and hardiness. The World Federation of Rose Societies has proposed renaming these roses—from hybrid teas to "large-flowered roses."

Grandifloras have all the characteristics of the hybrid tea from which they were bred except that they usually produce clusters of smaller hybrid tea-shaped blooms and the bushes in most cases are taller (see 'Queen Elizabeth').

Floribundas carry clusters of medium to small blossoms on bushes that grow from two and a half to six feet high. They produce almost constant flowers all season long and are marvelous for landscaping in which color is important. Credit for the first breakthrough in the group goes to the Poulsen family of Denmark, but it was the work of American Gene Boerner (see entry) that brought them to prominence. Unfortunately, the hybridizing of floribundas has not continued to any great extent in the United States, and most of the new roses in the class now come from British and other European growers. The World Federation of Rose Societies has proposed renaming these roses—from floribundas to "cluster-flowered roses."

Polyanthas prove that there are fashions in roses as in everything else. This class of rose first appeared in the 1880s, and breeders raced to produce these attractive cluster-flowered, compact bushes that generally grow lower than the floribundas. Polyanthas reached the height of their popularity in the 1920s when some 120 varieties were introduced, but after that they dropped quickly out of commerce. Only fifteen were introduced in the 1980s. Polyanthas were the petite roses that were popular before the miniatures took center stage. Only one polyantha ever really achieved fame in the United States: 'Pinkie', which gained an All-America Rose Selection award in 1948 for Herb Swim. 'Pinkie' can still be found in some catalogs today, and there is a climbing version (with almost thornless canes) that can climb to eight feet. Other little treasures from this group that are still well worth growing include 'The Fairy', 'White Pet', 'Cecile Brunner' (nicknamed the sweetheart rose), 'Marie Pavie', and 'Yvonne Rabier'.

Miniature roses raced to popularity through the work of California breeder Ralph Moore (see entry). The name comes mainly from the size of the blossom rather than the size of the bush. One variety, 'Si', is said to be the smallest rose in the world, with a blossom the size of a small pea and blooms on a bush only inches high. Some varieties, on the other hand, have bushes as high as three feet. The range of miniatures today is extensive, from ground huggers to climbers, from classically shaped little blooms to floribunda cluster types. One branch of the miniature classification has roses that are slightly too big to be miniatures, but are too small to be floribundas. These roses are known variously as patio roses, sweetheart roses, macrominis, cushion roses, and in-betweeners. The first of these is said to be a group of roses from J. Benjamin

Williams of Silver Spring, Maryland, who, in the mid-1980s, patented the name mini-flora for the grouping. He offered the name to the American Rose Society, but it was turned down, and this group of roses still is not officially classified. Mini-flora seems an appropriate name for this grouping, offering a helpful distinction within the grouping of miniatures-patio roses and polyanthas.

Climbers, as the name suggests, have long canes and heavy growth. They usually produce a mass of early bloom with only intermittent flowers to follow, although many new varieties now produce a second flush of flowers. Most of the climbers reach seven to ten feet—but some can mass themselves in trees fifty feet high. Climbers do not have tendrils to hold them upright, so they require the support of wire, trellis, wall, or fence. The huge interest in breeding climbers in the early part of the twentieth century (see *Rosa wichuraiana*) has not continued since about 1960, when gardens began getting smaller and had less space for large specimens.

Ground-cover roses are ground-clinging in most cases and are good for large surface areas, embankments, and walls. European breeders have been in the forefront in recent production, but these roses have a long history in the United States (see ground-cover roses).

Hybrid perpetuals are the great delight of those who search for forgotten roses. Unidentified varieties are constantly being found around old homesteads and cemeteries. These roses were such a mixture of genes that the class included a wide variation of types, from normal-size bushes to ones that straggled and spread. The hybrid perpetuals generally carried large, full, and fragrant flowers, and they were easy to grow and quite hardy. They never deserved the term "mongrel" that has been applied to them; all roses today are inter-bred and are none the worse for it. In 1844, Robert Buist (see entry) regarded hybrid perpetuals as a new race that would bring pleasure "to the northern grower and amateur, which had hitherto been reserved only to the fanciers of more favored climes." G. A. Stevens, rose researcher and leading commentator, wrote that "in the fifty years from 1840 until 1890, hybrid perpetuals attained complete dominance of the rose gardening of Europe and America." Stevens went on to say: "If we may trust the writers of that period, they [Hybrid Perpetuals] developed into marvels of incredible beauty. The pictures in their quaintly illustrated books are not entirely convincing, and the few actual roses which have come down to us are not the paragons of beauty we might expect; but, in spite of all, the Hybrid Perpetuals are impressive roses of noble stature and dignified bearing, and almost all of them possess that ineffable perfume which we associate with old-fashioned roses." They were the immediate ancestors of the hybrid teas. Among the most famous hybrid perpetuals were 'General Jacqueminot' (see entry) (dark, dark red with a great fragrance), 'Paul Neyron' (often remembered as the "grandmother's rose" of full, rich-pink, fragrant blooms), 'Frau Karl Druschki' (for many years the most popular white rose in the world and also known as 'Snow Queen' and 'White American Beauty'), and 'American Beauty' (see entry). The arrival of the hybrid tea, with its diversity of colors and more adaptable bush size, generally spelled the end of the popularity of the hybrid perpetual.

Tea roses have a place in history as the true aristocrat of the garden. The name is said to go back to the arrival in Britain in 1769 of the rose known as 'Hume's Blush Tea-Scented China'. It is said that the roses picked up the name because they were carried with crates of tea, but certainly not all tea roses had a tea-scented bloom. It was once suggested that only one variety—'American Banner', a sport of 'Bon Silene', discovered in the 1870s—had the real scent of tea leaves . . . but like most fragrances it all depends on the nose, and numerous modern roses are said to have a tea-leaf smell. The roses were first grouped by the suggestion of tea fragrance and then by the delicacy of the flower which, after much hybridization, changed into the high-centered hybrid tea bloom we know today. They were anything but hardy, needing southern climes to be at their best. The first varieties may have arrived in the United States about the same time they became known in England. Texas rose historian Pam Puryear points out that in 1831, a tea rose was mentioned for an award at the Charleston Horticultural Show. The tea rose was dearly loved by those who grew up with them, and they received glory in America for many years. By the 1920s, this most delicate of rose beauties had fallen out of favor. The tea rose is still much valued today, however, in parts of the country where it can be grown without fear of freezing.

Old garden roses and **heritage roses** form a grouping that takes in the famous roses that brighten American history, such as damask, bourbon, alba, species, and centifolia. They vary widely in bush dimension and bloom size, and many bloom only once a year. Most of them are fragrant, because through the years the nonfragrant ones have been eliminated. They are a marvelous addition to any garden. Following is a brief introduction to groups within the classification of old garden roses.

Species roses are the wild or original roses. Often known only by their botanical names, some have familiar names as well. For instance, the rose botanically called *Rosa x odorate pseudindica* is far better known as 'Fortune's Double Yellow', and even appears under the glamorous names of 'Beauty of Glazenwood' and 'Gold of Ophir'.

Alba roses are large, generally hardy shrubs. Some varieties are thornless, such as 'Mme Plantier', with its snowy-white, elegant bush and little flowers like powder puffs. Generally they are once-flowering roses. Other well-known and useful varieties are 'Konigen von Danemark' and 'Great Maiden's Blush'.

Bourbon roses are robust shrubs that bloom throughout the season. They are the result of a chance cross found on the Isle de Bourbon (later Reunion) in the Indian Ocean. Seeds were sent to France, where a galaxy of roses was bred, including such great varieties as 'Souvenir de la Malmaison', 'Zephirine Drouhin' (often called the thornless rose), 'Louise Odier', and 'Madame Isaac Pereire'. These roses do particularly well in the southern United States.

China roses are the most constant blooming roses, with full bushy growth and dainty foliage, but unfortunately they are not all that hardy. Their existence proves that the Chinese were breeding single roses into double-flower forms before the idea ever reached the West. Blooms are generally thin-petaled and cupped, with color deepening in the bloom as it ages.

Best known in the group are 'Old Blush' (see entry), 'Hermosa', and the Green Rose (see entry). 'Rouletii', begetter of most of the modern miniature roses, is believed to have been a China rose, even though it was discovered in Switzerland.

Noisette roses, which are climbers or good vigorous shrubs, are at their best in the South and need protection in colder zones. The Noisettes, found in a big range of bush shapes and growth, are fragrant and almost always rebloom. A rose from John Champneys (see entry) in Charleston, South Carolina, began this wonderful group. The French later took over the group and greatly expanded it. The best-known Noisettes are 'Champneys' Pink Cluster', 'Blush Noisette', 'Lamarque', and 'Amiee Vibert'.

Gallica roses, generally known as "French roses," are once-blooming roses (in May-June). They are found throughout the United States, where they exist happily except in the very coldest climates. Among Gallica roses are 'Tuscany' (often called the velvet rose because of its dark maroon-red blooms), 'Cardinal de Richelieu' (purple), and 'Belle de Crecy' (pink to mauve and often showing a green button in the center). Also included in this group is 'Rose Mundi' *(Rosa gallica versicolor),* dating from about 1850. The flowers are blush pink, splashed and striped irregularly with deep carmine; they are the earliest-known striped rose.

Damask roses have been known since the sixteenth century and may go back as far as ancient Rome. They were grown in monasteries for medicinal purposes. Their grayish, serrated foliage presents a bush of moderate vigor, with lax growth and lots of prickles. The most likely damask roses to be found today are 'Autumn Damask' (bright pink and thorny), 'Bella Donna' (bright rose pink), 'Belle Amour' (light pink), 'Botzaris' (a superb white), and 'Celsiana' (pale pink). Their delicious fragrance makes them irresistible.

Moss roses have modified types of bristles growing over the hips and the sepals. When rubbed, these glands give off a distinctive perfume. Many roses carry a mossiness: miniatures, centifolias, damasks, and even some hybrid teas. Moss roses have built characteristics of hardiness, fragrance, and interesting blooms throughout the United States, where breeder Ralph Moore (see entry) includes them in his hybridizing work. 'Chapeau de Napoleon' is an unusual rose with a high-crested bud just like a hat that Napoleon was said to have worn; it is also known as the crested moss. Moss roses likely to be found include 'Old Pink Moss', 'William Lobb' (which is purple), and 'Perpetual White Moss' (also known as 'Quatre Saisons Blanc Mousseux'). □

CLIMATIC ZONES

Nᴏʀᴛʜ ᴀᴍᴇʀɪᴄᴀ ɪs ᴀ ʟᴀɴᴅ ᴏғ ᴅɪsᴘᴀʀᴀᴛᴇ climates and growing conditions. Recognition of the various hardiness zones is vital. This information is provided in a map from the United States Department of Agriculture. Originally issued in 1960, it has been updated occasionally since then; the 1990 map is the result of data gathered over the previous ten years at 14,000 government weather stations. It indicates the average minimum winter temperatures in all areas of North America, including Hawaii and Canada. It also lists various woody plants with their hardiness zones.

To order this map, write to Superintendent of Documents, U.S. Government Printing Office, Washington, D.C. 20402-9325. □

CONARD-PYLE COMPANY

With its interest in imports, this company brought great roses from Europe to the United States.

Aʀᴏᴜɴᴅ 1850 ᴀʟғʀᴇᴅ ᴄᴏɴᴀʀᴅ sᴛᴀʀᴛᴇᴅ ᴀ business in horticulture. He took on various partners—the company became Dingee & Conard, then Conard-Jones, and eventually Conard-Pyle in 1897. In 1906, on the death of Conard, Robert Pyle, who had been employed as a helper in 1899, and his father purchased a large share in the business.

Robert Pyle decided in the early 1900s that the company should specialize in roses. "We will thrive if we specialize," he said. Roses became the dominant interest of the company, which trademarked the name "Star Roses." Perceiving a large market for new roses, Pyle began his travels to Europe in 1911 and made nearly annual visits until 1950. He established Conard-Pyle as the nation's most forward-looking importer of roses. In 1931 he was the first person to bring miniatures into the United States. He made friends with the famous French growers, Meilland, and imported the greatest of all twentieth-century roses, 'Peace' (see entry), as well as most other Meilland-bred roses.

Pyle was president of the American Rose Society from 1921 to 1923 and was a leader in establishing the All-America Rose selections. He also helped establish the magnificent rose gardens at Portland, Oregon, and at the

Conard-Pyle facility in West Grove, Pennsylvania. Pyle and his close friend J. Horace McFarland (see entry) collaborated on publishing the catalogs of Conard-Pyle.

Pyle died in 1951 and was succeeded by Sidney B. Hutton, Sr., who in turn was succeeded by his sons Sidney B. Jr. in 1964, and by Richard J. in 1974. □

CONFEDERATE ROSE

A single rose can tell a beautiful story.

THE LOVELY AND LONG-LASTING LEGACY OF an old rose is chronicled in this story from the *American Rose* magazine, February

1986. The writer, Donna Smoot, of Charleston, West Virginia, told of being given a spray of an old moss rose. She then recounted the story that went with it.

John Vardaman was a farmer and rural schoolteacher in Alabama when the Civil War broke out. He served in the Confederate Army of Tennessee, Hilliard's Legion, as a wheelwright, wagon maker, blacksmith, and provender-forager, and at war's end in April 1865, he started the long walk home.

It was spring in Tennessee when he stopped somewhere at a mountain home for a drink of water from a front-yard well. Beside the well a profusion of color swelled from a rosebush, and the leg-weary soldier delighted in both the refreshing water and the colorful abundance of blooms.

He begged and was granted a rooting from the bush. Wrapped in leaf mold and moss, the sprig of root and stalk rose traveled in his pack all the way to mid Alabama, watered daily by the traveler whenever he drank from spring, stream, or well. When he arrived home, Mr. Vardaman planted the rose root where the front yard of his new home was to be built and homesteaded a section of land near Goodwater, Alabama.

In 1906, Mr. Vardaman's

daughter, Mrs. Maggie V. Webb, took a rooting from the 41-year-old moss rose and planted it in her new home in Alexander City, Alabama, where it flourished for many years and probably still grows and blooms. Her nephew, a grandson of Mr. Vardaman, saw and admired it in his childhood visits there, where he first heard the story of its origins. In 1950 the nephew, Adrian Gwin, brought a rooting of the moss rose to his home in St. Albans, West Virginia. Here it has provided lacy leaves and old lavender blooms each spring in the yard—a familiar memento of a war-weary soldier's love of beauty.

The spray of blooms from that bush is a sort of memorial to the greenthumb care of a country dirt farmer, who later became his county's superintendent of education, and a tribute to the robust vivaciousness of a simple antique rose. ☐

COOK, JOHN (1833–1929)

More than two dozen rose varieties are credited to this German-born hybridizer.

M ENTION THE NAME OF JOHN COOK TO A rose enthusiast, and the immediate response will be 'Radiance'. This is the name of the pink rose that Cook introduced in 1908—a rose that has been called a world rose, a rose

to grow anywhere and under any conditions. 'Radiance', with its globular, sweet-scented, clear pink blooms, is still sold in the United States today. At the time he introduced 'Radiance', Cook had already hybridized ten top roses, beginning in 1888 with 'Souvenir of

Wooton', regarded as the first American-bred hybrid tea.

Cook came to America from Germany as Johann Koch in 1853 and found a job with a florist. As soon as he learned English he moved to Baltimore, where he worked for a florist and later managed gardens and estates. Cook married a native Maryland woman, Elizabeth Pfeiffer, in 1860. He purchased land for his own nursery, and he and his wife conducted a wholesale florist business before moving into the city with a retail floristry. Cook took an interest in hybridizing roses — and eventually twenty-eight varieties were listed to his name.

A rose garden was planted in Baltimore in Cook's honor in 1941 but fell into disrepair. In 1989, family members moved the garden to Druid Hill, Baltimore, where it includes plantings of some of the roses for which he was responsible, such as 'White Maman Cochet', 'Radiance', 'Enchantress', and 'Pearl of Baltimore'.

The Maryland Rose Society is searching for other Cook varieties to add as fitting memorial to the man who, said rosarian J. Horace McFarland, "thought roses as well as dreamed them and to the end of his life kept close to his greenhouses in which he could test both thoughts and dreams." □

DAWSON, CHARLES P. (1904–1987)

"Uncle Charlie" was a firm believer in horticultural miracles.

CHARLES DAWSON WAS THE COMMON SENSE Gardener to thousands of readers of the *American Rose* magazine from the 1960s through the 1970s. "My learning process began," he once wrote, "before age 12, mostly from my grandmother, whose rose garden was the one (possibly only) thing our neighborhood had to brag about." He continued his education through other family members—his brother was a greenhouse supervisor—and Dawson was a member of a group formed in

1935 in Simpsonville, Kentucky, to promote and study roses.

The man known as "Uncle Charlie" eventually began his magazine column, offering advice that was always punchy and to the point. He said that his idea in writing was to help growers, and that he did. He insisted that roses should be fun and said that he never was a perfectionist.

"My years with roses," he wrote, "have made me a firm believer in miracles—and most of them we don't even notice. We take for granted things which man has never been able to duplicate: sun, energy, oxygen, rainfall, soil microorganisms, and thousands of other processes we don't know about. We need to use these miracles of nature and learn to take care of them. We're only helpers."

Dawson was a great helper to generations of American gardeners. He told them, "If there is any easy way of doing things in this world, I have never found it. Guess that's why I stay poor in money, rich in spirit, strong in muscle and weak in the head!" □

De VINK, JAN (BORN 1888)

The backyard hybridizing of Dutchman Jan de Vink was world-class.

JAN DE VINK IS CREDITED WITH BRINGING THE miniature rose into the world as a result of his backyard hybridizing. De Vink was a hobbyist with roses, who at first was rather haphazard, never totally sure which roses were the parents of his seedlings. He might have gone unknown but for the foresight of Robert Pyle, of the Conard-Pyle Company (see entry). On a visit to the Netherlands, Pyle saw a little plant of de Vink's that bore a red rose with a white center. De Vink called the rose 'Peon'. The moment he saw it, Pyle realized its potential.

The plant eventually reached Conard-Pyle (some say Pyle took the plant home; others say a cutting was sent) and it was propagated. Pyle took a patent on the rose, renamed it 'Tom Thumb', and introduced it to the public in 1936. This was the beginning of the amazing rise of the miniature rose in the United States. So successful was this first rose that it had to be taken out of the Conard-Pyle catalog the following year because there wasn't enough propagation material to meet the demand.

More roses came from Jan de Vink. With the royalties he built a greenhouse in which to hybridize more roses, but even then he was doing it only on a small scale in his backyard. Among the later roses he produced were 'Bo Peep', 'Baby Bunting', and 'Cinderella', still a leading miniature.

Disability marked the end of Jan de Vink's work as a hybridizer. His story appeared in the August 1973 edition of the American Rose Society magazine, in a letter he wrote from Holland.

> I herewith beg to inform you that I wish to discontinue my membership of your society.
>
> I regret this very much but by some ailment of my eyes I cannot read anymore.
>
> It may interest you, my joining the society dates back to 1923 when I was 35 years old.
>
> I have given my 50 annuals to the Horticultural Experimental Station in Boskoop, having bought the copies I missed during the war.
>
> My best wishes accompany your staff and society for the short time I still have to live.

The letter, tucked away in a bottom corner of a magazine, was published without comment. It was only thirty-seven years since the Dutchman had revolutionized the world of roses, but already his contributions had been almost forgotten. □

DICKENS, CHARLES (1812–1870)

IN 1842, ON HIS FIRST VISIT TO AMERICA, Charles Dickens attended a party in his honor in Cincinnati wearing a large red rose in a buttonhole of his coat. A young woman asked the world-famous writer for the rose. Dickens thought for a second and then said that if he gave it to her, the other women would be unhappy. The women, who were surrounding him, then suggested that he divide the rose. "But that way," he said, "the rose would be unhappy." Under the press of the group of women, the rose fell, breaking apart as it hit the floor—and every woman got a petal. □

DISEASES

Good care and timely treatment can spare roses from some of their common diseases.

THE PRINCIPAL DISEASES OF ROSES ARE caused by fungi. Black spot, mildew, and rust start with tiny growths that penetrate the surface cells or enter through pores. Early infections are not noticeable, but by the time they have begun to spread and produce spores, it may be too late to stop the infection, particularly with black spot. Preventive spraying can be the answer. Most modern fungicides work against all three diseases, although rust may require separate treatment later on.

The prevention of fungal disease begins with removing old leaves and clearing the ground around the bush early in the season so that the area will be free of overwintering spores. Tea rose growers used to prune very hard, often to within three inches of the ground, in the belief that this would keep down disease. Hard pruning can reduce the source of spores, but it is a harsh remedy: cutting so much wood reduces the number of blooms.

Fungicides work on three levels: by contact, which protects the foliage surface to prevent spores from germinating; by penetrative action, which prevents germination and penetration of the spores; and by systemic action, which takes the fungicide into the plant's sap stream and stops the disease from spreading.

If spraying begins as soon as the first foliage shows (which is very soon after pruning) and is repeated about twelve days later, it will then be necessary to spray only once a month. This preventive spraying should control the three diseases. A delay in your spraying campaign can allow black spot to take hold.

The advice for early preventive spraying does *not* apply to insecticides. Plant pathologist Eldon W. Lyle avoids using insecticides until he sees the aphids. "Otherwise," he says, "you will kill the beneficials and possibly bring on other problems." (See the Pests entry.)

Many old varieties of roses do not take well to fungicide (test some foliage before spraying), but Lyle (see entry) says they appear less troubled by diseases and have a greater tolerance for them than modern roses. "For instance," he says, "the 'Radiance' varieties show black spot very quickly but do not have as fast a defoliation as newer varieties. The 'Blaze' climbers have the same trait. 'Dorothy Perkins' can have loads of mildew and yet not suffer, it must have something to do with genetic factors."

Black spot, powdery mildew, and certain other diseases are better controlled now than in the 1930s. Black spot, rampant in the greenhouses of that time, is seldom seen now because growers have learned not to syringe plants with water.

To control mildew, space bushes so that they have good air circulation. Spray when the first signs of the disease become apparent. If you have begun preventive spraying against black spot, you will find that this fungicide also keeps down mildew (and vice versa). One method of controlling downy mildew is to spray with a solution of baking soda; researchers at Cornell University reported in 1991 that tests using sodium bicarbonate were effective in not only preventing the disease but also clearing up infected plants. The recommended formulation is seven tablespoons of baking soda dissolved in five gallons of water, sprayed weekly.

Rust is a killer. It debilitates the plant and spreads rapidly. If you see little orange pustules on a leaf, use the commercial preparations to clear it up. The organic approach is to dig out the rust-susceptible roses and plant varieties that are known to be resistant. You might also move the problem bushes to another part of the garden, as rust seems to set itself in pockets. In my garden, some bushes of 'Pink Favorite' are among the first to get rust, yet others of the same variety, only yards away, never suffer.

You can also go a long way in the fight against fungal disease by giving roses a little bit of special care. In 1929, before fungicides were available, J. Horace McFarland (see entry) observed,

> While it is true that the rose is attacked by many insects and diseases, it is also true that healthy plants, like healthy humans, are resistant to these troubles. Furthermore rose sanitation, which means cleanliness of the plant and the ground about the plant, likewise tends to protect and resist the attacks of insects, just as sanitation similarly provides favorable conditions for human beings.

McFarland advised gardeners to fertilize plants during the growing season and not allow weeds. The position of rose beds, he rightly noted, has a lot to do with the health of the roses. Roots that are starved because of proximity to a hedge or large tree cannot sus-

tain good health. Free air circulating around plants is vital while roses should be given a place away from cold winds, air currents, and fog. And let them have sun.

I have a five-point plan that I have been advising for years: give your roses food, water, air, sun, and a little bit of love, and they are in for a good life.

Rose breeders are continually seeking roses that are hardy enough to fight off diseases by themselves. A 1992 All-America Rose Selection winner—'All That Jazz' by Jerry Twomey (see entry)—is considered almost totally disease resistant. A bright orange, it carries great vigor in its waxy, polished foliage. AARS judges noted its disease resistance, great foliage, and flowering ability. One judge wrote that "it could break the myth that all roses need spraying." □

DOBSON, BEVERLY R. (BORN 1927)

One of the most vital publications to rose lovers is the annual Combined Rose List *created by Beverly R. Dobson.*

A CRITICAL NEED FOR TIMELY ROSE INFORmation led Beverly Dobson to begin publishing the annual *Combined Rose List* from her Irvington, New York, home in the mid-1970s. This booklet contains an international list of roses that are in commerce and cultivation, details on roses that have been registered, and a very valuable list of hard-to-find roses and where to find them.

The job of providing such information originally was handled by J. Horace McFarland and subsequent editors in *Modern*

Roses, the "stud book" of roses. But *Modern Roses* was published only occasionally, and its information was soon out of date. This problem inspired Dobson, an American Rose Society judge. She needed information to validate rose varieties for awards and ribbons at rose shows, and she decided to do something about it. She produced her *Combined Rose List,* adding greatly to the basic information that rose lovers need. The booklet has become an international "must have" for rosarians. She now works with Ohio rosarian Peter Schneider on the publication, with the idea of eventually turning the work over to him.

Dobson also produces, six times a year, the widely read *Bev Dobson's Rose Letter,* a personal potpourri of information, reviews of rose literature, letters, and articles. She lectures widely in the United States and Canada and consults on rose and gardening books. ◻

'DR. HUEY'

This dark red rose won lasting fame as a stock for propagation.

THE NAME OF LEADING PHILADELPHIA AMAteur rosarian in the 1920s, dentist Robert Huey, remains very much alive today because of this rose. It was bred in 1914 by Captain George C. Thomas (see entry) and named in honor of the man who started him in roses. At the time of its national introduction in 1919, it was regarded as the darkest red of all climbing roses. J. Horace McFarland (see entry) wrote that it was a "unique variety which carries its abundant June flowers without any fading into blueish shades." And although 'Dr. Huey' was widely accepted for itself, it became famous in a very different way.

A search was on for suitable understock in a budding trial in California, and 'Dr. Huey' was included in the trial by mistake. But it was the easy overall winner and has since been used to propagate millions of roses. Ironically—as Trenholm N. Meyer pointed out in the American Rose Society annual of 1991—just before this special use of 'Dr. Huey' was discovered, Captain Thomas had written an article for the American Rose Society (1922) in which he entered the debate on the best way to propagate roses, by budding or from cuttings. Thomas believed that while a great many roses could be successfully propagated on their own roots, all roses could be successfully budded. But he pointed out that "the best stock for every variety has not yet been listed." Little did he know that his own dark red rose would solve the problem for the majority of American rose growers. ▢

DOORYARD ROSES

The wonderful concept of dooryard roses has gone out of favor. Has the world become too sophisticated to allow a rose bush to twine itself lovingly around a doorway?

THE IDEA OF DOORYARD ROSES HAS ALWAYS appealed to me, conjuring up romantic visions of a whitewashed Cape Cod cottage with roses around the door. Walter Van Fleet (see entry), at the beginning of the twentieth century, was the man who set out to produce roses that would become a familiar sight on every doorstep. He produced a host of roses aimed at the dooryard ideal—from the very first of them, 'Mary Wallace', through a galaxy of varieties such as 'American Pillar' (see entry) and 'Silver Moon' (once a great rose in the Virginia countryside), right on to the important rose that carries his own name. Van Fleet lived in an era when climbers were a dominant type emerging from hybridizers, and most of his roses were climbers.

The idea of dooryard roses caught on. One comment about 'Dorothy Perkins' (see entry for Jackson & Perkins) says it all: "She has thrown her wands of light pink beauty across ten thousand doorways in eastern America. Dependable, delightful, cluster flowered." The long-stemmed rambling roses from Van Fleet, Michael H. Walsh (see entry), and others had an informality to accompany the architecture of the time. The five-petaled pink magnificence of early varieties was a marvelous sight.

If you look back at old pictures, you can see roses tumbling informally over fences and in yards and by doorways. It's not a sight often seen today. Modern roses don't lend themselves to the same treatment, and the dooryard ideal of Van Fleet is no longer a common reality. In my own garden I grow a bed of roses near the front door, but modern architecture has decreed that there is no way I can get through the concrete surrounds to plant a rose right by the door. I know the arguments against the roses taking up half the entrance: they snag skirts, trousers, and stockings, and they have to be carefully looked after. But remember the words of Elizabeth Barrett Browning:

> From the moss-rose and the
>   musk-rose
> Maiden blush and royal-dusk
>   rose
> What glory for me
> In such a company?

To meet the dooryard ideal today, you have to search out the roses. Hybrid teas are too stiff, miniatures are too small, old garden roses are generally too big. Floribundas come closest to the need. I have seen elegance on a San Francisco streetside, with bushes of 'French Lace' growing where architects had left room for little but concrete. What a sophisticated and welcoming sight they made! But maybe even this rose is not informal enough. Perhaps we should go back a few decades to another age. The hybrid musks are very good; look to a 'Buff Beauty' for a welcoming rose. Or perhaps we need to go back to the roses from Van Fleet to regenerate the idea of the rose as a beautiful host on the doorstep. I hope the readers of this book will take the time to find a place to create the most welcoming sight of all, a dooryard rose. By doing so we would be fulfilling the dream of the marvelous hybridizers of a century ago. □

'DOUBLE DELIGHT'

This sensational rose depends on warm weather.

ONE OF THE MOST SPECTACULAR ROSE novelties of the late twentieth century, 'Double Delight' was an All-America Rose Selection and was voted one of the world's favorite roses by the World Federation of Rose Societies. The bloom is big, magnificently colored in red and white petals that merge toward a soft yellow at the center. The fragrance is magnificent.

When 'Double Delight' came from the master hand of Herb Swim and his assistant Arnold Ellis (see entry) in 1977, it was a sensation. With its unique coloring, nothing had been seen like it before. But for all its wonder it has never become an international garden favorite. Everyone loves the bloom, but it is a warm-weather rose. In California, it is magnificent; in England, it often sulks. More than anything else it needs heat and warmth to grow and to beat off the scourge of mildew. □

DREXEL, MOTHER KATHERINE

Roses bloomed at a Navajo mission thanks to Mother Katherine Drexel.

KATHERINE DREXEL WAS HEIRESS TO THE fortune of the Drexel and Morgan bank but turned her back on it to become a nun. She dedicated her life to providing Catholic education on the Navajo reservation at Cienega Amarilla, Arizona.

In the late 1800s, Mother Drexel bought a site for a Navajo school and, according to rosarian and historian Hallie Beck, hired a caretaker with a Winchester to discourage claim jumpers. By October 1898, the reconditioned buildings already on the site (about eight miles southwest of Window Rock, present-day capital of the Navajo Nation) were ready for occupancy. St. Michael's Mission won fame for the dictionary and grammar books it published in 1912, which are believed to have saved the Navajo language. But in the midst of the learning and teaching, Mother Drexel did not forget the need for the softness of roses, and she had a hedge of 'Harison's Yellow' planted. The roses still grow on the site. □

EDMUNDS, FRED, SR., AND FRED, JR.

Father and son created a tradition of roses in the state of Oregon.

THE EDMUNDS NAME HAS LONG BEEN CONnected with Oregon and today is one of the few rose companies left in a state that for many years was the leading producer of roses for the United States. Big companies eventually found it necessary to produce their roses in more hospitable climes, but the Edmunds family has hung on.

English-born Fred Edmunds, Sr., was apprenticed in 1885 to the famous firm of Frank Cant Roses in Colchester, Essex. He emigrated to the United States and worked in various jobs, from seeking gold in Alaska to mining in Montana. In the Yukon he turned briefly to horticulture in Dawson City, where he grew onions and radishes under glass in a place where few fresh vegetables were available. He was in the city at a fortunate time: electricity had just arrived and everyone was throwing out their carbide lamps. He collected them and used them to heat the greenhouses.

This ingenuity followed him to Oregon, where he became curator of the famous rose gardens in Portland. He was a prolific writer and a valuable source of information for visiting nurserymen. It was here on the knee of his father that Fred Jr. began to meet the most famous rosemen of his time. On one occasion, when Charlie Perkins visited the family, young Fred, who had just won a first prize for a rose in a show, was left with the giant of the business (see entry for Jackson & Perkins). It was Prohibition time and Fred Sr. had gone to search for a drop of whiskey for his distinguished visitor.

"When he came back," reminisces Fred Jr., "I had told Charlie Perkins, the biggest rose grower in the world, all there was to know about roses." His father admonished him, but Charlie Perkins said that if Fred Jr. ever wanted to grow roses, to come see him. He did, and he worked for Jackson & Perkins for some years. Fred Jr. later branched out on

ELIZABETH PARK
HARTFORD, CONNECTICUT

The nation's first municipal rose garden became a prize-winning place of roses.

W HEN CHARLES POND OF HARTFORD, CON- necticut, died in 1894, he willed his 100-acre West End estate and half his liquid assets to the city for development of a horti- cultural park to be named for his wife, Eliza- beth. The city hired Swiss-born Theodore Wirth as superintendent and designer. Wirth began with a rose garden of about a hundred bushes, and within five years the total had grown to a thousand. Wirth pleaded with park commissioners for funding for a large munici- pal garden. His reason was simple: "Roses brought joy to the public." He got the money.

The year 1904 saw the opening of Elizabeth Park, the first municipal rose garden in the country. Donna Fuss of Bloomfield, Con- necticut, described that first garden for me: "It was a perfect square, one and a half acres in area. In the center the land was raised four feet and on this rise was constructed a rustic ga- zebo. This was to permit a perfect vista of the entire garden. The banks around the gazebo were planted primarily with polyantha roses. There were eight sets of arches leading into the gazebo and these were covered with ramblers. The diagonals were covered with 'Dorothy Perkins' and 'White Dorothy' while the com- pass points were covered with 'Crimson Ram- bler' and 'Excelsa.'"

The new garden must have been a marvel- ous sight, especially as 132 beds radiated from the gazebo and the perimeters were fenced to

his own, and the famous firm Roses by Fred Edmunds was born.

The large hybrid tea 'Fred Edmunds', intro- duced in 1944 by the French firm of Meilland, still holds a place in many American catalogs. Its long-stemmed, coppery-colored buds and spicy fragrance always attract attention. Being named for an Oregon resident, it's appropriate that it needs a little shade and some cool weather to be at its best. Another rose is named for Wini, wife of Fred Jr., whose writ- ten comments always made reading the com- pany catalog a pleasure and an education. 'Wini Edmunds' is a striking red-blend hybrid tea that came from Sam McGredy in 1973. The firm is now under the guidance of Fred and Wini's son, Phil, and is still based just out- side Wilsonville, south of Portland. □

allow ramblers, climbers, and shrubs to grow. In 1912, a section was provided in which new roses could be tested. A further addition was made in 1937. The garden began a decline in the 1960s when most of the original gardeners had retired, and there was little money for a labor-intensive display. That was when the group known as The Friends of Elizabeth Park was formed. And the gardens came alive again—a place for weddings, walks, and picnics, where sports could be played, children could have fun, and roses could bloom. Elizabeth Park won the plaque as Most Outstanding All-America Rose Selection garden in 1990. And even better news is that many of the garden's original roses survived and now are part of a planting of 15,000 bushes. ◻

ELLIS, ARNOLD

ARNOLD ELLIS WORKED QUIETLY AWAY AS A rose breeder for many years in the top two nurseries in the United States, Jackson & Perkins and Armstrong's (see entries). Ellis was hybridizing at a time of big changes at Jackson & Perkins: Gene Boerner had just died, Dennison Morey had left, and William Warriner had been appointed to head research (see entries). At Armstrong's, Herb Swim was brought out of retirement to do rose breeding. Swim went poaching among the various hybridizers and brought in Ellis alongside a young and promising Jack Christensen (see entry). The expertise of Swim and Ellis was retained by the firm for a number of years in the 1970s, during which time they produced some top-class roses. ◻

ELLWANGER, HENRY B. (1816–1906)

The writings and nursery work of Henry B. Ellwanger helped make hybrid perpetuals highly fashionable in the late nineteenth century.

HENRY B. ELLWANGER WAS A NURSERYMAN at Mount Hope Nurseries in Rochester, New York, who introduced a publicity campaign to deal in roses on a national scale. From that time on, the whole market took on a different slant. Certainly the nation's nurserymen did not like the look of a giant coast-to-coast company giving them competition. The Ellwanger business stretched from New York to California, where he began to sell plants in 1870 as his partner Patrick Barry drummed up business in competition with local nurserymen.

Ellwanger hybridized some roses himself, though they made little impression. But he was responsible for bringing into commerce 'Crimson Rambler', a rose that became the most planted rambler in America until the arrival of varieties from Walter Van Fleet (see entry), Michael H. Walsh (see entry), M. V. Horvath, and James Farrell. 'Crimson Rambler' came to Ellwanger and Barry from England, but it was in truth an old Chinese variety that had attracted the attention of a visitor to China, who sent it back to England. 'Crimson Rambler' became the parent of a great race of climbers.

It was in the area of the hybrid perpetual that Ellwanger became famous. His book *The Rose* is devoted almost entirely to this class of rose, the most fashionable of its time. This class was said by one nurseryman to be "like Moses's serpent" as it swallowed up many other roses. Hundreds of hybrid perpetual varieties were introduced—Ellwanger listed 1,086—and his descriptions have been vital to rose researchers as more and more of the old, neglected varieties are being found in cemeteries and old gardens. □

A FAMILY ROSE

The echoes of history come into many American gardens by way of a small cutting or piece of a rose bush that has traveled through generations.

FROM MANY PARTS OF THE COUNTRY I HAVE heard stories of old roses that bring back memories of happiness, travails, wars, and—more than anything else—family love. One of the most evocative stories I have received comes from Sharon Van Enoo, a dedicated rose enthusiast from Torrance, California. Here is a condensed version of the story she gave me.

In my garden in Torrance, I have a rose, 'Mme Plantier', a white Alba from 1835 that I received as a rooted division from my maternal grandfather's second wife, Merna Davenport DeSpain. Upon her marriage to my grandfather, she brought with her a rooted division of 'Mme Plantier', a rose that had been passed down in her family for many generations.

Merna received her original bush from her mother, Genie Davenport, who lived in Egin Bench, Idaho. Genie received her rose from her sister, Mary Winegar, who had received it from their mother, Pamela Bullock Mason, who had brought it to Idaho in 1884.

Pamela Bullock was born in 1842 in Staffordshire, England, and married James Mason, who was born in 1841 in Lincolnshire, England. They eventually made their home in Utah, where James ran a nursery of sorts. By the early 1880s, Mason had taken a second wife, in keeping with the Mormon practice of polygamy. In 1884, Pamela settled in Egin Bench, Idaho, while the other wife established a home in a neighboring settlement.

When Utah became a state, the Mormon Church declared polygamy illegal. James Mason chose the younger of his two wives, leaving Pamela alone in the backwoods of Idaho with her children, her roses, and, eventually, the loss of her eyesight. In her last years nothing pleased Pamela more than to have a granddaughter arrive with a bouquet of her favorite fragrant roses. Among her favorites was the 'Mme Plantier' she had received from her father, Thomas Bullock.

Thomas Bullock was an exciseman for Her Majesty, the Queen; in other words, a tax collector. While still a young man he converted to Mormonism. Because of his religious conversion, he lost his job. He then immigrated to Nauvoo, Illinois, where he became personal secretary to Joseph Smith of the Mormon Church. After Joseph Smith was murdered, Thomas became secretary, clerk, and church historian to Brigham Young, whom he accompanied on his trek to Salt Lake Valley. It is Thomas's diaries of that trip that are the official historical record of the Mormon migration.

About 1858, Thomas Bullock wrote to his cousin Ralph Bullock in England, asking for plants, seeds, and cuttings for Utah. Thus it was Ralph Bullock who sent the original plant of 'Mme Plantier' to Thomas Bullock from England.

Our 'Mme Plantier' is a rose that has had many lives and will certainly outlast many more generations. The end of the twenty-first century will, most likely, see our 'Mme Plantier' still blooming profusely, with no end in sight. ◻

FEAST, JOHN AND SAMUEL

The work of these early hybridizers influenced the efforts of rose breeders for more than a century.

BALTIMORE NURSERYMEN JOHN AND SAMUEL Feast were among the clutch of hybridizers who began to breed roses in the 1830s and 1840s. Using the species *Rosa setigera* (see entry), the Prairie Rose, they produced some hardy seedlings, including 'Baltimore Belle', which brought its loose, double-blush blooms in a Noisette style into the gardens with a noted fragrance and helped establish hardier large-flowered climbers.

The other still-remembered Feast seedling is 'Queen of the Prairies', the hardiest pink climbing rose until it was supplanted by 'Crimson Rambler'. 'Queen of the Prairies' is still grown in places where truly hardy roses are needed. The work of the Feasts, coming at a time when Americans were just starting to breed roses, encouraged many others to begin work with native species. ◻

'FLEUR COWLES'

THIS CREAMY-WHITE FLORIBUNDA ROSE bears the name of Fleur Cowles, a painter, writer, publisher, and U.S. ambassador to the coronation of Queen Elizabeth II. Among her many books is *The Life and Times of the Rose* (1991), an evocation of the rose in history through myth and mystery, music and romance. She has rose gardens at her homes in Spain and England. Her rose was produced by the English firm of Gregory Roses. It can be seen in many international gardens, including that of the late Princess Grace at the palace in Monaco. ◻

FLORIDA

An old rose from China proved to be the answer to growing roses in Florida.

THERE WAS A TIME WHEN FLORIDA WAS NOT highly regarded as a place to grow roses. Roses that were wonders elsewhere often did not respond to the southern conditions. Northerners coming to Florida, wrote Barbara Harding Oehlbeck, horticulturalist and rose writer, "brought some of their favorites with them. Much to their sorrow, most of the bushes did not grow and thrive as they had in former locations. The reasons, naturally, were many, including drastic changes in climate and soils, and the fact that in Florida, there is relatively little, if any, dormant period."

Then someone decided it was the understock, on which most roses are budded, that was wrong. There is no such thing as a best understock for all parts of the country. 'Dr. Huey', so effective in California, was not as effective in Florida. Neither were rose stocks like *Rosa multiflora* or *Rosa manetti*. Plant pathologist Howard Miller and Dr. Sam McFadden came to the rescue. They discovered that *Rosa fortuniana*, a species that sends out its double white flowers in February and March, could be the answer. *Rosa fortuniana* passed on great vigor even to weak varieties, transforming them into stronger bushes with flowers of eminent quality. Miller and McFadden also produced a method of vegetative production of the rose that made it more accessible to all.

Rosa fortuniana was not new. It had been found growing in a mandarin's garden in China in 1850 by Robert Fortune, who sent it to the Horticultural Society of London, where it was named in his honor. It adapted well to warmer climates but is not hardy. "When pruned as a shrub," commented Oehlbeck, "it is literally a fountain of white during this once-a-year blooming season." It had been used frequently as an understock, but its possibilities for Florida were not revealed until the 1960s. But better late than never; new roses of all types can now be grown to perfection there. □

FLORIST ROSES

Roses grown for the florist trade are far different from those grown in the amateur garden.

MORE THAN 20 MILLION ROSE BUSHES IN the United States bear blooms for the florist trade. It is further estimated that 800 million roses are sold annually to Americans—at a total price of about $2.5 billion! Roses Incorporated (1250 I Street, N.W., Suite 500, Washington, D.C. 20005) estimates that twenty-five percent of all flowers sold by florists are roses, which have always had a high place in the floral social order and been sold at a premium.

Florist roses are generally varieties that will perform well only in greenhouse conditions. Few of them have a place in the garden. They are said to be the most difficult roses of any to breed, taking all of ten years from seedling to marketplace. Growing florist roses requires very different techniques from those used in the garden. A florist rose has to be a super producer of blooms, bright enough to catch the public attention. It must be able to crop well under difficult light conditions, blooms must last far longer than one would expect of a garden rose, and the petals must be tough and always crisp.

E. Gurney Hill (see entry), the father of greenhouse growing in the United States, tabulated his ten qualities for a rose before it could secure a place as a forcing variety—a variety suitable for use as a florist's rose, one that can be forced into growth under greenhouse conditions.

1. A strong, clean, free growth.

2. A long, shapely bud, erect and pointed.

3. Not too many petals (or it will not open well in dull weather).

4. A resistant texture that will make it a good keeper and shipper.

5. A strong stem and good foliage.

6. A true color (if pink, it must not shade into lavender; if red, it must never "blue"; if yellow, the tone must be intense).

7. Lots of blooms.

8. No tendency toward going dormant in winter.

9. A fragrance.

10. Popularity among people who buy roses.

This list gives an idea of how hard it is to get the perfect rose for the florist trade. And it is easy to understand that when a good rose arrives, the highest security is maintained to make sure no one propagates it illegally. Before plant patents came into force, remembers Raymond C. Allen (see entry), dentists' drills were used to remove the eyes on the cut stems before they were shipped to retailers, thereby preventing propagation.

One of the best of the American-bred greenhouse roses has been 'Samantha', an outstanding red developed by William Warriner at Jackson & Perkins (see entries). It was registered in a new grouping from J&P called 'flora-tea' (that was in everyone else's eyes basically a grandiflora). The forty-petaled blooms have an urn-shaped effect and last longer than all other red roses.

Other top American-bred greenhouse roses have come from Robert G. Jelly (see entry), with 'Sassy' and 'Royalty'; Jack Christensen and Tom Carruth (see entries), with 'Crystalline' and 'Scarlet O'Hara'; Gene Boerner (see entry), with 'Bridal White'; O. L. Weeks (see entry), with 'Disco'; and G. K. McDanial, with 'Cara Mia'. One of the greatest greenhouse roses of recent years has been the French-bred 'Sonia'. Of course, none of these created anywhere near the sensations caused by 'American Beauty' and 'General Jacqueminot' (see entries).

Rose fanciers who wish to grow greenhouse florist flowers in their gardens should be prepared for disappointment. A couple of examples will illustrate the problem. In 1990, a new yellow greenhouse rose called 'Frisco' was introduced, with the promise that it would hold its flower shape for almost a month. But unless you live in an area of almost continual sunshine, you will experience great disappointment if you try to grow it under garden conditions. Seventy-five years ago, one of the great indoor roses in America was a variety called 'Jonkheer J.L. Mock', which, according to Jean Henri Nicolas (see entry), had a great vogue in America as a cut flower before escaping into the garden. But Nicolas never met anyone who could grow the rose to perfection outdoors. He pointed out that one American catalog described it as "a massive rose of massive substance, noted for its great size, doubleness and strong coloring. It is likely to ball in all but the most favorable weather and the midsummer bloom is rather shy. Nevertheless it is a marvelous rose in some gardens."

"That description," wrote Nicolas, "reminds me of the answer given to a stranger inquiring about a young man of the town: 'He is a very fine fellow when sober but nobody ever saw him sober.'" J. Horace McFarland (see entry) used much the same description when he said it was a rose of "great distinction when and where it finds itself agreeably placed." That is the sort of advice that all people who want a greenhouse variety in their garden should heed.

The French-bred 'Sonia' has provided some success for gardeners, making an impact in gardens in warmer and sunnier parts of the United States with its long, elegant, satiny-pink blooms. Grown as a grandiflora, it can be cultivated outdoors and has been a big winner for show exhibitors. ◻

FOSSIL BEDS

FOSSIL BEDS SHOWING FOLIAGE OF THE ROSE have been discovered from Oregon to Montana and Colorado, proof that roses bloomed on this continent as long as 38 million years ago. Fossil beds such as those at Florissant, Colorado, formed when volcanic eruptions buried animals and plants in layers of fine-grained ash that hardened into shale. Erosion has revealed detailed impressions of the trapped insects and foliage. The Ruby Range of southern Montana is another area in which rose foliage has been found among fossil imprints. ◻

FRAGRANCE

Why do roses smell? The answer is part science, part poetry.

NO ONE EVER HOLDS A BLOOM OF THE ROSE without sniffing it. That moment when the soft, sweet perfume, even of the gentlest kind, fills the nostrils is the moment you know the rose has a special extra dimension, one that reaches into the very soul. It brings with it moments of romance, poetry, memory, and sweetness not presented as generously by any other flower.

Why do roses smell? They smell, says the poetry in me, that we might love. In her book *To Everything There Is a Season* (1973), Boston garden writer and broadcaster Thalassa Cruso wrote, "For many people the scent of certain plants can revive memories with a vividness that can be extraordinarily evocative, bringing back pictures as sharp as photographs of scenes that have left the conscious mind." People with a scientific interest will tell us that fragrance is merely a question of gland secretions, having to do with pheromones, fatty acids, releaser odors, and even a volatile sex attractant called seducin. When we smell a rose, I was told by a doctor who is a nose specialist, tiny bits of the rose—actually molecules of vapor—land on the cilia in our noses and send an electrical signal to the brain.

The more fragrant a rose, the more perfume

emitters there are on the surface of the petals. And the petals with the most emitters damage the most easily, which may help explain why cut roses in florist shops are frequently low in scent. Florists need tough-petaled roses to stand the strain of travel and handling.

Edith M. Updike of Medford, Oregon, wrote in the American Rose Society magazine that "the nature of perfume in roses is capricious. . . . In the same species and even on the same bush there are not found two roses absolutely identical in scent." In his book *Look to the Rose,* Sam McGredy wrote: "No two people get the same fragrance from a rose."

Why, nearly everyone asks, do modern roses not smell as sweet as roses used to? But the truth is that they do. More fragrant varieties are being bred today than at any time in the history of the rose. The answer to this question lies in the nature of memory.

Our memories often tell us that school days were the best days of our lives, that it never rained in summer, and that Granny's garden was always a haven of the sweetest-smelling roses. Louise Beebe Wilder, a gardening writer from the 1920s, knew this feeling well: "The gardens of my youth were fragrant gardens and it is their sweetness rather than their pat-terns or their furnishings that I now most clearly recall."

Old roses seem to have built up their own special wonders of scent. But then there is definitely no other rose in the world with the same perfume as 'Fragrant Cloud'—and it is certainly a modern variety. Other modern roses have gathered the various fragrances of the whole rose world together and seem to flood their blossoms with them (often hiding them, however, except for certain moments when the weather is right and the nose is clear).

It is frequently said that old roses are more fragrant than those offered in modern catalogs. This is true—to the extent that some modern varieties may be without a scent, but will most likely be cast aside in future years. As we go through the generations of roses of the twentieth century, we will find that the fragrant roses—like 'Fragrant Cloud', 'Double Delight', 'Sutter's Gold', and 'Mister Lincoln'—will remain.

We will forgive them any small inadequacies in return for their lovely fragrance. They have the style and class and perfume that earn them a place in the memory, where beauty always remains. □

GARBO, GRETA

Photographer cecil beaton, obsessed for many years by thoughts of film star Greta Garbo, finally met her in 1932, at a party. As they were looking at a vase of yellow roses, Garbo said, "A rose that lives and dies and never again returns." Then she picked a bloom from the vase, kissed and caressed it, then raised it above her head. Beaton got the rose from her and kept it pressed in his diary before having it framed. After Beaton's death, the rose was auctioned at Christie's for £750 (about $1,700 U.S.). □

GARDENS

Canada and the United States are rich in beautiful gardens open to the public.

––––––––––––– *Canada* –––––––––––––

Alberta
Calgary: Botanical Gardens
Calgary Devonian Gardens

British Columbia
Namaino: Rose Gardens
Vancouver: Elizabeth Park
Vancouver: University of British Columbia
   Gardens
Vancouver: Van Dusen Gardens
Victoria: The Fable Cottage Garden
Victoria: Butchart Gardens

Nova Scotia
Annapolis: Royal Antique Rose Garden
Halifax: Public Gardens

Newfoundland
St. John's: S.J. Memorial University Botanical
   (Native roses)

Ontario
Hamilton: Royal Botanical Gardens
Niagara Falls: Botanical Gardens
Niagara Falls: School of Horticulture
Ottawa: Dominion Arboretum
Sudbuty: Laurentian University Gardens
Thunder Bay: Lakehead University Gardens
Toronto: Edwards Gardens (Civic Center
   garden)
Toronto: Humber Arboretum
Whitby: Cullen Gardens
Windsor: Jackson Park

Prince Edward Island
Charlottetown: Gardens

Quebec
Montreal: Grand Metis
Montreal: Botanical Gardens
Quebec: Laval University
Ste-Anne-de-Bellevue: Morgan Arboretum

Saskatchewan
Indian Head

————— *United States* —————

Alabama

Birmingham: Botanical Gardens
Fairhope: City Rose Garden
Mobile: David A. Hemphill Park of Roses
  and Mobile Public Gardens
Mobile: Battleship Memorial Park
Theodore: Bellingrath Rose Garden

Arizona

Glendale: Sahauaro Historical Ranch Rose
  Garden
Glendale: Dr. Field's office at 4491 West
  Northern Avenue
Green Valley: Rose Society Garden (Social
  Center)
Mesa: Pioneer Rose Garden
Phoenix: Valley Garden Centre
Sun City: Sun Bowl Rose Garden
Tucson: Gene C. Reid Park

Arkansas

Little Rock: State Capitol Rose Garden

California

Arcadia: Los Angeles State and County
  Arboretum
Beverly Hills: Virginia Robinson Gardens
Carlsbad: McGee Park (Coastal Rose Society)
Citrus Heights: Fountain Square Rose Garden
Corona Del Mar: Roger's Gardens
Corona Del Mar: Sherman Library and
  Gardens
Delano: Bella Rosa Winery
Encinitas: Quail Botanical Garden
La Canada: Descanso Gardens
Long Beach: Los Cerritos Rancho Old Rose
  Garden
Los Angeles: Exposition Park Garden

Malibu: J. Paul Getty Museum
Oakland: Morcom Amphitheatre of Roses
Palos Verdes Peninsula: South Coast Botanic
  Garden
Pasadena: Rose Bowl Garden
Pasadena: Tournament of Roses Wrigley
  Garden
Riverside: Fairmount Park Rose Garden
Riverside: Botanic Rose Garden (University
  of California)
Riverside: White Park
Sacramento: McKinley Park Rose Garden
Sacramento: Capitol Park Rose Garden
San Diego: Inez Curant Park Rose Garden
San Diego: Casa de las Companas
San Fernando: Sepulveda Garden Center
San Fernando: Homestead Acre (Los Angeles
  County Park)
San Fernando: Orcutt Ranch
San Francisco: Golden Gate Park Rose
  Garden
San Jose: Municipal Rose Garden and Old
  Rose Garden
San Marino: Huntington Botanical Gardens
San Simeon: Hearst San Simeon State
  Historical Monument
Santa Barbara: A.S. Postel Memorial Rose
  Garden
Wasco: Community Garden
Westminster: Civic Center Rose Garden
Whittier: Pageant of Roses Garden
Whittier: Rose Hills
Woodside: Filoli House and Center

Colorado

Denver: Botanical Garden
Durango: Four Corners Rose Gardens
Littleton: War Memorial Rose Garden
Longmont: Memorial Rose Garden

Connecticut
Hartford: Elizabeth Park Rose Garden
Norwich: Norwich Memorial Rose Garden

Delaware
Wilmington: Hagley Museum and Library

Florida
Cypress Gardens: Florida Cypress Gardens
Lake Buena Vista: The Walt Disney World
  Rose Garden
Largo: Sturgeon Memorial Rose Garden
Okeechobee: Giles Rose Nursery

Georgia
Athens: Elizabeth Bradley Turner Memorial
  Rose Garden
Atlanta: Atlanta Botanic Gardens
Thomasville: Rose Test Garden

Hawaii
Honolulu: University of Hawaii

Idaho
Boise: Julia Davis Memorial Rose Garden

Illinois
Alton: The Nan Eliot Memorial Rose Garden
Chicago: Marquette Park
Evanston: Merrick Park Rose Gardens
Glencoe: The Bruce Krasberg Garden
Highland Park: Park District of Highland
  Park
Libertyville: Lynn J. Arthur Rose Garden
Lisle: Morton Arboretum
Peoria: George L. Luthy Memorial Botanic
  Garden
Rockford: Rockford Park District

Springfield: Washington Park Rose Garden
Wheaton: Cantigny Gardens

Indiana
Fort Wayne: Lakeside Rose Garden
Richmond: Richmond Rose Garden

Iowa
Ames: Iowa State University Horticultural
  Gardens
Bettendorf: Bettendorf Park Board Municipal
  Rose Garden
Cedar Rapids: Noelridge Park Rose Garden
Clinton: Bickelhaupt Arboretum
Davenport: Vander Veer Park Municipal Rose
  Garden
Des Moines: Greenwood Park Rose Garden
Dubuque: Arboretum and Botanical Gardens
Muscatine: Weed Park Memorial Garden
State Center: Public Rose Garden

Kansas
Topeka: E.F.A. Reinisch Rose Garden
Topeka: Lake Shawnee Rose Gardens

Kentucky
Louisville: Kentucky Memorial Rose Gardens

Louisiana
Baton Rouge: Louisiana State University
  Rose Variety Test Garden
Baton Rouge: Independence Park Rose
  Garden
Delcambre: Jefferson Island Gardens
Jennings: Interstate-10 Park Rose Garden
Lafayette: University of Southwestern
  Louisiana Rose Gardens
Lake Charles: Tourist Center Garden
Many: Hodges Garden

New Orleans: Longue Vue
New Orleans: Botanical Gardens
Shreveport: American Rose Centre
Shreveport: Centenary Rose Garden

Maine
Portland: City of Portland Rose Circle

Maryland
Annapolis: William Paca Rose Garden
Baltimore: Maryland Rose Society Heritage
   Rose Garden
Monkton: Ladew Topiary Gardens
Wheaton: Brookside Botanic Gardens Rose
   Garden

Massachusetts
Boston: The James P. Kelleher Rose Garden
Jamaica Plain: Arnold Arboretum of Harvard
   University
Stockbridge: Berkshire Garden Center
Westfield: The Stanley Park

Michigan
Ann Arbor: Matthaei Botanic Gardens
Bloomfield Hills: Cranbrook Gardens
Detroit: Anna Scripps Whitcomb
   Conservatory
East Lansing: Michigan State University
   Demonstration Gardens
Lansing: Frances Park Memorial Rose Garden
Niles: Fernwood Botanic Gardens

Minnesota
Chanhassen: Minnesota Landscape
   Arboretum
Minneapolis: Lyndale Park Municipal Garden
St. Paul: Como Park Conservatory

Mississippi
Biloxi: Beauvoir (one-time home of Jefferson
   Davis)
Gulfport: Grass Lawn Rose Garden
Hattiesburg: University of Southern
   Mississippi Rose Gardens
Natchez: Stanton Hall
Starkville: Mississippi State University Rose
   Research Garden

Missouri
Cape Girardeau: Rose Display Garden
Kansas City: Laura Conyers Smith Municipal
   Rose Garden
St. Louis: Gladney & Lehmann Rose Garden

Montana
Missoula: Memorial Rose Garden

Nebraska
Boys Town: AARS Constitution Rose Garden
Lincoln: Municipal Rose Garden
Omaha: Hanscom Park Greenhouse
Omaha: Memorial Park Rose Garden

Nevada
Reno: Municipal Rose Garden

New Hampshire
North Hampton: Fuller Gardens Rose
   Gardens

New Jersey
East Millstone: Rudolph W. van der Goot
   Rose Garden
Lincoln: Lambertus C. Bobbink Memorial
   Park
Morristown: Freylinghuysen Arboretum

Summit: Reeves-Reed Arboretum
Tenafly: The Jack D. Lissermore Rose Garden

New Mexico
Albuquerque: Prospect Park Rose Garden

New York
Bronx: The Peggy Rockefeller Rose Garden
Brooklyn: The Cranford Rose Garden
  (Brooklyn Botanic Garden)
Buffalo: Joan Fuzak Memorial Rose Garden
Canadaigua: Sonneberg Gardens Rose
  Garden
Flushing: Queens Botanical Gardens
Fort Tryon Park: The Cloisters
New York City: United Nations Rose Garden
Old Westbury: Rose Gardens
Rochester: Maplewood Rose Garden
Schenectady: Central Park Rose Garden
Syracuse: E.M. Mills Memorial Rose Garden

North Carolina
Asheville: Biltmore Estate
Chapel Hill: The Gene Strowd Community
  Rose Garden
Clemmons: Tanglewood Park Rose Garden
Fayetteville: Fayetteville Rose Garden
Raleigh: Raleigh Municipal Rose Garden
Winston-Salem: Reynolds Rose Garden of
  Wake Forest University

North Dakota
Dunseith: International Peace Garden

Ohio
Akron: Stan Hywet Hall and Gardens
Bay Village: Cahoon Memorial Rose Garden
Cleveland: Mary Anne Sears Sweetland Rose

Garden (at the Garden Center of Greater
  Cleveland)
Columbus: Park of Roses
Mansfield: Charles E. Nail Memorial Rose
  Garden (at Kingwood Center)
Westerville: Inniswood Metro Gardens
Wooster: Secreast Arboretum (Ohio State
  University)

Oklahoma
Muskogee: J.E. Conrad Municipal Rose
  Garden
Oklahoma City: Charles E. Sparks Rose
  Garden
Tulsa: Municipal Rose Garden

Oregon
Coos Bay: Shoreacres Botanical
  Gardens/State Park
Corvallis: Avery Park Rose Garden
Eugene: George E. Owen Memorial
  Rose Garden
Grants Pass: Victor Boehl Memorial
  Rose Garden
Hillsboro: Harold Eastman Memorial
  Rose Garden
Jacksonville: Old Rose Garden in a
  churchyard
Medford: Home of commercial growers
  Jackson & Perkins
Medford: Hawthorne Park
• Portland: International Rose Garden
Salem: Public Rose Garden on the grounds of
  the capitol

Pennsylvania
Allentown: Malcolm W. Gross Memorial
  Rose Garden

Hershey: Hershey Gardens
Kennett Square: Longwood Gardens
Philadelphia: Marion Rivanus Rose Garden
 (Morris Arboretum)
West Grove: Robert Pyle Memorial Gardens

Rhode Island
Bristol: Blithwold Gardens and Arboretum
Newport: Rosecliff

South Carolina
Orangeburg: Edisto Memorial Gardens

South Dakota
Rapid City: Memorial Rose Gardens

Tennessee
Chattanooga: Warner Park Rose Gardens
Memphis: Municipal Rose Garden
Nashville: Cheekwood Botanical Gardens

Texas
Austin: Mabel Davis Rose Garden
Dallas: Arboretum and Botanical Gardens
Dallas: Samuell-Grand Municipal Rose
 Garden
El Paso: Municipal Rose Garden
Fort Worth: Botanic Gardens
Houston: Municipal Rose Garden
Tyler: Municipal Rose Garden
Victoria: Rose Garden

Utah
Farmington: Utah State University/Utah
 Botanical Garden
Fillmore: Territorial Statehouse State Park
 Rose Garden

Nephi: Federated Women's Club Memorial
 Rose Garden
Salt Lake City: Municipal Rose Garden

Vermont
Brandon: Edgeview Antique Rose Garden

Virginia
Alexandria: River Farm
Arlington: Bon Air Memorial Rose Garden
Lynchburg: Confederate Cemetery
Mount Vernon: Woodlawn Plantation
Norfolk: Botanical Garden Bicentennial
 Rose Garden

Washington
Bellingham: Fairhaven Rose Garden
Bellingham: Cornwall Park Rose Garden
Chehalis: Municipal Rose Garden
Hoquiam: Ross Memorial Rose Garden
Kennewick: Lawrence Scott Park Rose
 Garden
Longview: Public Library Rose Garden
Olympia: Centennial Rose Garden
Seattle: Carl S. English Jr. Botanical Garden
Seattle: Woodland Park Rose Garden
Spokane: Manito Gardens (Rose Hill)
Tacoma: Point Defiance Rose Garden
Tumwater: Centennial Rose Garden (1989)
Walla Walla: Pioneer Park

West Virginia
Huntington: Ritter Park Rose Garden

Wisconsin
Hales Corners: Boerner Botanical Gardens
Madison: Longenecker Gardens of the
 University of Wisconsin Arboretum

Madison: Oldbrich Botanical Gardens
Milwaukee: Alfred Boerner Botanical Garden
  (Whitnall Park)
Oshkosh: Paine Art Center and Arboretum
Waukesha: Frame Park
Wild Rose: Community Historical Rose
  Garden

Washington, D.C.
George Washington University
United States Botanic Garden
Dumbarton Oaks □

'GENERAL JACQUEMINOT'

'General Jack' is what everyone seems to call this
rose, which was a great favorite in the old gardens of
America.

'GENERAL JACQUEMINOT' IS A ROSE FRE-
quently found by those who search out
historic roses in old homesteads and graveyards. Like many roses of the late 1800s, there
are different versions—some only slightly
different in the color of the prickles, some
with a slightly different petal color. No one
can put their finger precisely on the true rose.
Any rose that receives the nod of an expert
who says "that is General Jack, I suppose" is
regarded as good enough to carry the name.
Writer Ethelyn Emery Keays (see entry) had
various versions of the rose. Asked by friends
if she had the really true old 'General Jacqueminot', she replied, "Probably." Even the
people at gardens as respected as the Brooklyn
Botanic Gardens expressed doubts that the
rose they have in their collection of hybrid
perpetuals is the "real" 'General Jack'.

'General Jack' (or a rose very like it) bears
red, intensely fragrant blooms on a vigorous
but not too tall bush (though it can reach six
feet). The bush falls easy prey to mildew, but
even that fault did not stop the gardeners of
America from planting it by the thousands. It
was called a free and responsive garden rose
that bloomed in great splendor for six weeks
in spring and early summer. Florists added it
to their lists and it held a very high place—
once selling for $18 a bloom in New York—
until the arrival of 'American Beauty'. Rosarian
Georgia Torrey Drennan wrote in 1912 that
the "intense glow and radiance of the rich
crimson-lake roses of velvety substance would
give it distinction among the roses of
Kashmere or the blooms of Damascus."

'General Jack' is also famous for its role in
hybridizing. A survey by the Iowa Experimental Station in Ames, Iowa, by Clark D. Paris
and T. J. Maney in 1941 showed that there
were 468 direct-line seedlings and 62 sports
from the rose.

Legend says that the real-life general, who
was one of Napoleon's favorite officers, had a
daughter, Marguerite, whom he loved dearly.
One day the general found his daughter with a
young officer on a seat in the general's garden,
their arms around each other. He stabbed the
boy to death, and his daughter later died of a
broken heart. In the arbor where the lovers
had been seated under a large pink rose bush,
there appeared a short time afterward a stem,
deep red and quite different from the original
rose. The gardener wanted to cut it out but the
general, brokenhearted at the death of his
daughter, told him to leave it. "A flower of
God," he called it. And that, says the legend, is

how the red rose called 'General Jacqueminot' was born—from the blood of a young lover's heart. □

GLOSSARY OF ROSE TERMS

ERE IS A BRIEF LIST OF SOME ROSE TERMS, aimed at those who don't want to be left out of the conversation when rose lovers get together.

Anther: the part of the flower that produces pollen, found at the upper section of the stamen.

Axil: the angle between the upper surface of the leaf stalk and the stem.

Bareroot: roses dug from commercial fields, usually from late fall to early spring. They have been budded onto wild stock and have spent eighteen months growing before they reach the customer.

Basal break: a new cane coming from the bud union or from a bud at the very base of an old cane.

Blind shoot: a mature stem that fails to carry a bloom, often because of frosting.

Bloom: the flower after it passes the bud stage and is open or about to open.

Bud: a small, unopened bloom; a growth bud (or eye) that is found in the axil of a leaf stalk.

Bud union: the line where the roots meet the top growth. The roots in this case will be the wild stock; the top growth is provided by the new rose. Often called the knuckle.

Budding: the method by which most roses are now produced. A bud (the one found in the axil of the leaf stalk) is taken from a rose and inserted into a T-shaped cut in the understock, which itself is a hardy wild or species rose.

Cane: a main stem on a rose plant.

Canker: a disease that causes purplish spots on canes, usually causing the death of the cane.

Chlorsis: yellowing of the normal green growth, usually caused by a lack of iron.

Cluster: a group of blooms connected by their footstalks on one stem; a term often used with floribundas but seen in many other types of roses. Also known as a truss.

Cross: the term applied to the offspring of cross-pollination.

Cultivar: another word for rose variety; not a commonly used term.

Cutting: a piece of stem cut for the purpose of propagation.

Dying back: the dying of a cane or shoot from the tip downward, usually caused by frost or incorrect pruning.

Earthing up: drawing up soil around the base of a bush as winter protection.

Eye: the center of a bloom, often a slightly different color from the rest of the petals; also see *bud.*

Fertilization: the placing of pollen on the stigma to induce production of seeds.

Foliar feed: a fertilizer capable of being sprayed on and being absorbed by the foliage.

Guard petals: the outermost ring of petals; they are tougher than the other petals and can keep some insects from entering into the bloom.

Hardy: term to describe a plant that can

withstand winter in a particular area without protection.

Heel in: to place plants temporarily in the garden before permanent planting.

Hip (or hep): the seed pod of the rose.

Hybrid: a rose whose parents are genetically distinct (the parent plants are different varieties).

Infloresence: the arrangement of flowers on a stem, particularly important in the showing of floribundas.

Maiden: a rose bush in its first year after budding.

Node: the part of the stem where a leaf or bud is attached.

Own root: a rose grown on its own root, not budded. Most miniatures and many old roses are sold this way.

Ovule: the part of the female organ of the bloom that becomes a seed after fertilization.

Pollen: the yellow dustlike material, produced by the anthers, that is used to fertilize the ovule.

Pollination: the placing of the pollen on the stigma of the flower.

Root stock: a wild rose, rooted from a cutting or grown directly from seed, onto which a hybrid rose is budded.

Rosaceae: the family to which the rose belongs; it includes other plants with roselike flowers, such as apple, cherry, plum, hawthorn, strawberry, and many more.

Shoot: a stem or cane, though generally referring to young growth; a stem refers to more mature growth.

Single rose: a bloom with five to twelve petals.

Sport: a mutation or a change in the habit of a plant or, more generally, in the color of the bloom.

Stamen: the male organ of the flower; it consists of the anthers and filament (the supporting leg or column).

Stigma: the part of the female organ that catches pollen. □

'GRACE de MONACO'

"The most wonderful of all my wedding presents" was how Princess Grace of Monaco described the soft, light pink hybrid tea named in her honor in 1956 by Meilland Roses of France. A second rose, Princesse de Monaco, was launched by the same firm in 1981 at the first International Rose Show in Monaco. Grace had chosen the rose because it was nearest in color to the Monaco flag, a rouge and cream. It is registered as a pink blend and is more widely available now than the original rose named for her. Since her death in a car accident in 1982, blooms from these roses have been placed regularly on her crypt in the Cathedral of Monaco. □

GREEN ROSE

Every age of the rose produces its own curiosities, but none so extraordinary as the Green Rose.

There have been many green roses — from 'Green Ice' to 'Peppermint Ice' — but the Green Rose is nothing like a normal rose. In fact, there are people who will not accept that it is a rose at all.

What makes it different is that instead of the blooms being made up of normal petals, they open with leaves just like foliage. Botanically it is called *Rosa chinensis viridflora.* But because of its irregularity, it has been called—even in *Modern Roses,* the official stud book for all roses—monstrous.

Digging into the history of the rose, Lee Jeremais of Newberry, South Carolina, found that the Green Rose was brought from Charleston to the great English rose figure Thomas Rivers in 1837, and from there it was widely distributed. Jeremais found a letter to *Gardener's Chronicle* in England in the mid-1800s from Robert Buist of Rosedale Nurseries, Philadelphia, saying: "There appears to be some uncertainty in regard to the origin of this rose. It is a sport from *Rosa indica* (the China Rose of England and the Daily Rose of America). It was found in Charleston, South Carolina, about 1833 and came to Baltimore through Mr. R. Halliday from whom I obtained it, and presented two plants to my old friend Thomas Rivers in 1837." Nurseryman Buist listed the Green Rose as one that blooms the whole season.

While the Green Rose may be called a monstrosity by some, it is a member of the rose family to be cherished as any other rose. I enjoy growing it. The summer "blooms" take on a reddish hue that distinguishes it anywhere in the garden, and its well-greened real foliage is very good, too. American growers recognized its potential in the 1800s and saw that it was a thing of a certain beauty. And still today, whenever it is shown, it excites interest. In a letter to the American Rose Society in 1992, Angel Ibanez of Waianae, Hawaii, said the flower is used in the Hawaiian headband lei. □

GROUND-COVER ROSES

The modern ground-cover rose fits any sort of landscape.

THE FIRST GROUND-COVER ROSE WAS ONE called 'Max Graf'. It was spotted by J. Horace McFarland (see entry) when he visited the garden of W. C. Egan at Highland Park, Chicago. Wrote McFarland: "It was a mass of splendid single pink flowers amid glossy green leaves that were in themselves highly decorative." McFarland believed that 'Max Graf' had come from James H. Bowditch of Connecticut in 1919 and that it combined either *Rosa rugosa* or *Rosa wichuraiana*—or perhaps both—with *Rosa setigera.* McFarland, using the words ground cover, said, "I have seen no similar rose quite so persistently beautiful and dependable."

Notable detective work in recent years now suggests that 'Max Graf' was originally a rose called 'Lady Duncan', which was raised by Jackson Dawson of the Arnold Arboretum (see entry) and introduced by the arboretum in 1900. The rose then traveled to Germany, where Wilhelm Kordes raised a new race of roses from it. Today it is found in the background of most modern ground-cover roses. Jackson Dawson was not the only one producing this type of rose. So, too, were the Brownells, at their Rhode Island Research gardens. Among their ground-cover roses, now sadly missing from commerce, were 'Coral Creeper', 'Little Compton Creeper', 'Frederick S. Peck', 'Carpet of Gold', and 'Creeping Everbloom'.

Changes came in the concept of ground-cover roses via the help of a little rose called

'Temple Bells', bred in California by Dennison Morey (see entry). It excited top breeder Sam McGredy, and he produced the dwarf white 'Snow Carpet', which gave tiny flowers in masses and foliage with few thorns. It was a carpet, tough enough to take people walking over it, and the start of the modern ground-cover rose with a flower that fits in with any kind of landscape. In recent years, European rose breeders have searched intensely for the perfect ground-cover rose. While they have produced many interesting varieties, they have not yet been able to win over the hearts of the rose lovers of America. □

HAIRY ROSE

See Rosa stellata.

HARDINESS

Rose breeders are always looking for ways to improve the hardiness of roses against the extremes of weather.

ROSES GLORY IN SUNSHINE, BUT NOT ALL CAN take the tough winter conditions in parts of America. To be hardy means a plant is tough. Subzero temperatures are a fact of life in some areas where there are people who love roses and want to grow them. To save roses from the elements, growers in these areas often resort to covering the bushes with artificial boxes or mounding a cover of soil or leaves over them.

Hardiness has always been a factor among rose hybridizers. Unfortunately, someone breeding roses in a mild climate, such as that in Southern California, has to wait a long time before word gets back about the ability of a rose to stand up to low temperatures. The same goes for rose imports. Most French and British roses have not been tested in conditions as severe as they are likely to face in parts of Canada and the United States. The result is often disappointment when new roses fall victim to cold or drought before they get a chance to perform as they do under better conditions.

Walter Van Fleet, Michael H. Walsh, Captain George C. Thomas, Jr. (see entries), and other rose breeders hunted for hardiness in their seedlings. Connecticut rose grower James Bowditch deserves thanks for spreading the word about the rose 'Max Graf', a cross between *Rosa rugosa, Rosa wichuraiana,* and *Rosa setigera* which eventually produced a fertile area for breeders in search of hardy roses.

The Brownells in Rhode Island made hardy roses their main concern. Beginning work in the early part of the twentieth century, the Brownells sought to create roses with resistance to subzero temperatures and immunity from fungus infections. In half a century of hybridizing, they made significant progress toward bushes that would resist subzero weather. In more recent times, the work of Griffith Buck, William Radner in Milwaukee, Robert E. Bayse in Texas, and Jerry Twomey in San Diego produced a number of hardy, disease-resistant varieties. Climbing roses produced with *Rosa wichuraiana* (see entry) have achieved a high degree of hardiness.

A 1991 report on hardiness from the Old Garden Rose Committee of the American Rose Society, under the chairmanship of Bunny Skran, Saginaw, Michigan, found 'Rosa Mundi' to be the real survivor, among old roses, in every sort of weather. Other top old roses were the white damask 'Mme Hardy', followed by 'Charles de Mills', 'Salet', and 'Baronne Prevost'. In European surveys on hardiness, the modern American-bred 'Sutter's

Gold' always gets top marks. Fred Edmunds, Jr., offered an Oregon grower's definition of hardiness when he said, "If a rose is to be called winter hardy then it has to take the chills of winter like a grizzly bear!"

Research on hardiness in roses has received much attention in Canada, where only the toughest species and varieties can survive in many areas. The most popular roses can be grown successfully only in a few parts of British Columbia, southern Ontario, and southern Nova Scotia. Even in these places, heavy winterkill often occurs. Canadian rose breeders such as Frank Skinner of Manitoba, Percy Wright (see entry) in Saskatchewan, and the Alberta hybridizers Robert Simonet and Georges Bugnet set out to improve the roses available to Canadian gardeners. They had success with roses like 'Red Dawn' and 'Suzanne'. 'Therese Bugnet', introduced about 1950, had become by 1975 the most popular hardy rose in the prairie provinces. The lilac pink buds open to lovely fragrant blooms, and it is still a favorite with many American growers.

One part of the hardiness search has been for climbing roses that can survive Canadian conditions. The best of these so far seems to be "Ross Rambler", found in a plantation of pines at the Forestry Nursery Station at Indian Head, Saskatchewan, when Norman Ross was superintendent. Percy Wright, in the 1969 Canadian Rose Annual, reported, "The pines had been grown from seeds from the region of the Himalayan mountains, so it was assumed that a seed of the rose had somehow got into a sample of pine seed." In later years the rambler became a parent to many of the prairie roses produced at Canada's experimental stations.

As far back as 1886, the Canadian government set up a scheme in conjunction with its experimental farms to test for winter-hardy roses. In 1922 they had some success when William Saunders, director of the Central Experimental Farm in Ottawa, released 'Agnes', which was hardy and which also introduced amber yellow, a new color to the rugosa rose range. Rose breeding continued in Ottawa between 1920 and 1940 under the direction of Isabella Preston, who released some twenty varieties of shrub roses, mainly named for Canadian Indian tribes. One of her roses, 'Carmetta', was said to survive winter in subArctic conditions.

Research work was established in Manitoba at Morden Research Station, where Henry Marshall introduced a series called "Parkland" roses, which included 'Assiniboine' (1962), a hybrid of 'Donald Prior' and the native wild species *Rosa arkansana*. 'Assiniboine' is a deep pink semidouble repeat-flowering shrub that became the ancestor of all subsequent roses from Morden. Recent introductions under Morden breeder Lynn Collicutt include 'Winnipeg Parks' and 'Prairie Joy'. These are selected to grow on their own roots and are said to have the ability to produce new wood and flowers even if they are killed back to the ground.

In the 1960s, Felicitas Svejda arrived to take over the post that had been left vacant in the 1940s by the retirement of Isabella Preston. Svejda initiated the "Explorer" roses, beginning with hardy shrublike hybrid rugosa varieties that have earned wide praise, especially for landscaping. These included 'Martin Frobisher', 'Jens Munk', 'Henry Hudson', 'David Thompson', and 'Charles Albanel'. She brought in hardy roses produced by Skinner, Wright, Bugnet, and Simonet, as well as breeding material from Kordes in Germany. These produced significant breaks, especially when Skinner's 'Suzanne' and Simonet's 'Red Dawn' were used. New roses included the very hardy 'William Baffin', which is said to survive being tied to its supports over winter in most regions of southern Canada and is one of the few climbers to survive the frigid winters of the western plains.

Work in Canada is now being continued at L'Assomption Experimental Farm, Quebec, by Ian Ogilvie. One of the first crosses from here was 'Captain Samuel Holland', a medium red climber that is hardy, resistant to chewing insects, and a good producer of flowers. Ogilvie is using earlier roses produced in the programs and is aiming at a breakthrough in disease resistance.

Work by Canadian breeders has had a major impact on rose growing in most of the colder regions of the world. Ogilvie points out that "there are large areas where it is impractical to grow most of the currently available commercial cultivars due to the cost of providing winter protection." He feels that "new self-rooted repeat-blooming hardy roses will provide material which can be used as landscape plants in many places where roses would not otherwise be considered." □

'HARISON'S YELLOW'

If ever there is a Hall of Fame for great American roses, 'Harison's Yellow' is assured of a place.

'HARISON'S YELLOW' IS THE TRUE ALL-American rose. It belongs not to the rose garden, but to the vastness of America. It is nothing more than a small, wild-looking yellow flower, but it grows on a large bush, six to eight feet high, that makes a huge mass after some years. The phrase "mighty like a rose" could have been inspired by 'Harison's Yellow'. It is probably the most traveled rose in the country's history, vigorous, healthy, and still widely grown.

'Harison's Yellow' is regarded as one of the first artificially hybridized roses in America, although this point continues to be argued, with skeptics claiming that pollination was still being done only by nature when this rose entered the world. There will always be a hint of mystery about the rose and how it was born. But the credit for being its originator goes to a New Yorker, George Folliott Harison. Research published in the 1943 *American Rose Annual* by New Yorker Richardson Wright provided answers to many questions about Harison. He was not a minister, though the first edition of *Modern Roses* had so described him. Descended from an English family, Harison was admitted to law as an attorney of the Supreme Court of Judicature in 1798 and as a solicitor in 1817. He was a bachelor, not very robust, not overly involved in the law business, who enjoyed gardening. He lived in the country around what is now 43rd Street in New York City.

Family history says Harison produced this beautifully scented rose while he worked in his father's garden. It is suggested that when the family home was to be sold, he gave the rose to local nurseryman Thomas Hogg for propagation. For a time it was called Hogg's Yellow American Rose, but that name was dropped after a few years. The parentage of the rose was never recorded, but experts believe it to be a cross of two immigrant roses—probably *Rosa foetida persiana* and *Rosa spinosissima*.

'Harison's Yellow' is truly an enduring shrub, marking the trails of pioneers right across the United States from east to west and north to south. Clair Martin, curator of the Rose Garden at the Huntington Botanical Gardens in San Marino, California, tells one story that in its own way authenticates the rambling ability of 'Harison's Yellow', which came to the gardens with a well-documented history from a Los Angeles family. Notes on the accession card read, in part:

> The roots of this particular yellow Quaker rose are known to have been kept alive from generation to generation at least since 1809. . . . The first mention of the rose is from the George Hinshaw family genealogy sources in Warren County, Tennessee, where it may have been transplanted from their home in the Quaker settlement of North Carolina. The rose must have been regarded with special affection or the roots would not have been carefully carried by ox-cart by Polly Ann Hinshaw to their new home in Cheyne's Grove, McLean County, Illinois. It remained there through three generations. In 1913 the rose was again transplanted when Hattie Knight Harris took it to the plains of Brown County, South Dakota.

'Harison's Yellow' is found wherever pioneer mothers stopped along the trails of the nation.

A poignant story of pioneers and the rose is told in a 1943 essay in the *Oregon Historical Quarterly* by Mary Patricia Rawe. The essay began:

> The house is gone. A pile of rocks marks the spot where the fireplace stood. The log walls have crumbled into decay, but the yellow rose bush that stood by the door still blooms as gaily as it did that bright May day 100 years ago when, wrapped in a piece of old comforter, it started on a 2,000-mile journey over the Oregon Trail.

There are many stories in history that echo this one. Here was a rose that had a place among the most valuable items brought on wagon trains. All that had to be done to make it grow was to take a small cutting and place it in the ground. It was planted widely and grew as a marker of the way a wagon train had passed. Writing in the American Rose Society magazine, Edith C. Schurr recorded having found traces of it in every state west of the Mississippi and in most states east of it. "The Oregon trail is marked today," she wrote, "by naturalized clumps of 'Harison's Yellow' left around abandoned ranches, in ghost towns, and on farms."

'Harison's Yellow' is a part of the history of many states. At one time it was regarded as the Yellow Rose of Texas. A New Mexico history notes, "The roses came too—all the way from Pennsylvania in covered wagon. The roses were yellow." One woman wrote of her grandmother taking the rose with her when she moved as a bride, and how she and the other children ate the yellow petals, calling them "sweet butter." A resident of Nebraska related: "I have a yellow rose that was brought here in 1871 by my grandmother and when she died a slip was placed on her grave. It still grows there." A letter from a homesick traveler in Lincoln, Nebraska, read: "I feel better—much better. My little yellow rose started to bloom yesterday. Hallelujah!"

Hallelujah, indeed. The great little 'Harison's Yellow' did more to break the loneliness and the despair of early settlers than any other plant or flower. □

HAWAII

Roses like the sun and rain of the Aloha State.

FLOWERS ARE A PART OF EVERYDAY LIFE IN Hawaii. You expect orchids and other exotics—but roses? Yes, indeed, roses. Hawaii has a small but thriving interest in roses. The latest rose society to become affiliated with the American Rose Society was that of the town of Hilo, in 1992. There is a University of Hawaii rose and research garden and a rose called 'Hawaii' (an orange-red hybrid tea), introduced by Gene Boerner (see entry) in 1960.

With no shortage of rain and no shortage of sun, most roses do well in Hawaii, especially sun lovers like 'Double Delight'. But the other side of the coin is that there is no dormant season to allow bushes to rest and store up nutrients for the next season. The result is that bushes have to be constantly fed, but even then they may well deteriorate after a few years. Hawaii has some bugs that you don't get elsewhere, and there are other terrors like hurricanes that don't do roses (or people) any good. Even paradise has problems. □

'HELEN TRAUBEL'

A lovely rose was named for a great singer.

HERBERT C. SWIM (SEE ENTRY) BRED THIS beautiful apricot hybrid tea and saw it win the All-America Rose Selection award and the Rome Gold Medal, but no one could offer a suitable name for it. Then Awdry Armstrong, head of Armstrong's rose firm (see entry), decided to break the rules.

"In naming this rose," Herb Swim wrote, "Awdry Armstrong broke his own rule for the third time. The rule was that new varieties should not be named after living people. The naming of 'Charlotte Armstrong' and 'Mirandy' had already violated this rule. This one was named 'Helen Traubel' after the most famous female opera singer of the day. She was a neighbor of Awdry Armstrong's at the beach where she rented a house next door to his."

When Traubel was invited to sing in Japan in 1952, Awdry Armstrong shipped enough bushes there for a bed to be planted. A few

months later, when the singer arrived, the bed was in full bloom. The chief artist of the Noritake earthenware factory painted the rose, with Traubel's autograph superimposed. Five plates were made with the painting on them, and they were given to the singer, the artist, Awdry Armstrong, Raymond C. Allen (then executive director of the American Rose Society), and Herb Swim. □

HENNESSY, ROY (DIED 1962)

Oregon rose grower Roy Hennessy was noted for his single-mindedness.

THERE WAS NO HALFWAY WHEN IT CAME TO Roy Hennessy; people either loved him or hated him. Even many years after his death, his name brings sparks to a conversation. He seemed to have a constant feud with the American Rose Society and its officers. He told the world that the roses he grew were all prizewinners. He would fill orders as he thought they should be filled and not necessarily as the customer wished. He wrote one book, *Hennessy on Roses,* which he published himself in 1942. He had wanted the book published by the ARS, but the society wouldn't do it without first having it studied in committee, a requirement that annoyed Hennessy.

Hennessy's book does not show any signs of his renowned cussedness, and it is certainly worth having, if you can find a copy. The book begins with a tribute to his wife, which says, in part:

> I wish to thank you on behalf of the readers of this work . . . You took down from dictation floods

of rose information, and having sorted it out, you found it was phrased in such sternly technical language and was so compressed that you yourself could not understand it . . . You therefore pursued the author of this book through fields and over rows of roses, in storage houses and on tractors, in packing house and in garden, crying pathetically: "Roy, please come in this minute and stretch this subject out. Put more words in it, explain it, give examples, talk about it more. It's so frightfully technical I can't make head or tail of it myself." For your laudable feminine persistence and constant nagging I therefore tender my sincere thanks on behalf of myself and the readers of this book. □

'HENRY FORD'

THIS HYBRID TEA ROSE ISSUED IN 1927 caused something of a stir in the world because its name was considered something of a deception. It wasn't named for the car manufacturer but, as J. H. Nicolas wrote, "for a mediocrity somewhere in New Jersey who permitted the use of his name, probably for a consideration." Could it be that there was some sour grapes here — that maybe J&P, for whom Nicolas worked, wished they had thought of using the name! In 1954 another company, Howard and Smith of Montebello, California, did issue a rose for "the real" Henry Ford. This was a silvery-pink hybrid tea. □

'HERBERT HOOVER'

Introduced on the day Hoover was elected President in 1928, this fragrant orange, rose, and gold hybrid tea became famous as a greenhouse rose. In southern states, especially Texas, it could also be grown in gardens, where its large, open, free-flowering blooms were produced in great quantities all season long. It produced a notable sport in 1935 called 'Texas Centennial', which became popular for its vigorous growth, persistent bloom, fine form, and fragrance. Less spectacular was another sport in the same year, the yellow hybrid tea greenhouse variety 'Texas Gold'. 'Herbert Hoover' didn't last in commerce, but 'Texas Centennial' can still be purchased in England, Spain, France, Australia, and, as you would expect, Texas. (The complete name for this variety is 'President Herbert Hoover'.) □

THE HERITAGE ROSE FOUNDATION

Established in 1986, the Heritage Rose Foundation is the first nonprofit corporation devoted exclusively to preservation and study of heritage (antique) roses. Membership is open to anyone who is in sympathy with its purpose. Dues for U.S. members are $10 annually. Write to the Heritage Rose Foundation, 1512 Gorman Street, Raleigh, NC 27606. □

HERITAGE ROSE GROUP

Rosarians with their hearts firmly planted in the old-rose movement banded together to form the Heritage Rose Group.

The Heritage Rose Group began with a small advertisement in the American Rose Society magazine in 1974, placed by Miriam Wilkins of California, who has spent a lifetime encouraging rose lovers as well as writing about old roses, searching for them, and growing a great collection of roses from other ages. Wilkins felt that the American Rose Society was giving insufficient attention to antique roses.

Replies to the advertisement tumbled in, and eventually a small newsletter was produced. Names now internationally famous joined in: Carl Cato, from Virginia (who suggested the group name); the late Edith Schurr, one-time chair of the Old Garden Rose Committee of the American Rose Society; rose writer Lily Shohan; author and illustrator Leonie Bell; Mitzi VanSant, of Texas; and Charles A. Walker, Jr., now president of the Heritage Rose Foundation. Today the Heritage Rose Group is organized nationwide into six regions, some with their own newsletters in addition to the national rose letter. □

HILL, E. GURNEY (1847–1933)

The name of master greenhouse rose grower E. Gurney Hill of Richmond, Indiana, is one you will encounter in almost every book about the rose.

English-born E. Gurney Hill emigrated to the United States with his family when he was four years old. He founded his Indiana nursery in 1881, where initially he introduced only European roses. But when he began hybridizing, with the help of his son, his reputation was made.

Hill traveled the world in search of new roses. At Dickson's Nursery in Northern Ireland, he found 'Liberty', a brilliant red rose, very fragrant. He also found the French rose 'Souvenir de Claudius Pernet'. In England, he found the amazing 'Ophelia', which he saw in the rose field of William Paul. Hill was impressed with this beautiful, long-lasting, long-pointed bud of a medium-sized flower in salmon pink, flushed with lighter shades, growing on an upright plant. He realized 'Ophelia' deserved a chance to be seen by the world.

No one knew 'Ophelia's' pedigree. It was from a pod, said the Paul family, "gathered at hazard in the nursery." In later years there was speculation that parentage of the rose was deliberately concealed to allow the breeder to continue his own strain. But parents or not, Hill knew that even an orphan rose could produce wonders. 'Ophelia' begat a whole race of roses, many of them entering the cut-flower trade. 'Ophelia' sported with amazing indifference to its parenthood, giving the Hill firm the wonderful 'Mme Butterfly'. And the firm bred from it, too, turning up the top greenhouse rose 'Columbia', another rose that sported freely.

Hill had the reputation of being a happy man. J. Horace McFarland (see entry) wrote that the name of E. Gurney Hill would "always be written with a smile. He had that smile, and all who had to do with him felt better because he beamed that smile at fellow flower-lovers." A rose was named for him in his lifetime—'E. G. Hill', a rich, deeply fra-

grant, red hybrid tea. Among the roses he bred was 'Hill's America', a rose-pink hybrid tea. He wanted to name it 'America', but the name had already been given to a rose bred by Massachusetts hybridizer Michael H. Walsh (see entry). (Strangely enough there is today another rose called 'America', a climber bred by William Warriner; see entry.)

Hill also bred a rose, in 1905, called 'General MacArthur', which did well in England. Once on a visit to Kew Gardens in London, Hill saw a particularly good red rose and tried to learn more about it because he wanted to buy it for introduction to America. Imagine his astonishment when he was told that it was 'General MacArthur'. He delighted in telling how he then said that he had originated the rose. Hill, by the way, would never have said that he created the rose. Jean Henri Nicolas (see entry) remembered Hill protesting against use of the word "creation." "God alone creates," Hill said. "Man only assembles and transforms." □

HOLE, THE REVEREND S. REYNOLDS (1821–1904)

The Dean of Rochester Cathedral and "father of the English rose," The Reverend S. Reynolds Hole was one of the world's most influential rosarians.

THE REVEREND S. REYNOLDS HOLE WAS AN eminent clergyman, a writer, and a tireless apostle for roses. He helped organize the first national rose show in England, a huge success, in 1857. He wrote the wonderful anecdotal *A Book About Roses* (1869), which mirrors the rose in Victorian life. Anyone with interest in the history of the rose should read the book, which went into more than twenty printings. He became the first president of the British National Rose Society (later changed to Royal), a position he held until his death twenty-eight years later. "He who would have beautiful Roses in his garden," Hole wrote, "must have beautiful Roses in his heart."

His fame spread quickly to America. A reception and banquet in his honor was held on November 14, 1894, at New York's Savoy Hotel. Among the tributes to him was a rose that carried his name, an American-found sport of 'Mme Caroline Testout'. In 1904, Dickson's Nursery in Northern Ireland produced another rose, the one that is known today as 'Dean Hole'. Another variety, 'S. Reynolds Hole', appears as the frontispiece in the 1880 edition of *A Book About Roses.*

Hole's New York reception was a great success, with a guest list that read like a Who's Who of rose lovers. He later wrote the book *A Little Tour of America,* in which he noted that the most popular varieties of florist roses included 'American Beauty', 'American Belle', 'Bridesmaid', 'La France', 'Catherine Mermet', 'Niphetos', 'Safrano', and 'Kaiserin Auguste Viktoria', many of which are still available today. □

HUNTINGTON BOTANICAL GARDENS SAN MARINO, CALIFORNIA

O NE OF THE GREAT SHOWPIECE GARDENS IN the United States had its beginning in the late 1800s, when Collis P. Huntington moved from New York to share management of the Southern Pacific Railway. On his way to San Francisco, he visited the estate of San Marino (outside Los Angeles), which he later purchased. The Huntington family became an important collector of art, rare books, and manuscripts. In 1919 the family signed a deed to transfer the estate to a nonprofit educational trust. The Huntington today is a haven of libraries, pavilions, galleries, and magnificent gardens. The gardens cover 130 acres of the 207-acre grounds, and include a rose garden that shows the history of the rose over 2,000 years. The modern rose beds are changed frequently, and the gardens host an annual symposium on roses. □

HYBRIDIZING

Anyone can take a try at hybridizing roses simply by following some basic procedures.

H YBRIDIZING IS THE TECHNICAL TERM FOR plant breeding. No one really knows when human hands began moving pollen from rose to rose. The first American hybridization is said to have been carried out by John Champneys (see entry) in 1802. Since then, amateurs and professionals have altered the world of the rose by bringing together all different types to produce hybrids of just about everything. We are in an exciting and ambitious era of hybridizing, and it's open to anyone. Later in this section, I'll explain step by step how you can hybridize a rose.

The list of amateur rose breeders achieving success is growing all the time. First-class roses have been produced by hybridizers such as Joe Winchel, Jerry Twomey, Von Weddle, Frank Benardella, Robert Bayse, Astor Perry, A. J. (Pop) Warner, Tom McMillan, Carl Meyer, Paul Jerabek, Louis Stoddard, Robert

Rosa centifolia made the voyage from the Old World to grace the New and is the rose most likely to evoke memories of grandmother's garden. The name means, literally, "with a hundred leaves," actually, more than can be readily counted.

The wonderfully large and fragrant blooms of Rosa bullata make it the uncontested epitome of the cabbage rose. Blooms are coaxed to even greater-than-usual abundance when the long, arching stems are pegged down.

Found in Charleston, South Carolina, in 1833, the 'Green Rose' is considered monstrous by some because of its high irregularity; others see it as a curiosity and a proper member of the rose family.

Soon after 'Old Blush' was taken from China to Sweden in the mid-1700s, it was seen in America, where its survival in many cemeteries from the 1800s shows that it was a hardy traveler and well-chosen memorial.

John Champneys, a South Carolina rice planter, achieved the distinction of being the first to hybridize a rose in the United States. By crossing two immigrant roses (one of them most probably 'Old Blush'), he produced 'Champneys' Pink Cluster', an instant success.

'Mme Plantier' is an example of the sense of continuity—down through the generations and across the ocean to the New World—that families have long found in rose bushes. One such story is vividly told in the entry "A Family Rose."

'Marechal Neil', once popular in America as a climbing rose, has fallen out of favor with many because of its heavy demands for attention.

Legend has it that 'General Jacqueminot', frequently found in old homesteads of America, was born from the blood of a young lover's heart.

With stems said to be a yard long and a price to match, 'American Beauty' enjoyed a popularity in the United States in the early 1900s impossible to overstate—but was it really "American"? The original exists today only in garden museums; shown here is a 1992 specimen.

A New York firm was founded to raise grapes and berries, but 'Dorothy Perkins', hybridized in 1901 by the company's propagator, changed all that. The new flower was an immediate winner and started Jackson & Perkins on its way to becoming the dominant name in the rose industry.

Dr. Walter Van Fleet, king of the climbing rose breeders of his day, hybridized 'American Pillar' in 1902. It was nearly rejected when offered to the Conard-Jones Company, but head propagator Antoine Wintzer argued for its acceptance. Today, 'American Pillar' is one of the most popular climbers in the world.

'Charlotte Armstrong' won the All-America Rose Selection award in 1941, the second of several winners for hybridizer Walter E. Lammerts. This blood-red, fragrant rose had a significant influence on rose breeding.

In the mid-1940s, the Conard-Pyle Company wanted to give this rose a permanent name in the United States; nurseryman Clyde Stocking suggested 'Peace', a word then foremost in everyone's mind. Official acknowledgment of the name was received on April 25, 1945, the very day that Berlin was rescued from Nazi control.

'Sutter's Gold' was named an All-America Rose Selection winner in 1950. The award was introduced a decade earlier and has been granted to only those plants that pass rigorous tests of hardiness and resistance to disease.

The introduction in 1955 of 'Queen Elizabeth', with its unusual features, forced the creation of a new class of roses, the grandiflora. Hints of unhappiness among British growers that an American variety should be named for their queen soon gave way to feelings of gratitude for the fine compliment.

Bred by William Warriner and introduced by Jackson & Perkins in 1976, 'Pristine' immediately began winning prizes. It remains one of the finest hybrid tea roses in commerce.

When 'Double Delight' came from the master hands of Herb Swim and Arnold Ellis in 1977, it was an instant sensation. Nothing like its spectacular coloring had ever been seen. Although it really thrives only in warm-weather countries, it has been named among the world's favorite roses.

Unable to interest American rose companies in hybridizing a rose in honor of their favorite entertainer, determined fans turned to Harkness Roses in England. Hybridizing efforts were begun in 1970 and completed in 1978, and the 'Judy Garland' rose was eventually cleared for import to the United States.

Although lavender roses were considered out of fashion when 'Paradise' was introduced by Ollie Weeks, the flower was such an eye-catcher that it won the All-America Rose Selection award in 1979.

William Warriner made an incredible sweep of the All-America Rose Selection awards in 1980 with his entries of 'Love', 'Honor', and 'Cherish'.

'Dee Bennett', winner of the Big E Award in 1989, was produced by Harmon Saville. Long interested in roses as a hobby, in 1971 Saville went into the business of selling and hybridizing miniature roses.

The Canadian government's interest in roses can be traced back as far as 1886 when it entered into an agreement with its experimental farms to test for winter hardy roses. One find in its hardiness search is this sturdy flower, 'Frontenac'.

'John Davis' is one of the many hardy roses bred at the Canadian government experimental farms. Research on hardiness in roses has received much attention in Canada, where only the toughest species and varieties can survive in many areas.

June and Keith Laver produced this perfectly formed flower, 'June Laver', which has become a top American exhibition miniature.

'Sheer Elegance', winner of the All-America Rose Selection award in 1991, was bred by Jerry Twomey, who turned to roses after retirement and set a goal of developing hardy, low-maintenance garden roses that wouldn't need "poisons to keep them good."

In 1992, Jerry Twomey's 'All That Jazz' won the All-America Rose Selection award in an unprecedented feat: A rose amateur took the honor two years in a row. And Twomey attained his goal—this shrub rose is not only disease resistant but is also practically pest resistant.

Elizabeth Park in Hartford, Connecticut, opened in 1904 as the first municipal rose garden in the country. The garden fell into decline in the 1960s but has since been restored and was cited as the Most Outstanding All-America Rose Selection Garden in 1991. Many of the garden's original roses survived and now are part of a planting of 15,000 bushes.

Harvey, David Lowell, John Ohlson, Dr. Neil Adams, Dwayne Schramm, Joe Woodard, Dave Evans, and Dale Martin.

Many rose businesses in the United States have been started just because someone wanted to cross a pair of roses and see what happened. Harmon Saville (see entry), one of the top growers of miniature roses in the United States, began his operation after a life spent first as a commercial fisherman and later in the mail-order merchandising business. Miniature roses have been the starting place for many other hybridizers who found that some of their seedlings were worth putting on the market. Success stories include the names of people like the Taylor family of Chickasaw, Alabama; Dorothy Cralle and Laurie Chaffin of Yorba Linda, California; the Jollys of Galena, Maryland; the Bridges of Lawndale, North Carolina; the Williamses of Cross Hill, South Carolina; the Justices of Wilsonville, Oregon; and Gene King of Monroe, Louisiana.

A wonderful thing about hybridizing is that you need only two rose bushes to begin with. From them you could finish up with a few hundred seeds at the end of the year, which by the following summer might well produce a winning rose. It is as simple as that.

If you would like to try your hand at hybridizing, observe the following tips and procedures. The best way to start is with miniatures. Have two different varieties, growing in pots, that will come into bloom at the same time. You will need some cover for the operation, unless you live in a warm, dry part of the world (Southern California is the ideal place for an outdoor rose breeder). But don't be put off by the lack of an ideal place for growing your seeds. Breeder John Sheridan, who lives in Catford, London, grew his plants on the kitchen windowsill and has had a couple of international successes.

There are no rules about the roses that you select, but good advice is to "breed from the best to the best and hope for the best." With your two plants in bloom, place pollen from each one onto the other, and you are on the way to creating a rose of your own. Following are the steps to take.

1. Collect pollen from rose number one. From a bloom that is one-quarter open, gently remove the petals. Do not leave any bits behind. Then remove the anthers, which carry the pollen, using a small pair of scissors or tweezers. Lay the anthers on a sheet of paper marked with the name of the rose.

2. Collect pollen from rose number two, following all procedures in Step 1.

3. Place the sheets of paper bearing the anthers overnight in a refrigerator. Keep the sheets apart from each other.

4. The following day, the pollen should be ready. Shake the anthers gently to see that they are releasing the yellow pollen.

5. Transfer pollen from rose number one to the stigma of rose number two, using an index finger or a small brush. The stigma is the central column of the bloom leading to the pod where the seeds will form. Tag the rose bush with the names of the roses you have crossed.

6. Transfer pollen from rose number two to the stigma of rose number one, following all procedures in Step 5.

7. Place a small paper cover over the head of the rose. But if the pollination takes place in a greenhouse, there is no need to cover the rose.

8. After pollination, leave the resulting seed

pods (hips) on the bushes for twelve to fourteen weeks, in which time they should turn orange (though some varieties will become a darkish gray) and be ready for harvesting.

9. Open the hips individually, and give the seeds the water test. Put them in a cupful of water. Those that sink are fertile. Throw away the floaters. Keep the good seeds from rose number one separate from those of rose number two. The seeds must not dry out.

10. Wrap the good seeds from rose number one in a small piece of damp kitchen paper towel, put the towel inside a small plastic bag, and clearly label the bag with the name of the cross. Repeat this procedure with the good seeds from rose number two. Put the bags in the vegetable compartment of your refrigerator for about six weeks.

11. Plant the seeds in trays, using a recognized seed potting mix. Again, keep seeds from the two roses separate. Place the seeds about half an inch under the soil and about one inch apart. Keep the soil moist. Cover the soil with plastic.

12. In a matter of weeks the first seedlings should show through. When the first two leaves are established, the little bushes are ready to be transplanted.

What I've described here is a very basic hybridizing program. There can be much more to it, and there are any number of variations on the procedures I've outlined. You can try the pollen of any type of rose—large roses, old roses, climbing roses. There is no end to the experiments you can carry out.

During his first two years as a rose breeder, Herbert C. Swim (see entry) discovered the importance of "knowing one's self as it pertains to evaluating seedlings." He had heard it said about certain breeders and nurserymen that "pride of ownership was blinding"; they could not see the faults in their own seedlings. Swim found that some roses would look good at one viewing, even good at a second, but then eventually display weaknesses. "In the end a rose must be judged by its consistency of performance," he said. As you produce your own hybrids, it's important to see the flaws as well as the merits.

One vital piece of advice: never criticize another hybridizer's seedlings. This is worse than criticizing the person's children.

To learn more about hybridizing, join the Rose Hybridizers Association, 3245 Wheaton Road, Horseheads, New York 14845. ◻

IOWA STATE UNIVERSITY

A successful breeding program produced vigorous roses.

IOWA STATE UNIVERSITY ESTABLISHED ITS ROSE-breeding program in the late 1800s when Joseph Budd, head of the horticulture department, and graduate student N. E. Hansen, began hybridizing with the Japanese rose introduction, *Rosa rugosa,* and garden varieties. The goal was to produce roses that would withstand harsh Iowa winters. Among the earliest roses were a rich velvety red named 'Prof. N. E. Hansen' (1882) and the first in the 'Ames' series of roses. 'Ames 5', introduced in 1932, was a very vigorous, almost thornless rose that for a time was a frequently used understock.

'Ames 5' was produced through the efforts of Thomas J. Maney, who taught at the University from 1912 until his death in 1945. Among other Maney roses to achieve some success were 'Maytime', 'Prairie Moon', 'Lois Maney', and 'Tom Maney'. The roses, although hardy, were only once-blooming. The most successful phase of the Iowa State program was headed by Griffith Buck (see entry), who produced many fine roses, including the disease-resistant 'Carefree Beauty' and the almost-blue 'Blue Skies'. □

JACKSON & PERKINS

Under the hard-driving hand of Charlie Perkins, J&P became the dominant name in the rose industry.

THE NAME PERKINS ALWAYS DOMINATED Jackson & Perkins (very few people ever knew who Jackson was), but there was a family connection. A. E. Jackson was the father-in-law of the firm's founder, Charles E. Perkins. They came together as partners in 1872, and the name stayed for the lifetime of the firm. There weren't any other Jacksons to follow, but the Perkins family lineage never diminished.

The firm was founded to raise grapes and berries in Newark, New York, but a rose was destined to change all that. The rose was 'Dorothy Perkins', hybridized in 1901 by E. Alvin Miller, the company's propagator. Full, fragrant, rose pink, and very vigorous (and often a slave to mildew), it became an immediate winner and sent the company off in a different direction. It was named for the baby daughter of George Perkins, then head of the firm (or was it, as some contend, named for the mother of the founder of the firm?).

One rose changed the business, and one Perkins changed the image of the American rose world. This was the boss's nephew, named Charles but known as Charlie. Later on, Charlie's three brothers Clarence, Ralph, and Carroll followed him into the company. In 1928, they bought the company. It wasn't the

and gave distribution rights to J&P. The country was just pulling out of the Depression. The rose was called 'Better Times'. It couldn't have been better named. It was a remarkable variety that produced lots of tall, straight-stemmed roses from each bush. It won gold medals in New York, Philadelphia and St. Louis, as well as one from the American Rose Society. Everyone wanted a bush, and every florist wanted the flowers. It is reckoned that before the patent ran out, Joe Hill netted half a million dollars in royalties. And where is the rose today? The only nursery I could find still handling it is in France.

The Perkins brothers made some good moves. They allowed one of the young marketing men, Gene Boerner (see entry), to buy into the company. They brought in French hybridizer Jean Henri Nicolas (see entry), who developed roses that caught the public's fancy. The company was clear of debt by 1940. The truly big break would come when Boerner moved into the research and hybridizing end of the business.

A rose out of Europe in the 1930s caught Charlie Perkins's attention. It was hardy, and it carried trusses of large blooms on a single strong stem, almost like a candelabra. Some of the clusters had as many as sixty flowers. It was classified as a polyanthus hybrid—and Charlie Perkins hated the name. Nobody would buy a rose with a name like that, he said. He asked everyone, in his brash, outspoken way, for a suggestion for a name for the rose. Gardening writer Ed Seymour suggested: "Why don't you call it floribunda? That means many-flowered."

Charlie Perkins liked the name, and he stuck with it. Any company refusing to use the name

best time to go into business. The Great Depression was just around the corner, and the brothers were $875,000 in the red. But people didn't call Charlie gritty and hustling for nothing. He borrowed money, pushed roses, guessed right, and made it.

The gods must have been on Charlie's side, too, because just when times were looking bad, J&P received a red rose sport from the J.H. Hill Company of Richmond, Indiana. Joe Hill, son of master hybridizer E. Gurney Hill (see entry), set up business with his father's help in 1916, and the company still exists. Joe saw a different mutation on a bush of "Briarcliff" and propagated it. He took out a patent (only the twenty-third ever issued for a rose) was not given permission to use the color plates of the rose. The American Rose Society fought the name for three years, then gave in. The name has stuck, despite a 1990 effort by the World Federation of Rose Societies to change it to "cluster-flowered." The floribunda became the hallmark of J&P. Vigor and blooming quality and bright colors pushed the flowers into the public eye.

One great event in J&P history came at the 1940 World's Fair in New York, where the company planted a model garden of 7,000 bushes, most of them floribundas. At the time the company was only selling wholesale, but the public decided it wanted the bushes then and there. So J&P moved into direct-mail marketing. Within ten years they were sending out two million catalogs a year, and selling twice as many bushes as that.

Of course it wasn't all success. The J&P stand on floribundas was so strong that it turned down the chance to introduce the hybrid tea 'Peace' (see entry) to America, and Conard-Pyle got the flower. J&P eventually ended up growing the rose, but had to pay royalties to Conard-Pyle. But the J&P business continued strong. Over the years, the company moved from Newark to Texas, then to Arizona, and finally to California. The good years continued with a number of great successes including 'Simplicity', a rose from hybridizer William Warriner (see entry). It was selling five million bushes a year at one time— and it was nothing more than a simple little five-petaled pink rose, but what a hedge it makes.

Conditions changed as members of the Perkins family died and old associations disappeared. The company was bought by an Oregon fruit and mail-order company, Harry & David, which later sold it to tobacco giant R. J. Reynolds, which sold it to Shaklee, a pharmaceutical firm. In 1987, Shaklee also bought the other rose giant, Armstrong's. In 1989, a Japanese-based company took over the rose companies, which are now split into various units that deal with different aspects of the business. The unit known as Bear Creek Productions breeds roses (about 350,000 a year, under research director Keith Zary; see entry). Bear Creek Gardens sells the roses (about twenty million a year). □

JELLY, ROBERT G. (BORN 1915)

Cut-flower varieties are a specialty of hybridizer Robert G. Jelly.

IT WAS NO SURPRISE THAT FROM RICHMOND, Indiana, home of the master of greenhouse roses, E. Gurney Hill, should come a modern hybridizer to carry on the tradition. Although the ordinary rosarian would hardly have heard of him, Bob Jelly is one of the most distinguished hybridizers of greenhouse varieties in the world. Among his roses is 'Forever Yours', one of the most outstanding hybrid teas ever placed on the cut-flower market. Other famous cut-flower varieties include 'Can Can', 'Coed', 'Excitement', 'Jack Frost', 'Jr. Bridesmaid', 'Promise Me', 'Royalty', 'Sassy', and 'Stop Lite'.

Jelly achieved more general fame when his 'Charisma' became an All-America Rose Selection winner in 1977. It was an unusual winner in that it was a floribunda; most awards have gone to hybrid teas. 'Charisma'

offers intense coloring with ever-changing tones of scarlet, orange, and bright golden yellow blossoms carried in great clusters. It is a tough, compact plant, and high on anyone's list of decorative garden varieties. Although regarded as an outdoor rose, it was bred from a long line of greenhouse varieties. □

'JOHN F. KENNEDY'

PRESIDENT KENNEDY'S NAME IS HONORED IN this white rose with just a tinge of green showing through its large, hybrid tea flower. Bred by Gene Boerner (see entry) in 1965, it carries a strange licorice fragrance. It is still a

widely planted garden variety, especially in warm, dry climates. For the wedding of the president's daughter, Caroline, hundreds of perfect blooms were sent from California, where they are grown outdoors at Garden Valley Ranch. □

JONES, KARL (1894–1990)

Karl Jones built an inspiring rose garden after his retirement.

KARL JONES OF BARRINGTON, RHODE ISLAND, was one of the most widely known and honored rosarians in New England for almost a century. He was president of the New England Rose Society and received awards from horticultural groups throughout the area. And he founded the largest privately owned rose garden in the United States.

An engineer by trade, Jones began building the garden on retirement. At one time it carried 11,000 rose plants on its eleven acres. The garden is reputed to have cost $50,000 a year to maintain, but that never bothered Jones. "It was good fun," he said. True to his Welsh background, he gave the garden the Welsh name of Llys Yr Rhosyn (Royal Court of the Rose).

The garden was called awe-inspiring by Mike Lowe, a rose grower who had a great friendship with Jones. It was open to everyone, for wedding pictures, annual festivities, and meetings among the roses. Jones's eventual offer of the garden as a public park to the town of Barrington was rejected. When the property was sold in 1985 for $150,000, the loss created a wave of protest in the town. A group of citizens tried to save the garden, but the bulldozers got there first and a great American garden fell to "progress." ◻

'JUDY GARLAND'

One fan's determined effort brought the 'Judy Garland' rose to the United States.

WHEN JUDY GARLAND DIED IN 1969, HER fans decided to create a living memorial to her—a rose. Led by Pat Losiewicz of Oak Harbor, Ohio, they turned to the top American rose companies. But the companies were not interested. Then, through British fan club secretary Gwen Potter, she contacted Harkness Roses, a leading hybridizer in Eng-

land. The hybridizing effort began in 1970 and was completed in 1978 when the first 'Judy Garland', a yellow floribunda with just a touch of red, went on sale in Britain.

Pat Losiewicz then faced the difficulties of importing the rose to the United States. By the time that success was near, Harkness had decided to drop the rose from its catalog. Then English grower Rearsby Roses decided to offer it. Finally the rose was cleared for import to the United States, where several nurseries put it on sale. It is also planted at Disney World in Florida and at the Hershey gardens in Pennsylvania. A bed planted in Brooklyn Heights, New York, was vandalized—the roses uprooted and stolen. ◻

KEAYS, ETHELYN EMERY
(1871–1961)

Rosarians are grateful to Mrs. Keays for sharing with them her love of old roses.

ETHELYN EMERY KEAYS WAS KNOWN throughout the rose world simply as Mrs. Keays. Her classic book, called *Old Roses,* was published in 1936 by the Macmillan Company and reprinted in 1978. She was sixty years old before she began writing about roses, first with articles in the *American Rose Annual* and then with the book that opened up a new interest in old roses in the eastern United States, sending people out searching to rediscover and save old roses.

In her foreword to the 1978 edition, rose searcher Leonie Bell pointed out that Mrs. Keays had no idea what lay ahead of her when she began to search out the old roses around her Maryland vacation home. The property had some twenty-five kinds of roses, and neighbors grew other treasured roses that had been passed down from grandmother to granddaughter. "A classics major in college, Ethelyn Keays was quickly entranced by the history inherent in rose plants that were even then antiques," Bell wrote.

Mrs. Keays covered every sort of rose—cabbage, alba, brier, moss, climbing, hybrid perpetual, and tea—searching out the old bushes wherever she went and finding many. Quite a few remained unidentified and were given names associated with the people or places where they were found. Her book can still send chills of excitement up the spine of the rose lover who has an interest in history.

About one of her discoveries she wrote:

> Another plant we have found we believe to be 'L'Heritier'. It came from an old garden about a small cabin which we always speak of as "the cabin where the andirons were." Sometime in the long past the last colored occupant went out, leaving the old andirons, the three-legged skillets and pots, and the dead ashes of the hearth. This rose is interesting for its former popularity. Into gardens in various localities it probably was carried as a remembrance of home by pioneers going west and south.

When I read the book, I felt as though I was looking out a window where the net curtain had just been raised, showing me a garden of roses I never knew before. □

KERN, JOSEPH J.
(1905–1986)

Joe Kern used to say he never met a rose he didn't like. He proved this by growing a spectacular collection from every age.

JOSEPH J. KERN BEGAN GROWING ROSES AS A hobby in the 1930s while employed as a railroad worker for the New York Central

System. He took to them commercially in the early 1950s when he retired. In 1969, he donated some 1,500 rose bushes representing nearly 500 varieties to the Garden of Roses of Romance and Legend in Wooster, Ohio, which he designed. He also donated many bushes to the Columbus Park of Roses and to Williamsburg, Virginia. His storage house and office were located on the grounds of the Michael H. Horvath estate in Mentor, Ohio. Kern introduced a number of roses, including the famous show variety 'Uncle Joe' (see entry), 'Florence' (for his wife), 'Lemon Sherbet', and 'Nantucket'.

"Joe loved his roses," said Frank Koss, his field superintendent. "He always had a twinkle in his eye that tells of a man who does what he does because he loves it." On Kern's death, Milwaukee rose grower Floyd Johnson said, "Joe loved antique roses just like some people love antique furniture or antique glassware."

Kern was a national authority on roses, a consultant for the Time-Life book *Roses* (1971), and an honoree of many garden clubs and rose societies. □

LAMMERTS, WALTER E. (BORN 1904)

The Dean of American hybridizing has a host of great roses to his name.

WALTER E. LAMMERTS ACHIEVED NATIONAL acclaim when, as head of research for Armstrong's rose company (see entry), his rose 'The Chief' was named in 1940 as one of the first winners of the All-America Rose Selections. He came up the following year with the American wonder rose 'Charlotte Armstrong'. This blood-red, thirty-five-petaled fragrant rose had a significant influence on rose breeding. The petals were long, the center regular

and beautifully flexed before opening. The rose brought back some of the refined looks of a strong tea rose, taking over in a feminine way from the mannish form of hybrid teas up to then. The fact that World War II virtually stopped European rose breeding meant that American hybridizers were given free rein with 'Charlotte Armstrong', which was bred from a cross between the German 'Crimson Glory' and the French 'Soeur Therese'.

English rose authority Jack Harkness, in his book *Roses* (1978), compared the produce of the families of 'Peace' and of 'Charlotte Armstrong'. Those from 'Peace', the yellow French rose, were big and burly like 'Eden Rose' and 'Karl Herbst'. The American rose 'Charlotte', on the other hand, gave the elegance to 'First Love' and 'Sutter's Gold'.

Other All-America Rose Selection winners followed for Lammerts, who, Sam McGredy has said, was unusual in rose breeding because he was a trained geneticist who also had a commercial eye for a novelty. "I've known scientists," McGredy wrote, "to breed roses and be unable to see the flower for the chromosomes!" Among the top roses bred by Lammerts were AARS winners 'Mirandy' (1945), 'Taffeta' and 'High Noon' (1948), 'Golden Showers' (1957), 'Starfire' (1959), 'American Heritage' (1966), 'Bewitched' (1967), and 'Bahia' (1974).

Lammerts also produced 'Queen Elizabeth' (see entry), the 1955 AARS winner, which had 'Charlotte Armstrong' as its mother. At that time Lammerts was working as a plant breeder at Descanso Gardens in Southern California. The rose was introduced through Germain's Inc. and has proved to be one of the great roses of the twentieth century. It grows anywhere in the world and needs little or no pampering in rain, wind, or frost. 'Queen Elizabeth' was a crowning achievement of Lammerts's constant search for parents with divergent backgrounds, a search that took him all over the world. □

LANCASTER AND YORK PENNSYLVANIA

AMONG THE MANY TOWNS WITH ROSE ASSOciations and names, the towns of Lancaster and York in Pennsylvania stand out. Both are named for ancient cities in England. The story goes that before the War of the Roses in the fifteenth century, the heads of the houses of Lancaster and York chose roses from a bush that bore blooms of two colors: red for Lancaster and white for York. That rose, with a mixture of white and pinkish blooms, still exists. In Pennsylvania the tradition lives in the two towns; even their sports teams are called the Red Roses and the White Roses. □

LANGUAGE OF THE ROSE

When you are stuck for words, just reach for a rose.

OVER THE YEARS, TIME HAS GIVEN MANY meanings to different types and colors of roses. Following are some of the most memorable words in the language of the rose.

Red: "I love you," or "Good Luck."

White: Youthful innocence; innocence and purity; secrecy and silence; "You are heavenly."

White on red: Unity.

Dark crimson: Mourning.

Yellow: "Try to care," or "I'm jealous."

Old tea roses: "I will always remember."

Pink: Perfect happiness.

A rose bud: Beauty and youth; a heart innocent of love.

A full-blown rose: Forever.

A full-blown rose and a rose bud: Secrecy.

A withered rose: "You made no impression."

A rose leaf: "You may keep on hoping."

Roses at Christmas: "Ease my anxiety." □

LARGEST ROSE TREES

America's largest rose trees attain sizes almost beyond belief.

THE EXTRAORDINARY GROWING POWER OF the soil in the United States has produced some remarkable trees. More than 180,000 blooms were recorded on a rose tree at General Stoneman's estate in the San Gabriel Valley in California. The trunk was fifteen inches thick, the stems reared up to fifteen feet, and the plant brought visitors for miles around to see it in the 1800s. The rose variety was 'Lamarque', a Noisette, that owed its origins to the work of John Champneys (see entry) in Charleston, South Carolina. The pure white bloom with a creamy-yellow center has the added distinction of being marvelously scented.

Victoria Padilla, writing in *Southern California Gardens,* described a 'Beauty of Glazenwood' (one of the many names for 'Fortune's Double Yellow') growing near Los Angeles that covered a eucalyptus tree eighty feet high, "transforming the tree into a colossal pillar of blooms of exquisite rose-pink and pale yellow." The same rose—under the name 'Gold of Ophir'—was planted as a hedge in the town of Redlands and extended for over a mile, all grown from a single bush. Another spectacular plant was recorded in Ventura, where another 'Lamarque', grown from a slip planted in 1875, covered an area of nearly 2,000 square feet. Padilla commented that although wagonloads of cuttings were often carried away, the old bush managed to maintain its size for a long time. Intrepid guests at the Arlington Hotel in Santa Barbara could climb three at a time into the branches of the rose tree that had a spread of some sixty feet.

Even these remarkable roses pale into insignificance beside the size of the largest rose tree in the United States, on the grounds of the Rose Tree Inn in Tombstone, Arizona. This rose tree goes back to the year 1884, when Mary Gee came to Tombstone with her mining husband. She wrote to her mother in Scotland, asking her to send some cuttings from a rose that grew in a Scottish garden, "the one that smells of violets." Her mother sent cuttings, and Mary began her roses. Within very little time, one plant had almost taken over. Trellises had to be built to hold it up, and it was allowed to grow and grow. Today the Lady Banksia rose in Tombstone is easily America's largest rose tree, spreading its branches over 8,000 square feet and carrying millions of small, creamy white blooms every April.

Many modern roses grow to a huge size out of their normal environment. Irish hybridizer Patrick Dickson tells a great story of one of his varieties, the large red 'Precious Platinum'. Dickson was visiting a group of nurserymen in the 1970s who were looking for new roses to introduce. He suggested 'Precious Platinum' to Texas grower Joe Burks. Dickson, noting a quizzical look, asked Burks if he already grew it. "I do," replied the Texan. "For firewood." □

LAVER, KEITH AND JUNE

The Lavers produce thousands of new seedlings annually in the search for perfect roses.

CANADIAN PRODUCERS OF SOME OF THE world's leading miniature roses, June and Keith Laver began business in 1980 in Caledon East, Ontario. Their 'Potluck Yellow' was the start of something big, and now "Potluck" roses can be found in practically all colors. European growers showed interest in Laver roses, which have now spread around the world.

The Lavers also hybridized one of the top show roses in the United States. Named 'June Laver', it is a perfectly formed yellow that often receives the comment that it is short-stemmed—a fault with exhibitors. But June Laver points out that the rose was intentionally bred that way in an attempt to produce the perfect yello v pot rose, but instead of achieving that, they produced a top show variety.

Keith Laver's prime goal is to produce miniatures suitable for pot forcing. He has conquered the range of colors, but he still wants the "perfect" red and sees that as his major challenge. "It is hard," he says, "to find the perfect little rose that will not bolt, has great color, perfect form, produces many blooms with both substance and lasting qualities." Each year thousands of new seedlings are produced in the search for perfection.

As well as hybridizing roses, June Laver has produced a cookbook of rose recipes: *Cooking with Roses,* World Federation of Rose Societies, 1991. Keith is a former president of the Canadian Rose Society and has a special interest in genetic engineering, which he hopes may one day produce a rose perfect in all ways and hardy enough to grow anywhere in Canada. ◻

LOST-AND-FOUND ROSES

In the search for old roses, identification is the toughest part of the task.

EVERY ROSE LOVER IN TEXAS KNOWS MAGGIE, but no one knows who Maggie really is. She was discovered one day in 1980 and has puzzled the rose world ever since. No doubt Maggie had been growing in the South for over a century when William Welch, extension landscape specialist for Texas A&M University, found her at the home of his wife's grandparents in northern Louisiana. The large red rose with a distinctive peppery odor attracted his attention, but he could not identify it. So he gave the rose a study name, in this case the name of his wife's grandmother. It bloomed in the spring and was still blooming at Christmas. Since then, Maggie has been found in all the best places in the South where searching for old roses, or rose rustling, is a great pastime.

Charles A. Walker, Jr., one of the country's leading old-rose specialists, believes that Maggie is just one of several local names given to this particular rose. He also found it growing in Miami, Puerto Rico, and Bermuda. But does he know its real name? The search for the original name and identity of the rose must take into consideration many things: the detailed tint of blooms, the type of petals, the number of leaflets on the foliage, the color and feel of the leaves, the number and shape and size of prickles—all very much a part of the vital evidence of the individuality of a rose. So the temporary name Maggie may well last indefinitely.

Maggie isn't alone. Other famous Texas-found roses have temporary names pending true identification: Pam's Pink, Natchitoches Noisette, Monday Morning, Highway 290 Pink Buttons, Granny Grimmetts. Lily Shohan of New York talks affectionately of a rose she calls Old Red Runaround, so named because it sends suckers everywhere. The Antique Rose Emporium in Brenham, Texas, sells Maggie and Granny Grimmetts, while Heritage Roses in Branscombe and Fort Bragg, California, lists some fifteen, with study names like Mrs. Woods Lavender–Pink Noisette and Secret Garden Musk Climber.

Roses that have been "lost" must number in the thousands since artificial hybridizing began at the start of the nineteenth century. Many were lost because they failed to attract enough attention and were allowed to drift away. Others died because they were not resistant to weather extremes or became weakened from disease or lack of care. But many great roses still wait to be rescued from a cemetery or an old settlement—and then to be identified.

The identification of an old rose brings with it great excitement, especially when it is a rose that has not been known to still exist. This happened to Californian Sharon Van Enoo. In

1990, she visited the southern foothills community of Mount Pleasant, Utah, which had been populated by pioneer farmers. Old farms and gardens are plentiful there. She took cuttings from some roses. The ubiquitous 'Harison's Yellow' (see entry) was there, as was 'Austrian Copper' *(Rosa foetida bicolor)*, both probably brought by pioneers and now growing wild. But one rose was different. Long canes—almost thornless and five to six feet high—were swinging in the wind when she saw the rose bush. The cuttings she took home bloomed and gave small, cupped, semidouble dark-purple flowers with bright yellow stamens. After conferring with Clair Martin at the Huntington Botanical Gardens in Southern California, it was decided that it was an old Boursault from 1829 named 'Amadis'. "You can imagine my excitement when I found a real identification for this old rose," she says.

Identification is a delicate matter. It's mainly a process of elimination until the true characteristics can be discerned, but the finder might take three or four years to come up with a possible identification. You need the touch of a Sherlock Holmes to become a rose identifier. Thomas Christopher presented the perfect picture of rose hunters and identifiers in his book *In Search of Lost Roses* (Summit Books, 1989). He himself even found a rose. □

LYLE, ELDON W. (BORN 1908)

The diseases and other problems of roses are the specialty of plant pathologist Eldon W. Lyle.

FEW MEN HAVE HAD AS MUCH INFLUENCE IN field and garden growing of roses as Texas-born Eldon W. Lyle. Constantly on the move, impish in his wit, with no fancy airs, Lyle needs only a couple of sentences to explain what is needed to keep a rose at its very best.

Lyle was born in Corpus Christi, Texas, and lived his youth in California and Oregon. At Cornell University, in 1935, he made his initial mark on rose history by giving the first demonstration of black spot disease control in the greenhouse. This was a major step in the fight against this defoliating and debilitating disease of the rose, a disease that became highlighted as more and more hybrid roses were produced. After a short time working in greenhouses in Connecticut, he moved back to Texas, set up home in Tyler, and has never left.

Lyle became the first director of the Texas Rose Research Foundation, established in 1946 by a group of commercial rose growers with the aim of carrying out research into all aspects of rose growing, from climate to disease to flowering. The foundation under Lyle's guidance is credited with improvement in rose understocks, bringing about the change from dusting crops to spraying them, storage of budwood over winter so that work may be carried out early in spring, and a continuing search for new rose varieties. His success as a plant pathologist began with tests to control root knot nematode and a study of virus diseases. Research brought a new understock for roses, vital in the fields around Tyler, where half of the nation's commercial roses are grown. The understock was a multiflora/*Rosa blanda* hybrid from Prof. Thomas J. Maney of Iowa, and it proved resistant to root knot.

Lyle also was involved in efforts to produce machinery for the mechanical pruning of roses, tests of crop rotation, and tests on the use of overhead watering to control powdery mildew. He helped start the Tyler Rose Society and, with R. L. Sheldon of the Tyler Parks Department, the Tyler Rose Gardens and Rose Festival. Awarded the Gold Honor Medal of the American Rose Society in 1965, he went on to become its president from 1971–1973. He produced an excellent pamphlet for the Texas Rose Research Foundation in 1989, *Rose Growing Suggestions,* which succinctly covered every aspect of rose growing. □

'MARECHAL NEIL'

Time has taken its toll on this famous climbing rose born in France more than a century ago.

'MARECHAL NEIL', THE MOST FAMOUS OF all great climbing roses in American history, needs sun and warmth. And where it gets it, it is still a glorious rose. Writer Georgia Torrey Drennan praised 'Marechal Neil' in 1864 as "a proud triumph of nature that exceeds all expectation and defies criticism." H. B. Ellwanger, writing in 1882, called it "the best Noisette, the finest yellow, and the most beautiful variety of any class that has ever been sent out." John Weather, in 1903, said it was "the finest yellow rose in cultivation."

Even gardeners in the colder parts of the North grew it, although they might have had to replace the bush every year because of its lack of hardiness. But size, color, shape, texture, and fragrance combined to make it a truly great variety. It was said to have a short life even in warm climates, but I have seen it grown for many years in the garden of Ralph Moore (see entry) in Visalia, in central California. And in southern states it can still have a long life, and a glorious one. It played its part in breeding other roses, too, among them the All-America Rose Selection winner 'Diamond Jubilee', a soft yellow with large, leathery foliage that, unlike its father, survives in cooler temperatures.

To make the story of 'Marechal Neil' an especially good one, it offers a bit of mystery.

No authentication has ever been found of the rose's pedigree other than that it was introduced in France in 1863 and "received the name of Marechal Neil, who had recently presided at the opening of a botanical garden in the vicinity of Monttuban." No one ever really knew what classification to put it into. It is called a Noisette, the race of roses founded in Charleston, South Carolina, simply because it resembles other roses in that class.

Time has not necessarily been kind to this lovely rose. Nurserymen now find that it doesn't have its old vigor and that it is hard to root. Others have fallen out of love with it because of its constant need for care. Hallie Beck, writing from Arizona, told me: "I didn't lose 'Marechal Neil'. I got rid of him. He too-quickly outgrew his allotted space. I couldn't deal with him. He wore me out. I'd keep pruning and carting off parts of him and he'd only flex his canes and come back stronger. It was like you pulled out one gray hair and four came back. Then, too, dry spring winds crisped and withered the petal edges, turning them an unsightly brown, which ruined his looks as far as I am concerned."

From the Peaceable Kingdom School in Old Washington, Texas, Liz Druitt wrote that as yellow roses stand for the decrease of love, so people often picked on 'Marechal Neil' to symbolize disappointed hopes. She added that she has a terrible time getting it to grow. But at the rate that 'Marechal Neil' was grown throughout America over the years, it doesn't deserve too many harsh words. Gardeners with a warm spot in a warm part of the country, or a heated greenhouse, can still do wonders with it. □

McFARLAND, DR. J. HORACE (1859–1948)

McFarland holds an honored place in American rose history through his growing, writing, and printing.

THIS GREAT MAN OF THE ROSE WAS A VISIONary, a writer, a printer, and a famous grower. "Few other Americans, if any, have fostered the art of gardening with the earnestness and enthusiasm of Dr. J. Horace McFarland," wrote Raymond C. Allen (see entry) in his introduction to McFarland's *Memoirs of a Roseman.*

McFarland lived in Harrisburg, Pennsylvania, where he built a marvelous garden, Breeze Hill (see entry). He brought into print the first authentic color book of roses. There had been occasional color pictures before his, but to produce books like *Roses of the World in Color* (Houghton-Mifflin, 1936 and 1947) at a time when quality color printing was in its infancy was a great achievement.

McFarland was a man of wide interests. He worked constantly for better city planning, for state and national parks, and for the preservation of the beauty of Niagara Falls. His plant photography still impresses. He encouraged the development of new plant strains of all sorts. He built his garden at Breeze Hill, which became one of the best known in the United States. Here he watched over great roses and saw many that didn't measure up. As of 1930, more than 800 varieties had been grown at Breeze Hill. He was president of the American Rose Society from 1930 to 1932.

One of McFarland's major works was the creation, in 1930, of the first complete rose registration, with publication of *Modern Roses* (Macmillan, New York). It is the world's greatest rose publication for historical purposes. It took him fifteen years to compile. And he wanted just the facts, he wrote, in order to avoid the "sometimes pardonable pride or less pardonable commercial enthusiasm which leads to the use of many favorable words." To get the facts, he sent inquiry cards around the world and confined his list to the varieties that were then available. Despite his own admonition, in the first edition McFarland didn't necessarily stick to the facts. Now and again his enthusiasm about a rose or its history leaps from the pages. *Modern Roses* went into eight editions; a supplementary edition appeared some years later. *Modern Roses 10* is the latest edition, published by the American Rose Society in 1993.

"The rose has brought me some of the most lasting satisfactions of my life," McFarland wrote. "It has given me an interest in many sidelines of scientific research, in plant explorations all over the globe, in the organization and promotion and continuance of a society of kindred spirits. Perhaps best of all are the rose friends it has brought me in many lands and covering a span of generations. To know that the love of the rose is truly universal and deeply implanted in the souls of men is enough to make one hope that in many other matters the world may soon get together in common fellowship."

Reflecting from the vantage point of old age, McFarland once said that "a lifetime of almost ninety years has not been enough to teach me all there is to know about roses. I have grown, photographed, written about, and color-printed roses for most of these years, and I still want to shout about them from the roof-top!" □

McMAHON, BERNARD (1775–1816)

This pioneer American nurseryman counted Thomas Jefferson among his customers.

IRISH-BORN NURSERYMAN AND WRITER Bernard McMahon produced the most influential book in the early part of American horticulture when he wrote *The American Gardener's Calendar* (1806). He lived a short but influential life, and no record of American gardening would be complete without a reference to him. His book went through eleven editions and was the first horticulture book produced specifically for American growing conditions. McMahon was practical in his approach to planting, pruning, and other aspects of gardening. His directions would not send anyone wrong even today.

McMahon arrived in Philadelphia in 1796. Within ten years he had become a major distributor of seeds and plants. Everyone who wanted to know about gardens came to him. He knew that this was a new land bravely searching for its own roots, and he saw his work in a wide social and historical context. When his book was first published, he sent a copy to President Jefferson with a note: "I have much pleasure in requesting your acceptance of one of my publications on Horticulture which I forward to you by this mail. Should my humble efforts meet with your approba-tion, and render any service to my adopted and beloved country, I shall feel happy consolation of having contributed my mite to the welfare of my fellow man." Not only did Jefferson accept the book, but he also became a customer and friend. Jefferson recorded that in 1807 he "planted 6. scarlet Alpine strawberry roots from Mc.Mahon on the lower side of the peruvian tussock, within a few inches." And in return he sent McMahon currants and goose-berries.

McMahon's nursery catalog listed over eighty kinds of roses, including the Common Provence Rose, the Hudson Bay Rose *(Rosa blanda)*, a dwarf Austrian, and a Pennsylvania rose. Roses were a small part of the catalog's total offering of more than 3,500 species and varieties "of the most valuable and curious plants hitherto discovered." □

MEDICINAL USES

For hundreds of years, people have credited the rose with powers of promoting health.

AS FAR BACK AS PLINY IN A.D. 77, THE ROSE was considered a cure for some thirty diseases. Most of the prescriptions of that time are now disregarded, but it's interesting to note them. It was said that red rose petals placed next to the skin would cure heart troubles. Roses were prescribed for "purification of the mind," for curing the bite of a sea dragon, and—as a linament with bear grease—for curing baldness.

There was a time when a headache, tooth-ache, stomach pain, or inflammation of the eyes were thought curable with rose petals or rose hips. Roses supposedly could even help remove freckles. Of course rosewater was always in demand to cover up unpleasant smells. One recipe for rosewater said to take "two and a half pounds of petals from the most fragrant roses, dry them thoroughly in the shade and put them in a jar closed tightly with a quart of distilled water and a teaspoonful of salt. Stir every day with a clean stick, then filter. Petals should be picked before midday when they are most fragrant."

In the mid-1860s, the growers of Provins, France—home of the Apothecary's Rose *(Rosa gallica officinalis)*—exported almost forty tons of dried rose petals to the United States, where they were used many different ways. William Penn had offered this cure for insomnia: "Take a small pillow of dried rose petals to bed and you will have many pleasant dreams." Traveling medicine men of the early West made rose petals into a pill, held together with gum. Rose pills were sold as a cure for hemorrhoids, ulcers, and stomach problems.

Rose hips have long had a place in medicine. As a diuretic and as a treatment against colic, the value of concentrated hips has been proven. The Chinese brought with them the suggestion that the hips could be used against indigestion. Rose wine vinegar has been a proven treatment for tiredness and fainting.

Colonist John Josselyn, in the mid-1600s, found *Rosa carolina,* which he recorded as "wild damask roses that were single but very large and sweet but stiptick," which he may have been able to use to stop bleeding. Josselyn also mentioned recipes, mainly obtained from Indians, that included the use of roses for decoctions, conserves, ointments, syrup, and honey. These were good for everything from a cut on the finger to comforting a weak stomach.

Early California missionaries planted the damask rose, as they called the Rose of Castile

(see entry), because of its perfume and its medicinal properties. Missionaries used the rose in religious processions, then collected the petals from the dead flowers to make into oils and ointments. Mission dispensaries kept supplies of dried rose petals and hips.

In the 1930s, much research was done on rose hips for their vitamin C content, research that was sparked by Richard L. Meiling, an American medical student in a German hospital. Meiling's professor had suggested that he study, for his medical thesis, the use of vitamin C against such illnesses as pneumonia. Meiling, who later became Vice President for Medical Affairs at Ohio State University, told me that he used mice, guinea pigs, rabbits, and dogs in the study. To begin, the animals received a diet of food that had been sterilized to remove all vitamin C. The next step was to obtain a source of vitamin C in a nutritional substance grown in Germany. The answer was the rose hip (or hagebutton), which is very high in vitamin C.

Meiling said the rose hips were carefully prepared into marmalade, soup, and sauces, which were fed to test animals. "We soon learned that the daily requirements of vitamin C could be supplied from the various preparations of the hagebutton," he said. "It did not prevent pneumonia, but our animals with this vitamin C supplement could produce self-defense against infection." From the animal laboratories, the work was taken into general hospitals and was a success. Rose hips came into such demand that a plan went into effect to plant wild roses on unused land and along autobahn dividers. Since then, more research has validated Meiling's work. We now know that one wild rose, *Rosa mollis,* contains by weight five times more vitamin C than black currants and fifty times more than oranges. Just a word of warning about these special uses of roses: never use the hips, flowers, or petals of any rose that has been treated with an insecticide or fungicide, even of the mildest kind. □

MEYER, CARL
(BORN 1913)

This Cincinnati pipe fitter proved that an amateur can sometimes compete successfully with the big-name rose breeders.

CARL MEYER WAS THE FIRST AMATEUR ROSE breeder to produce an All-America Rose Selection winner. In 1972, his 'Portrait' was selected as a winner, along with 'Apollo', from a major producer, Armstrong's rose company. It was big news: a pipe fitter from a Cincinnati meat plant outdoing the world's top hybridizers. *National Geographic* magazine published a nine-page feature on the man and his rose.

Carl Meyer began breeding roses in the early 1950s after he saw some varieties created by a local nurseryman. "If he could do it, so could I," Meyer said. He bred a number of roses before he found one that he considered good enough to send to the Conard-Pyle Company (see entry) for evaluation. That year, Conard-Pyle had 600 roses under review. But it was Carl Meyer's rose—then distinguished only by a number, 975—that was selected for entry to the prestigious All-America Rose Selection trials. Forty-four roses competed in the final trials, and 'Portrait' became one of the two winning selections. It won because of its glowing pink blossom and its hardy, vigorous, and disease-free growth.

In the long run, 'Portrait' never made the top

grade throughout the country. It was best described by hybridizer Herb Swim (see entry) as being "technically a good rose but we do not see it as a blue ribbon winner in rose shows." And to be among the top blooms, a rose has to be a big winner on the show bench. 'Portrait' is still widely available around the world, however—a tribute to the amateur grower who took on the world's best, and won. □

'MISTER LINCOLN'

One of the finest dark red roses of all time, 'Mister Lincoln' is magnificent in size, shape, and perfume.

THE SEEDS FOR 'MISTER LINCOLN'—A CROSS of two famous reds, 'Chrysler Imperial' and 'Charles Mallerin'—were thought to have died in a refrigeration accident. Somehow they survived. Among the roses produced from these seeds in 1964 were two of the finest reds ever, 'Oklahoma' and 'Mister Lincoln'.

Herb Swim (see entry), who bred 'Mister Lincoln' in association with O. L. Weeks (see entry), wrote in his book *Roses—from Dreams to Reality* that he did not notice the original plant, which was growing at the end of a seedling row, until it was about six feet tall. It had fifty flowers on it in various stages of maturity, and he always remembered the thrill it gave him.

Swim budded some stock, entered the rose in the All-America Rose Selection trials, and it won. And the sister seedling 'Oklahoma' came in third. Years later, Swim told me that of all the roses he bred, 'Mister Lincoln' gave him the greatest satisfaction. (A rose called 'President Lincoln'—large, full, and dark red—was introduced from France in 1863, but it didn't make the impression that this one did.) □

MOORE, RALPH
(BORN 1907)

*When the talk turns to miniature roses, it will
be only a sentence or two before the name of Ralph
Moore comes up. Moore made the miniature rose
what it is today.*

RALPH MOORE CANNOT PUT A FINGER ON
the exact time when, in his home town of
Visalia, California, he began to work with
miniatures. But in his early twenties, he began
collecting hips from roses around his home
and grew small plants from the seeds. One of
the roses he used for seeds was the lovely little
'Cecile Brunner', a hybrid polyantha with very
small and beautiful blooms. This was the rose
that gave him a lifelong love of tiny roses.

Moore became so entranced by small roses
that he began his own nursery business in
1937, introducing some of his own roses along
the way. Some growers laughed at his "toy
roses." Others called them ugly ducklings. By
the end of the 1950s, this attitude was changing as his roses began to show their great ability to adapt to different situations. They were
small, healthy, and in a mass of colors never
seen before. His small roses were far in advance of anything that had ever been done
with miniatures. These early miniatures are
now found in the breeding lines of almost
every miniature in the world.

Miniature roses are tricky to handle. The
parts of the flowers that need to be worked
with are small and delicate. Moore realized
that he needed a robust growing rose that
would produce lots of seeds in the miniature
mold. He found the 1956 yellow blend 'Little
Darling', and although it was a floribunda, it
reacted so well to the miniature pollen that it
gave him a whole line of great small roses. It is
a line that has been followed by breeders ever
since. Most top hybridizers acknowledge that
their miniature breeding has been highly influenced by Moore. New Zealand's Sam Mc-
Gredy wrote in his book *Look to the Rose*,
"Whenever I think of miniatures I immediately
think of Ralph Moore. No one else has done so
much to improve the type and to make them
popular. . . . He had the vision and he was
dreaming his dreams of minis when none of
the rest of us bothered."

The past and the future of the miniature rose
lies for me in that "Alice in Wonderland" garden in Visalia where Moore plays with dreams
and pollen. He wants to breed unusual

things—roses that others have by-passed, roses that bring in the blood from older varieties. The moss rose fascinates him. It held an important place in the old-rose world, and he believes there is a place for it today. He is aiming toward a fully crested moss miniature like *Rosa centifolia cristata* (often called 'Chapeau de Napoleon'), the original plant of which was found on a convent wall in France in 1827.

He once talked to me about his efforts to get the fully crested moss rose in miniature. Imagine, he said, this beautiful green bud with fresh parsleylike growth on a thornless rose. I asked how far he was toward reaching this goal. He spread his arm toward a bench holding mossed roses he had been working on for twenty years. "Another ten years, that's thirty years in all; not bad to see a dream come true," he said.

Moore explained his approach to the long-term mission of developing a new strain of roses. "It is like engineering. You've got to see the finished concept in its entirety. . . . You've got to dream for your ruffled rose, for your climber, and learn how to engineer your way to it whether it takes two years, ten years, or twenty years. It's a mental thing first."

One of Moore's great interests is the introduction of older tea roses back into the miniature line. When he was a boy, his grandfather gave him a plant of a rose called 'Safrano', saffron colored and fragrant, from 1839. Only now is he bringing it into the breeding line, and he has had some success. His 'New Adventure' is a direct descendant of 'Safrano'.

Moore's efforts have opened other new windows on roses. He re-created interest in the single bloom with five to twelve petals. He gave breeders a route to stripes among their roses with his red and white 'Stars 'n' Stripes'.

He brought in the first climbing miniatures. The list of great Moore miniatures goes on and on, but among them are 'Rise 'n' Shine' (yellow), 'Magic Carousel' (red and white), 'Easter Morning' (creamy white), 'Little Buckaroo' (red), 'Baby Darling' (salmon-orange), 'Beauty Secret' (red), 'Earthquake' (red and yellow stripes), 'Lavender Lace' (mauve-lavender), and 'Over the Rainbow' (red and yellow). □

MOREY, DENNISON

Prolific hybridizer Dennison Morey produced a number of roses that have taken their places among America's best.

T OP ROSES PRODUCED BY DENNISON MOREY include 'King's Ransom' (described as the best yellow of the 1960s), 'South Seas', and 'Proud Land', all produced when he was working for the western division of Jackson & Perkins. At J&P his hybridizing was on a massive scale. He often made as many as 100,000 crosses in a year—about ten times what another top-ranking hybridizer might be expected to make. It was from these crosses that he made the great jump into yellow hybrid teas, which were then in short supply, when he produced 'King's Ransom'.

Another of Morey's roses was to excite the interest of breeder Sam McGredy. In his book *Look to the Rose,* McGredy wrote: "One year I noticed a most unusual weeper in the magnificent rose gardens of Portland, Oregon. It was planted at the top of a wall, cascading down some three metres and covered in tiny white flowers. I thought to myself there has to be something I could do with that." The rose was Morey's 'Temple Bells'. McGredy took 'Temple Bells' back with him to Ireland and through cross-breeding eventually produced 'Snow Carpet', the first step to something new in roses—a ground-cover rose that stays small, with miniature flowers. In the mid-1960s, Morey left J&P to set up his own rose-producing outlet. □

MOST POPULAR ROSES

THE MOST POPULAR ROSES IN NORTH America, as presented to the World Federation of Rose Societies meeting in Belfast in 1991, and based on a poll conducted by the American Rose Society, are as follows:

United States
1. 'Touch of Class'
2. 'Gold Medal'
3. 'Europeana'
4. 'Jean Kenneally'
5. 'Snow Bride'
6. 'Acey Deucy'
7. 'Pristine'
8. 'Charles de Mills'
9. 'Mme Hardy'
10. 'Agnes'

Canada
1. 'Garden Party'
2. 'Pascali'
3. 'Super Star' ('Tropicana')
4. 'Mister Lincoln'
5. 'Tiffany'
6. 'Maria Callas'
7. 'Just Joey'
8. 'Chrysler Imperial'

9. 'First Prize'
10. 'Europeana' and 'Dainty Bess' (Tie)

At the same meeting, the federation took a poll to establish a Hall of Fame for older roses. Four United States invitees voted this way:

Miriam Wilkins
1. 'Sombreuil'
2. 'Jacques Cartier'
3. *R. roxburghii*
4. 'Mme Hardy'
5. *R. centifolia muscosa*
6. *R. centifolia cristata*
7. 'Celsiana'
8. 'Schneezwerg'
9. 'Cecile Brunner'
10. 'Ophelia'

Dr. Charles Jeremias (then president of the American Rose Society)
1. 'Old Blush'
2. 'Souvenir de la Malmaison'
3. 'Safrano'
4. 'General Jacqueminot'
5. 'Crimson Glory'
6. 'Crested Moss'
7. 'Ophelia'
8. 'Sombreuil'
9. 'Baronne Prevost'
10. 'Frau Karl Druschki'

Charles A. Walker, Jr.
1. 'Mermaid'
2. 'Charles de Mills'
3. 'Mme Plantier'
4. 'Cecile Brunner'
5. 'New Dawn'
6. 'Crested Moss'
7. 'Mme Hardy'

8. 'Rosa Mundi'
9. 'Baronne Prevost'
10. 'Old Blush'

Patricia Stemler-Wiley

1. 'Souvenir de la Malmaison'
2. 'La Reine Victoria'
3. 'Salet'
4. 'Mrs. John Laing'
5. 'Rose du Roi'
6. 'Sombreuil'
7. 'Gloire de Dijon'
8. 'Baronne Prevost'
9. 'Reine des Violettes'
10. 'Ophelia'

The old roses eventually selected from nominations by twenty-four people gave the first Hall of Fame place to 'Souvenir de la Malmaison'. The entire list follows.

1. 'Souvenir de la Malmaison'
2. 'Cecile Brunner'
3. 'Old Blush'
4. 'Gloire de Dijon'
5. 'Mme Hardy'
6. 'Ophelia'
7. 'Mermaid'
8. 'Sombreuil'
9. 'Mutabilis'
10. 'Baronne Prevost'

A Handbook for Selecting Roses, a guide to the top-rated roses throughout the United States, is issued annually by the American Rose Society. □

NAMES OF ROSES

The story behind the naming of a rose can be as colorful as the rose itself.

WHATEVER HAPPENED TO MISS CALIFORnia? Or Sitting Bull? Or Mrs. Lovell Swisher? The list could go on endlessly of roses that promised everything but then faded into nothingness. Breeders often have no one to blame but themselves; after all, they gave a rose the name of Sitting Bull but indicated that it was not hardy! In 1926 'Mrs. Lovell Swisher' was said to be a beautiful silver pink, perfectly formed, fragrant, very vigorous, resistant to disease, notable for the size and lasting quality of bloom. No doubt the lady was pleased, but no one, it seems, even remembers the rose now. 'Miss California' was billed as intensely fragrant, high-centered, long-lasting, very hardy, with a brilliant, glowing, even color; everything was going for her, but she too disappeared.

Even a famous name doesn't guarantee continuation of a rose. No longer will you find 'Clara Bow'. 'Sophia Loren' and 'Ginger Rogers' have disappeared. It's one thing to have a rose named for you, but quite another to have it last more than a decade or two.

It has been estimated that almost a third of given rose names are for people, while another third are general descriptive names such as the sun-bright 'Rise 'n' Shine', the colorful 'Over the Rainbow', and the shattering little striped red, orange, and yellow 'Earthquake' (named soon after a quake hit the town of Coalinga, California). And 'Pandemonium' perfectly registers the look on the wild striped orange and yellow rose.

"Rose names reveal the entire gamut of human emotion," Jean Henri Nicolas (see entry) said in 1937. "We find joy, pathos, allusions to art, literature and history, love and romance." And also embarrassment, as Francis Lester reported in *My Friend the Rose*. He wrote that a "tanned and well-built woman of ample proportions" once arrived in his rose yard. He missed her name, but as they were discussing roses, she asked: "How do you like 'Marion Cran'?"

"Well," he said, "she doesn't seem to like Californian conditions. For me she is such a very weak grower that I am going to get rid of her. But I imagine she is well named; she's a pretty slip of a girl, artful and dainty even if she is a weakling."

The lady, much taller than Lester, looked down at him. "I am Marion Cran," she said.

That sort of thing does happen, and it is always better to take care in describing a rose as a good bedding type or effective against a wall unless you are absolutely sure that it won't be taken the wrong way. Rose breeder Dee Bennett (see entry) conveyed an unintended meaning when she named a rose 'Angel Dust', unaware it is also the name of a dangerous psychedelic drug.

There are some 20,000 roses, each with a

name. Roses are named for people, places, emotions, events, ideas—a practice that has been going on for hundreds of years. The first commercial naming of a rose was said to have been made by a French milliner, Mme. Caroline Testout, who picked a rose to help promote her business. The rose with her name went on to fame, and it's available yet today. The lady's name lives on.

The famous have always had roses. Today, Whoopi Goldberg has one. So too has Barbara Bush. And Nancy Reagan. And also some women of lesser fame: Arabella Sprunt and Mrs. Percy V. Pennybacker and Gertrude Schweitzer.

In 1990 reporter Charles Hillinger, in the *Los Angeles Times,* told the story of the naming of one rose. Breeder Ralph Moore (see entry) entered his bank in Visalia, California, carrying a yellow and pink miniature rose in a small pot. He stopped by the desk of bank vice president Mary Hill, who exclaimed, "What a gorgeous rose!"

"It's one of my newest miniatures," Moore said. "I want to name it for a friend, but I must get her permission first."

"What a lucky person," Hill responded. "I'm sure she will love it."

"So you will give me your permission then?" Moore asked.

Mary Hill said afterward that she was flabbergasted. "After all," she said, "it immortalizes you." And so the bank's vice president became one of a small group of people who have had roses named for them. Moore has honored other friends with a namesake rose. 'Mary Marshall' was named for one of America's most loved rosarians. Moore named his first rose for a friend, Shelby Wallace, who died

young. 'Little Mike' is one of Ralph's grandsons; 'Anita Charles' is a friend who sings in his church choir; and 'Rose Gilardi' is American Rose Society District Director for California.

Breeders of roses search everywhere for good names—good, sound, commercial names. Grower Jerry Justice in Oregon says that a good rose without a good name doesn't stand a chance. Harmon Saville (see entry) has come up with a great list of names, such as 'Good Morning America', 'Acey Deucy', 'Centerpiece', 'Rainbow's End', 'Happy Go Lucky', 'Cheers', 'Hokey Pokey', 'High Spirits', 'Wedded Bliss', and 'Live Wire'. Texas hybridizer Ernest Williams used the word 'glo' with many of his roses, such as 'Dreamglo' and 'Gloriglo'. William Warriner (see entry) picked a great threesome in 'Love' (red and silver), 'Honor' (white), and 'Cherish' (pink). Female names are popular. New Jersey hybridizer Frank Benardella (see entry) has 'Jennifer' among his top roses, but spreads his net wide with names like 'Old Glory', 'Figurine' and 'Pirouette'.

My own contribution of names for my roses includes, 'You 'n' Me', 'Ain't Misbehavin'', 'Kiss 'n' Tell', 'Kiss the Bride', 'Lovers Only', 'Lady in Red', 'Someday Soon', and 'Stolen Moment'. I named 'Wit's End' for humor columnist Erma Bombeck.

Cities and other places sometimes serve as rose names. In 1980, at a rose testing program in Toledo, Ohio, a rose attracted the local growers. They approached its breeder, Jack Christensen (see entry), who was delighted to name it 'Holy Toledo'.

Griffith Buck of Iowa (see entry) wanted to relate his roses to that state and came up with the Prairie series, including 'Prairie Princess', 'Prairie Sunset', and 'Prairie Harvest'. He didn't neglect the state's name, and we have 'Iowa Belle'. Next he moved on to country dancing, the inspiration for 'Country Dancer', 'Square Dancer', 'Virginia Reel', 'Barn Dance', and 'Do-Si-Do'.

Rose names may change from country to country, but the way to determine which is which is by looking to the code name which becomes part of the rose's name. It is a coined word usually taking the first three letters of the hybridizer's name and then a name to denote a more general name. Thus you find Mor for Ralph Moore, Mac for McGredy, Buc for Griffith Buck roses, and Jac for Jackson & Perkins. □

NATIONAL FLORAL EMBLEM

The rose became the National Floral Emblem in 1986, but not without a fight.

IT WAS ALMOST THE MARIGOLD. OR THE SUN-flower. Or the Shasta daisy. Someone even suggested a stalk of corn. But in the end the rose triumphed.

The efforts to make the rose the national floral symbol began during the presidency of Teddy Roosevelt. Such champions as Senator Margaret Chase Smith, who always wore a rose and whose bill to the Senate in 1955 sought to name the rose as the national flower, prompted much debate but no action. The next major move began in 1978 when Mary Johnston, wife of Louisiana Senator J. Bennett Johnston, approached Harold S. Goldstein, executive secretary of the American Rose Society, for backing for new rose legislation. A campaign was organized, but it wasn't until 1985 that Senator Johnston introduced a joint Senate-House resolution to designate the rose as the national floral emblem.

The resolution said that fossil study shows that the rose in America goes back thirty-five million years. It pointed out that the rose is grown in every state, said the rose is the favorite flower of the American people, and called George Washington the nation's first rose breeder. "The rose has long represented love, friendship, peace, and the devotion of the American people to their country," it said.

The resolution then went to debate. Opponents first pointed out a very simple fact: George Washington was *not* the first American rose breeder. That part of the resolution was incorrect. Opponents argued that the rose already was the emblem of England and of the Virgin Mary. Most opponents conceded that the rose was a spectacular flower, but contended it should not be the national flower. Some so-called experts said incorrectly that old American roses are rarely used in gardens or for breeding purposes. They complained that modern roses are hybridized from Chinese and European roses, which is only partly true. They claimed incorrectly that modern roses have lost the beauty, fragrance, form, and fruit of the old roses.

It was also argued that the rose is no longer an especially native American plant, having changed so much since the original settlers. But doubting Thomases got one answer from a congressman who asked: "What's wrong with evolution? America has evolved." In the end, the rose won. In 1986 the rose was named the national flower in a proclamation signed by President Reagan. □

Federal Register

Vol. 51, No. 226

Monday, November 24, 1986

Presidential Documents

Title 3—

The President

Proclamation 5574 of November 20, 1986

The National Floral Emblem of the United States of America The Rose

By the President of the United States of America

A Proclamation

Americans have always loved the flowers with which God decorates our land. More often than any other flower, we hold the rose dear as the symbol of life and love and devotion, of beauty and eternity. For the love of man and woman, for the love of mankind and God, for the love of country, Americans who would speak the language of the heart do so with a rose.

We see proofs of this everywhere. The study of fossils reveals that the rose has existed in America for age upon age. We have always cultivated roses in our gardens. Our first President, George Washington, bred roses, and a variety he named after his mother is still grown today. The White House itself boasts a beautiful Rose Garden. We grow roses in all our fifty States. We find roses throughout our art, music, and literature. We decorate our celebrations and parades with roses. Most of all, we present roses to those we love, and we lavish them on our altars, our civil shrines, and the final resting places of our honored dead.

The American people have long held a special place in their hearts for roses. Let us continue to cherish them, to honor the love and devotion they represent, and to bestow them on all we love just as God has bestowed them on us.

The Congress, by Senate Joint Resolution 159, has designated the rose as the National Floral Emblem of the United States and authorized and requested the President to issue a proclamation declaring this fact.

NOW, THEREFORE, I, RONALD REAGAN, President of the United States of America, do hereby proclaim the rose as the National Floral Emblem of the United States of America.

IN WITNESS WHEREOF, I have hereunto set my hand this twentieth day of November, in the year of our Lord nineteen hundred and eighty-six, and of the Independence of the United States of America the two hundred and eleventh.

Ronald Reagan

[FR Doc. 86-26605

Filed 11-21-86; 11:02 am]

Billing code 3195-01-M

NATIVE ROSES

The wild roses of America have a long and fascinating history.

LEGENDS SAY THAT INDIAN TRIBES GREW roses and used them for medicinal purposes and to beautify their camps. Captain George Weymouth, upon landing "on an island towards the northward of Virginia" in 1605, found "Gooseberries, Strawberries, Pease and Rose Bushes." William Strachey, in *The Historie of Travell Into Virginia Britania,* said he found, by the dwellings of the Indians, "Bay trees, wild roses and a kynd of low tree." The native roses were soon joined by roses from Europe, and there are many written references to roses being sent to the colonies.

The native roses were good enough on their own to delight and thrill many. Henry David Thoreau, living in a cabin at Walden Pond from 1845 to 1847, loved the wild roses that grew in New England. He found "not wildness" but a certain noble and delicate civility about them, and commented on their rich color, size, and form.

Native roses that decorated the American landscape asked for little and got less. Growing as they did from the Arctic Circle to the Gulf of Mexico, they adapted themselves to the varying conditions so that they could flourish. They carried unsophisticated blooms by today's standards—small, delightful, generally fragrant flowers of few petals having great informality. Eventually they took on names with a horticultural flavor, like *Rosa acicularis,* simply known before then as the Prickly Rose. Although the Prickly Rose is often regarded as being native only to America, it has been found in parts of Europe and Asia. It is re-

garded as the only completely circumpolar rose species and the hardiest rose in the world.

Rosa blanda presents a vision of peace (it was often known as the Meadow Rose), but it had its hardy side, too, and is also known popularly as the Hudson Bay Rose and the Labrador Rose. The old general names survive, so that you will still find the Bald Hip Rose *(Rosa gymnocarpa),* the Virginia Rose (either *Rosa virginiana* or *Rosa lucida),* the Bristly Rose *(Rosa setigera),* and the Prairie Rose *(Rosa nitida).*

Many other native roses have adorned the American landscape. *Rosa ridiscula,* which grows from Oklahoma to Wisconsin, is noted for its wondrous hips in the fall. The Arkansas late-flowering *Rosa foliolosa* has wonderful foliage and doesn't mind the weather, whether it be frost or drought. *Rosa woodsii* grows from British Columbia to Texas. *Rosa nitida*—small, compact, lilac-pink—asks for nothing more than a place to grow, whether it be good soil or bad, well-drained or not; its hardiness takes it from the cold of Newfoundland right down along the northeast coast of the United States. *Rosa stellata,* a fairly large pink flower with a hint of yellow at the heart of the bloom, is more particular about where it will grow because it needs sun and well-drained soil, although it is very hardy. Its homeland is from West Texas to Arizona.

The historical influences of these roses go deep into the past of America. One small pink-flowered species, *Rosa minutifolia* (see entry), is considered one of the most primitive roses surviving in the world today. Yet it was only discovered in 1882, by botanists traveling in Baja California. The stories of all these American native roses have been documented by rose societies and other groups that continue to find more of these hidden links to our past. No longer are these just "wild roses." They are the ancestors of famous modern roses and have helped to raise the rose to its place of honor in America. ◻

NICOLAS, JEAN HENRI (1875–1937)

The 1930s was a time of great new American roses, and many of these can be attributed to Jean Henri Nicolas.

A GROUP OF COTTON MANUFACTURERS headed by his father sent Jean Henri Nicolas to the United States to buy cotton for their mills. He had no intention of staying, but in 1902 fate took a hand. "In New Orleans," he wrote, "I met a young lady from Chicago wintering in the south with her family. The inevitable happened. Before giving his consent, her father exacted my promise that I would not take his daughter to France and that I would become an American citizen."

Nicolas had been a keen amateur rose grower from the age of ten, when his father taught him to bud roses. But the cotton business and then World War I interrupted any thoughts of becoming a professional roseman. When the war ended, he decided that "my avocation should become my vocation," and he joined Jackson & Perkins (see entry). Roses were big business for the firm, and although climbing/rambling roses were sweeping America, Nicolas was not keen on them. "I had seen the tea rose slide gradually from the height of popularity to complete oblivion, the lovely climbing teas replaced . . . by the coarser *wichuraiana* hybrids." He began to produce new roses.

"When it comes to the rose," he wrote, "God gave us wild roses in their primitive stage scattered all over the upper hemisphere. But were it not for men of genius, vision, and infinite patience, the world would still be today as it was created, with only a few wild roses to adorn our gardens." But Nicolas also said, "Man cannot do God's work, only cooperate along the way."

Among the roses he produced as head of research for J&P was 'Eclipse', given its name because it was first seen on a day in August 1932 when there was an eclipse of the sun. 'Eclipse' received one of the highest rose honors of that time, the Bagatelle Gold Medal in 1936. J. Horace McFarland (see entry) wrote of the rose: "If the word aristocratic can properly be applied to a rose, the long yellow buds of 'Eclipse' deserve that adjective." It also won gold medals in Rome and in Portland, Oregon, and is still widely available in the United States, Canada, France, Switzerland, and South Africa. Nicolas also was a rose writer, author of three books: *A Rose Odyssey, The Rose Manual,* and *A Year in the Rose Garden.*

In the history of the floribunda, most credit is given to Gene Boerner (see entry). But it seems possible that Nicolas preceded even Boerner with 'Rochester', a beautiful buff cluster-flower rose that was even then registered as a hybrid tea, and later as a polyantha—but certainly from photographs of the time looks like a beautiful floribunda.

Nicolas was a great traveler in search of new roses. In England he met W. E. Chaplin, head of the famous rose firm run by Chaplin and his seven sons. Nicolas said that Chaplin, then about 80, could have been a character from a Dickens novel. "He is gruff, outspoken, and his remarks would not always be welcome in a

Victorian salon. I called on him in 1928 with an American wholesale florist. He had a beautiful climbing rose that we would have liked to buy for exclusive American distribution. . . . The old man listened to us, then said: 'Gentlemen, my mother was a very religious woman. She taught me to pray mornings and evenings and to trust Americans for cash only. What is your cash proposition?'" They couldn't agree—which was lucky for Nicolas as the rose, Chaplin's Pink Climber, eventually turned out to have a dislike of the American climate.

Nicolas died in 1937 but he left behind a rose that he had hybridized himself. Labeled a climber, it is reluctant to climb very high but it does make a good pillar rose with fragrant, rose-pink double blooms. Issued in 1940, 'Dr. J. H. Nicolas' is still widely available in America. □

OKLAHOMA ROSE ROCKS

Creation of a rare rock formation is explained by both geology and folklore.

In a narrow, eighty-mile strip of Oklahoma between Paul's Valley and Guthrie, an area of reddish-brown rock is formed in clusters that uncannily resemble a fully opened rose with anywhere from five to twenty petals. The rocks, composed of sandy crystals of barite (barium sulfate), generally measure from half an inch to four inches in diameter. The rocks are believed to have been deposited some 250 million years ago. Erosion produces the rose-like design, and weathering has caused many of the stones to become detached from the main rocks.

A legend goes with the rocks. During the 1800s, Indians were driven westward into Oklahoma, and many died on this "trail of tears." Folklore says that as the blood of braves and the tears of maidens fell to the ground, they formed the rocks into the shape of the Cherokee Rose. □

'OLD BLUSH'

This pink rose is more than two centuries old and still blooming magnificently throughout the land.

English rose authority Graham Stuart Thomas wrote that "there are few garden plants of so great value in cultivation today as the 'Old Blush.'" But you don't have to turn to an expert to discover the prevalence of this old China rose. Look in any old graveyard, especially in the southern United States or in the Gold Country of California, and you are almost certain to find 'Old Blush' blooming away. If anything survives in an old garden, it is likely to be 'Old Blush'.

This rose survives so widely because of its ability to root and grow from the tiniest slip or cutting taken from a bush. It thrives anywhere except in very cold areas, and in southern sheltered spots it can grow up to ten feet high. Its color is in its name—blush pink—and the flowers are small, semidouble, and produced over a long period. The fragrance is, to those with a good nose, "true perfume." To others (and this is the official description), it is scentless. 'Old Blush' has many other names: Parson's Pink China, the Common Monthly, Old Pink Daily, or Old Pink Monthly.

Who can even guess how long the rose bloomed in China before being brought to Sweden to Carolus Linnaeus in the mid-1700s? Soon it was seen in America, and its growth on many graves from the 1800s shows that it was a rugged and versatile traveler. Mary Austin Halley's 1835 diary, edited by J. O. Bryan and held at the University of Texas in Austin, records that 'Old Blush' grew at her brother's house in Brozonia, Texas. 'Old Blush' may not have traveled as widely as 'Harison's Yellow', but it certainly got around. It became a great favorite because the flowers would bloom in spring and come again for the fall, often blooming until Christmas. 'Old Blush' also became known as one of the great stud roses, so promiscuous that its pollen was responsible for those marvelous races of roses the Bourbons and the Noisettes. □

OLDEST ROSE SOCIETY

Rose shows were a vital part of early activities.

THE TITLE OF THE OLDEST LOCAL ROSE SOCIety affiliated with the American Rose Society (see entry) generally goes to the Syracuse, New York, Rose Society. The first rose show was held in Syracuse in June 1910, and the society was organized the following winter. The first president was Dr. Edmund M. Mills, who later became president of the American Rose Society. The Syracuse Rose Society became an affiliate of the American Rose Society in 1911. In 1936, the Syracuse society established a garden in honor of Mills, with 10,000 plants.

The main challenge to the longevity claim by Syracuse comes from Portland, Oregon, where the local society was incorporated in 1888 and affiliated with the ARS in 1919. The Portland society was formed by Mrs. Henry B. Pittock, who had just returned from England where she attended a rose show. She wanted to encourage amateurs to cultivate and exhibit roses, and the society's first show, in 1889, was held in a large tent in the garden of the Pittock home. □

OREGON MISSION ROSE

A rose from Boston brought beauty to a wilderness mission.

AT THE HISTORIC 1841 PARSONAGE OF MISSionary Jason Lee, in Salem, Oregon, a tall, lank, green rose bush still grows. Jeannie Hansen, of Salem, says the rose came to Oregon in 1837 with Anna Maria Pitman, whose story is told in the book *With Her Own Wings* (written by Vera Joyce Nelson and edited by Helen Krebs Smith).

Pitman sailed around Cape Horn from Boston to reach Oregon in 1837 to help build a mission in the wilderness. On that same boat, the Oregon Mission Rose also traveled—as a bush, cuttings, or seeds.

In July 1837, Pitman married Jason Lee. In June, a year later, she gave birth to a child who died after only two days.

Anna Maria herself died just a short time later. The rose, a small light pink, still blooming at the parsonage, also grows throughout the state. It has never been formally identified. □

PARKMAN, FRANCIS (1823–1893)

This great American historian is also famous as an expert on roses.

THE BOOK OF ROSES (1866) BY FRANCIS Parkman, frail son of a wealthy New England family, was one of the most interesting books on roses published in the last century. In it he describes his own garden world, writing of the varieties that did well. The book discusses all matters of cultivation, propagation, and hybridizing. Parkman was adamant about the need for pure blood in roses, and devotes a lot of attention in the book to the species and their immediate offspring. His list of recommended roses still makes interesting reading, although most of them are now extinct.

Parkman also gained lasting fame from his history books, notably *The California and Oregon Trail* (1849), now titled *The Oregon Trail*. He set out in 1846 to journey along this trail, returning home physically exhausted. Despite failing eyesight, he wrote his memoirs of the journey.

Parkman was married in 1850 and fathered three children. In 1857, his wife and infant son died. Parkman held a variety of distinguished university positions, including professor of horticulture at Harvard. In 1967, the U.S. Post Office issued a three-cent stamp in honor of Francis Parkman. □

PATENTING OF ROSES

THE FIRST ROSE TO BE REGISTERED UNDER the U.S. Plant Patent Act of 1931 was named, appropriately, 'New Dawn'. When the five-thousandth plant was registered in 1983, it also had an appropriate name: 'Milestone'. Plant patents, lasting seventeen years, bring royalties to breeders for every registered plant sold. The patent act was instrumental in nurseries setting up research departments to produce new roses. Most modern growers patent new varieties, but some now trademark the names instead, receiving a form of legal protection that can remain in force indefinitely. □

'PEACE'

The story of 'Peace' has become one of the most romantic rose stories of our time.

I HAVE NEVER SEEN ANOTHER ROSE LIKE IT. IT is certainly the most beautiful rose in the whole world." So spoke the Duke of Windsor just before World War II as he walked the rose fields of the Meilland family in Tissan, France. The rose has even earned a book devoted to it, Antonia Ridge's *For Love of a Rose*.

A yellow rose with the slightest touch of pink on the tips of the petals, 'Peace' is full, vigorous, and glowing. Grown the world over, it owes a lot of its fame to the United

States. Cuttings of the rose were sent, in the last diplomatic bag to be shipped from France before World War II, to the Conard-Pyle Company (see entry) in Pennsylvania. One day, several years after Conard-Pyle had begun growing the rose, Robert Pyle was lunching with Ramona and Clyde Stocking at their nursery in San Jose, California, and mentioned his interest in giving the rose a permanent name for the United States. (The rose already had several names in Europe, where its production was being delayed by the war: 'Mme A. Meilland', for the breeder's mother, was the name in France; 'Gloria Dei' was the name in Germany; 'Gioia' in Italy.) Clyde Stocking suggested the name 'Peace', a word foremost in everyone's mind at that time.

Official acknowledgment of the name of the rose was received by Conard-Pyle on April 25, 1945, the very day that Berlin was rescued from Nazi control. At the organizational meeting of the United Nations, in San Francisco, the Stocking nursery provided thousands of 'Peace' roses to decorate the tables. "We picked every rose, from bud to full bloom," said Ramona Stocking, "so that every delegate should also have a bud in their rooms." A card went with each rose: "This is the Peace Rose, which was christened at the Pacific Rose Society's Convention in Pasadena on the day Berlin fell. We hope the Peace Rose will influence men's thoughts for everlasting world peace."

Francis Meilland later wrote of the rose he had developed: "If circumstances have decided that it should be known as different names in different countries, this at least is true, that each of these names remind men of goodwill that the love of flowers, and in particular the admiration of this rose, will forever provide them with the occasion to praise God." Robert Pyle wrote, "Even the most skilled of hybridists would count it a triumph if once in a lifetime his fingers and brain might evolve a creation like this. It is a rose vivid with the colors of a dawn of a new era." □

PERRY, ASTOR (BORN 1924)

Astor Perry already was a dedicated exhibitor at rose shows when he began hybridizing roses in 1965, concentrating on large hybrid tea roses. Perry, a peanut specialist for North Carolina University, named

almost all the roses he produced for peanut-growing towns, such as 'Dothan', 'Koppies', 'Lewiston', 'Stokes', 'Suffolk', and 'Dublin' (a peanut town in Georgia). For a long time his roses were not appreciated in the United States; the only place you could find a plant of 'Dublin' was in India. Now it is a top winner at shows in the United States, thanks to a peanut sheller in that town who received 'Dublin' as a gift and helped promote its reputation. □

PESTS

The history of rose growing is also the history of gardeners' battles against pests.

Is it possible to grow beautiful roses without damaging the environment with dangerous insecticides, miticides, and fungicides? As early as 1806, Bernard McMahon (see entry) in his *American Gardener's Calendar* advised gardeners to pull off leaves that looked to be in trouble and, if the ends of shoots were infected, to prune away the infected part. Then he advised them to "dash the branches with water in dry weather . . . which will do a great deal in preventing the mischief from spreading considerably." McMahon also recommended a popular remedy of the time: "Get some tobacco dust, or fine snuff, and scatter some of it over all the branches, but most on those places where the insects are troublesome. This should be strewed over the trees in the morning when the twigs and leaves are wet and let it remain. It will greatly diminish the vermin, and not injure the leaves or fruit."

His remedies sound much like the integrated pest management practices advocated for today's chemical-free garden. But from to-bacco people moved on to stronger stuff: dusting the leaves with quicklime, sulfur, soot, and dust impregnated with the oil of turpentine. William N. White in his *Gardening for the South* (1866) warned that "insects are on the increase in American gardens, partly from the fact that the destruction of forest trees and wild plants has driven them to cultivated ones." White's remedies included sprinkling or washing the plants with hot water or with "infusions of aloes, tobacco, quassia, China berries" or with "soapsuds (especially those made from whale oil soap)" or "guano dissolved in water." Then fumigate with tobacco smoke, he said. Another suggestion from White: set a bonfire of brush just after dark, "which will attract and destroy immense numbers of moths and beetles."

Following are some more examples of old remedies: the good news is that some of them are still valid.

Early Virginia gardeners took tobacco dust and sprinkled it to keep away the aphids and other pests. And it worked. Today tobacco is still used—as shreds for burning as a fumigant and as a rose spray in the form of nicotine sulfate. In another example of coming to grips with garden pests by looking to the past, a number of biodegradable soaps that can be used as sprays have been produced from tobacco.

In the early 1800s, an extract of chrysanthemum flowers was used successfully as an insecticide, and today pyrethrum is still being produced from the same source. In the early 1900s, a tobacco and kerosene mix was said to be an insecticide harmless to foliage. Other old remedies called for one tablespoon of kerosene to a gallon of soapy water, or two parts kero-

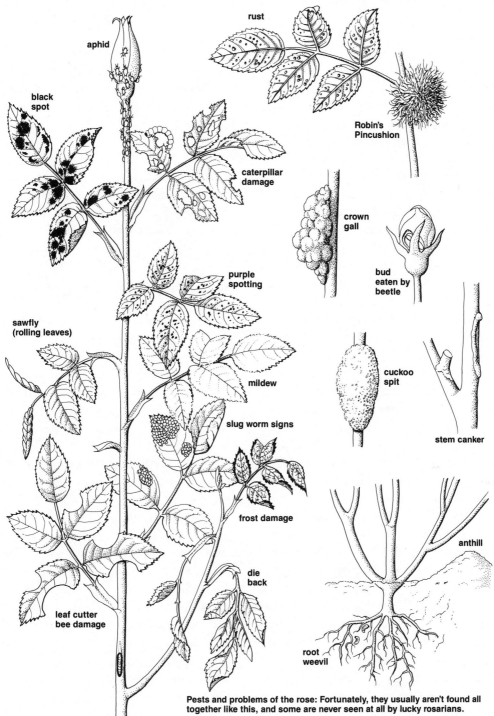

aphid

rust

black
spot

Robin's
Pincushion

caterpillar
damage

crown
gall

bud
eaten by
beetle

purple
spotting

sawfly
(rolling leaves)

cuckoo
spit

mildew

stem canker

slug worm signs

frost damage

anthill

die
back

leaf cutter
bee damage

root
weevil

Pests and problems of the rose: Fortunately, they usually aren't found all
together like this, and some are never seen at all by lucky rosarians.

sene to two of sour milk, shaken together with twenty parts of water. Sabadilla, made from the seeds of a plant of the lily family found in Central and South America, has been a long-time favorite and is still used by organic gardeners. Canadian rose grower Tony Frick has suggested using a tea made from tomato leaves against insects and diseases. The ancient Chinese used derris root, but it was not until 1895 that its insecticidal ingredient was isolated. It is still being used as an extract from the roots of *Derris elliptica, Lonchocarpus utilis,* and other species. Proponents of companion planting contend that if you plant garlic with your roses, the bushes will absorb certain garlic root secretions that keep the bushes clean. Awareness of the dangers of chemical pesticides has led to the development of insecticides that replicate natural extracts; some people call them "synthetic organic" formulations.

The methods of integrated pest management help organic gardeners grow beautiful roses. The George E. Owen Municipal Rose Garden in Eugene, Oregon, with some 4,000 plants of 400 different varieties, once was said to use more fungicide, insecticide, and miticide than all the other gardens in Eugene combined. Then came IPM—with marvelous savings in both time and money. The garden's roses now grow vigorously without yesterday's barrage of sprays. The program, initiated by head gardener Glenn Thompson, has dramatically reduced pesticide use. Beneficial insects are allowed to thrive and control the more harmful ones. Aphids are washed away by normal sprinkler watering or, if they persist, by soap washes. A thorough pruning in January, when weak growth that will not support a bloom is removed, helps control disease.

A monthly fertilizer program and early morning irrigation encourages vigorous growth, which itself is the foundation for healthier roses. The garden won an Outstanding Garden Award from the All-America Rose Selections in 1987.

Growers who resort to chemical sprays should remember that preventive spraying against pests is futile. Wait until you do see the first pests. Wear protective clothing to avoid contact with the chemical, and use it sparingly and in strict accordance with the directions. □

PLANTING A ROSE BUSH

A few basic considerations in planting of a rose bush will help your roses get off to a good start.

WHEN PLANTING A POTTED ROSE, BE CAREful to keep the root ball intact. A few special rules apply to bareroot roses.

• Soak the plant in a bucket of water for at least three hours.

•Cut the canes back to ten inches or so. Make each cut above an outward-facing eye, which appears as a little red bud on the cane. (This is more easily done before planting.)

•Prepare a planting mix that contains rotted compost, a cup of bonemeal or superphosphate, and fine soil.

•Dig the hole big enough to accommodate the roots easily—at least eighteen inches deep and wide. You may also trim back some of the longer roots.

•Place the plant in the hole so that the bud union (where the canes and the roots meet) sits about one inch below ground level.

•Fill the hole halfway with planting mix. Water thoroughly. Then fill in the hole.

Mound the soil up around the canes to protect them.

Don't plant new roses where old roses have been growing for some years. Give that soil a rest, or bring in fresh soil for the planting hole. □

PORCELAIN ROSES

American artists Jean du Tilleux and Edward Marshall Boehm created treasured likenesses of the rose in porcelain.

JEAN DU TILLEUX (1903–1991), THE QUEEN OF porcelain roses, was interested in roses before she began creating porcelain art. "It isn't surprising that Mother chose to duplicate the rose, because of my father's interest," said Mae Jean Eschenfelder, who continues the family business in Shreveport, Louisiana. "Dad always had a few rose bushes growing in the yard, and if one was in bloom, he would cut it and take it to her, alongside a cup of coffee. What a lovely way to start the day!" The roses grown in the Tilleux family garden were 'Red Radiance', 'Pink Radiance', 'Dainty Bess', and 'Talisman', and most of them came to be featured in the Tilleux porcelain work.

It was not until the 1960s that Eugenie Josephine Tilleux (always known as Jean) followed up an interest in antiques by creating her first work in ceramics. She tried both pottery (nontranslucent earthenware) and porcelain (translucent chinaware), and decided that porcelain would be her medium. She purchased a small kiln and, after creating her first bouquet, undertook art training with Elizabeth Harris of Shreveport.

She completed her first ceramic rose ar-

rangement in 1962 and entered it in the San Francisco Ceramic Show. The show's clerk told her that only the vase was eligible for entry because artificial flowers were not permitted. She explained that the flowers were created totally of porcelain, and the amazed clerk accepted them into competition. The surprise of the clerk was echoed by the judges, who awarded the arrangement best in show. From there the roses of Jean du Tilleux (she used the European version of her husband's family name for the business) became famous. And Jean shared the fame with her husband, Oscar, who selected containers for the arrangements and grew roses for the models.

In 1972, American Rose Society secretary

Harold Goldstein commissioned her to create an arrangement of twenty-five 'Garden Party' roses to commemorate selection of First Lady Pat Nixon as the first patroness of the society. For her own golden wedding anniversary in 1972, Jean created an arrangement in porcelain of the rose 'Golden Anniversary', with 24 large roses, 25 buds, and 500 leaves.

Writing in the brochure for a showing of her roses at Shreveport's Norton Art Gallery in 1973, Goldstein said: "To create such lifelike roses, Jean Tilleux had to study the rose as God created it. Love of the rose as well as love of work played their respective roles." The exhibit included bouquets of porcelain roses depicting such famous varieties as 'Angel Wings', 'Redgold', 'Show Girl', 'Cecile Brunner', and a wild rose similar to the Cherokee Rose. And, of course, there was a reminder of those early garden roses that came with the morning coffee—'Dainty Bess'.

Boehm porcelain, renowned worldwide, began in a basement in Trenton, New Jersey. Still headquartered in Trenton, Boehm now has a sister company in England and studios in New York, Chicago, Los Angeles, Dallas, and Houston. Edward Marshall Boehm (1913–1969) and his wife, Helen, knew nothing about porcelain and little about painting when they began learning those arts in 1950 and started a porcelain art business in Trenton, ceramics center of the United States since the mid-nineteenth century.

As early as 1951, Boehm porcelain was gaining an international name, with the Metropolitan Museum of Art acquiring two of the first pieces, a Percheron stallion and a Hereford bull. Within a few years, Boehm work had been taken up by many museums as well as being placed in Buckingham Palace, Elysee Palace, and the Vatican. President and Mrs. Eisenhower began to use Boehm porcelain as gifts to other heads of state. Every American president since Eisenhower has commissioned Boehm gifts for visiting dignitaries.

Boehm porcelain eventually included representations of the rose. Among roses selected for porcelain work were 'Mountbatten', 'Grace de Monaco', 'Princess Margaret', and, in 1992, the new rose from Jackson & Perkins for First Lady Barbara Bush. □

PORTLAND, OREGON

Portland, Oregon, is home to an international rose trial garden that has bestowed coveted gold medals since 1919.

PORTLAND'S INFATUATION WITH THE ROSE goes a long way back. The Portland Rose Society was incorporated in 1888 and held its first show the following year. In 1904, Portland celebrated the 100th anniversary of Lewis and Clark's explorations by planting an early hybrid tea rose, 'Mme Caroline Testout', along fifty miles of its streets. The lady for whom the rose was named was a French dressmaker who wanted to promote her business and paid "a big price" to Pernet for this rose. Pernet said afterwards that he was delighted to sell the rose, as he had already discarded it! But the lady had the last laugh—today it is one of the few roses remaining that carry the name of Pernet in catalogs. From these beginnings came the annual Portland Rose Festival, now regarded as one of the top ten community festivals in the nation.

Portland has a magnificent international rose trial garden, with ten acres of bloom, established in 1917 by famous American rosarians E. Gurney Hill (see entry) of Indiana, Robert Pyle (see entry for Conard-Pyle Company) of Pennsylvania, and George Morris of Ohio. One of the city's leading businessmen, Jesse A. Currey, helped make the test garden a reality.

In the early years, the test garden was surrounded by a wire fence and gates to foil thieves looking for specimens of new roses. In those days, there was no Plant Patent Act, and anyone who got a rose, in whatever manner, could market it. In September 1925, rose pirates stole the Gold Medal-winning 'Cascadia', which had been judged ninety-six percent

perfect. History seems not to have agreed; the rose is not found in commerce today.

There is no longer a need for a fence, and the garden is the longest continuously operating test garden in the United States. One of its most famous curators was Fred Edmunds, Sr. (see entry), who was always enlarging and improving the plantings. His own explanation was that, "like Topsy, they just growed."

Despite all the rose attention on this city, only three roses had been named for it as of 1992, and two of them are Irish. 'Portland Trailblazer' is a big red hybrid tea (known as 'Big Chief' in Britain), from Pat Dickson in Northern Ireland. The miniature 'Portland Dawn' was raised by me in Dublin. In 1992, a

French-bred rose was registered as 'Portland Rose Festival', a red-blend hybrid tea. (The old race of Portland roses has nothing to do with the Oregon city. They emanated from the garden of the Empress Josephine, who called the first of the race 'Duchess of Portland'.)

These are the Gold Medal winners from the Portland International Test Garden:

YEAR	WINNERS	COLOR	CLASS	ORIGINATOR
1993	Sally Holmes	white	shrub	Robert Holmes
1992	Prima Donna	deep pink	grandiflora	Takeshi Shirakawa
1991	Maid of Honour	yellow blend	hybrid tea	Von Weddle
1990	Sexy Rexy	medium pink	floribunda	Sam McGredy
1989	Class Act Playboy	white red blend	floribunda floribunda	William Warriner Anne Cocker
1988	Touch of Class Las Vegas	orange-pink orange blend	hybrid tea hybrid tea	Michel Kriloff Reimer Kordes
1987	Keepsake	pink blend	hybrid tea	Reimer Kordes
1986	Tony Jacklin	orange blend	floribunda	Sam McGredy
1985	Olympiad Sun Flare The Sun	medium red medium yellow orange blend	hybrid tea floribunda floribunda	Sam McGredy William Warriner Sam McGredy
1984	French Lace Viva	white medium red	floribunda floribunda	William Warriner William Warriner
1982	Matangi	orange blend	floribunda	Sam McGredy
1981	Silver Jubilee Trumpeter	pink blend orange-red	hybrid tea floribunda	Alex Cocker Sam McGredy

YEAR	WINNERS	COLOR	CLASS	ORIGINATOR
1980	Bobby Charlton	pink blend	hybrid tea	Gareth Fryer
	Love	red blend	grandiflora	William Warriner
1979	Liverpool Echo	orange-pink	floribunda	Sam McGredy
	Paradise	mauve	hybrid tea	O. L. Weeks
	Pristine	white	hybrid tea	William Warriner
1978	Razzle Dazzle	red blend	floribunda	William Warriner
	Honor	white	hybrid tea	William Warriner
1977	Evening Star	white	floribunda	William Warriner
	Princess Margaret of England	medium pink	hybrid tea	M. L. Meilland
1976	Charisma	red blend	floribunda	Bob Jelly
1975	Prominent	orange-red	grandiflora	Reimer Kordes
	Handel	red blend	climber	Sam McGredy
1974	Cathedral	apricot blend	floribunda	Sam McGredy
1973	Electron	deep pink	hybrid tea	Sam McGredy
1972	Medallion	apricot blend	hybrid tea	William Warriner
1971	Dortmund	medium red	kordesii	Reimer Kordes
	Sparrieshoop	light pink	shrub	Reimer Kordes
	Molly McGredy	red blend	floribunda	Sam McGredy
	Paloma	white	hybrid tea	Swim and Weeks
1970	Europeana	dark red	floribunda	G. de Ruiter
	Ice White	white	floribunda	Sam McGredy

YEAR	WINNERS	COLOR	CLASS	ORIGINATOR
1970 cont.	Irish Gold	medium yellow	hybrid tea	Pat Dickson
	Red Devil	medium red	hybrid tea	Pat Dickson
1968	Lady X	mauve	hybrid tea	M. L. Meilland
	Redgold	yellow blend	floribunda	Pat Dickson
1967	Bewitched	medium pink	hybrid tea	Walter Lammerts
	Pascali	white	hybrid tea	Louis Lens
1966	Summer Rainbow	pink blend	hybrid tea	Bob Jelly
	Miss All-American Beauty	medium pink	hybrid tea	Fred J. Armbrust
	Fragrant Cloud	orange-red	hybrid tea	Mathias Tantau
1965	Mischief	medium pink	hybrid tea	Sam McGredy
	Orangeade	orange-red	floribunda	Sam McGredy
1964	Matterhorn	white	hybrid tea	Armstrong and Swim
	Wendy Cussons	medium red	hybrid tea	Charles Gregory
	Silver Lining	pink blend	hybrid tea	Pat Dickson
1962	My Choice	pink blend	hybrid tea	Edward Le Grice
	Chicago Peace	pink blend	hybrid tea	Stanley G. Johnston
1962	Royal Highness	light pink	hybrid tea	Swim and Weeks
	Tropicana	orange-red	hybrid tea	Mathias Tantau
1960	Golden Slippers	yellow blend	floribunda	Gordon Von Abrams
	Memoriam	white	hybrid tea	Gordon Von Abrams
	Royal Sunset	apricot blend	climber	Dennison Morey
1959	El Capitan	medium red	grandiflora	Herb Swim

YEAR	WINNERS	COLOR	CLASS	ORIGINATOR
1959 cont.	Angel Wings	pink blend	hybrid tea	Robert V. Lindquist
	Pink Parfait	pink blend	grandiflora	Herb Swim
1958	Kordes Perfecta	pink blend	hybrid tea	Reimer Kordes
	Little Darling	yellow blend	floribunda	Carl G. Duehrsen
	Sarabande	orange-red	floribunda	Francis Meilland
1957	Audie Murphy	medium red	hybrid tea	Walter Lammerts
	Burnaby	white	hybrid tea	Gordon Eddie
	Golden Showers	medium yellow	climber	Walter Lammerts
	Pink Favorite	pink	hybrid tea	Gordon Von Abrams
	Montezuma	orange-pink	hybrid tea	Herb Swim
1956	Mrs. Sam McGredy	orange blend	hybrid tea	Sam McGredy
	McGredy's Yellow	medium yellow	hybrid tea	Sam McGredy
1955	Ena Harkness	dark red	hybrid tea	Albert Norman
	Carrousel	dark red	grandiflora	Carl G. Duehrsen
	Spartan	orange-red	floribunda	Eugene Boerner
1954	Queen Elizabeth	pink	grandiflora	Walter Lammerts
	Tiffany	pink blend	hybrid tea	Robert V. Lindquist
1953	Independence	orange-red	floribunda	Wilhelm Kordes
1951	Chrysler Imperial	dark red	hybrid tea	Walter Lammerts
1950	Vogue	pink blend	floribunda	Eugene Boerner
1949	Fashion	pink blend	floribunda	Eugene Boerner
1947	Forty-Niner	red blend	hybrid tea	Herb Swim

YEAR	WINNERS	COLOR	CLASS	ORIGINATOR
1946	Sutter's Gold	orange blend	hybrid tea	Herb Swim
1945	Rubaiyat	light red	hybrid tea	Sam McGredy
1944	Lowell Thomas	deep yellow	hybrid tea	Charles Mallerin
	Peace	yellow blend	hybrid tea	Francis Meilland
1942	Fred Edmunds	orange blend	hybrid tea	Francis Meilland
	Pinocchio	pink blend	floribunda	Wilhelm Kordes
1941	Charlotte Armstrong	light red	hybrid tea	Walter Lammerts
	Heart's Desire	medium red	hybrid tea	Fred H. Howard
	Dainty Maid	light pink	floribunda	Edward Le Grice
	Dickson's Red	dark red	hybrid tea	Alex Dickson
	Grande Duchesse Charlotte	medium red	hybrid tea	Ketten Bros.
	Neville Chamberlain	orange blend	hybrid tea	Louis Lens
1940	Matador	dark red	hybrid tea	G. A. Van Rossem
	Poinsettia	medium red	hybrid tea	Howard and Smith
1939	Mme Henri Guillot	red blend	hybrid tea	Charles Mallerin
	Holstein	red	floribunda	Wilhelm Kordes
1938	Charlotte E. van Dedem	yellow	hybrid tea	G. A. H. Buisman
	Sterling	medium pink	hybrid tea	E. Gurney Hill
	Saturnia	red blend	hybrid tea	Luigi Aicardi
1937	Signora	orange blend	hybrid tea	Luigi Aicardi
	Golden State	deep yellow	hybrid tea	Francis Meilland
	Christopher Stone	medium red	hybrid tea	Herbert Robinson

YEAR	WINNERS	COLOR	CLASS	ORIGINATOR
1936	Feu Pernet-Ducher	medium yellow	hybrid tea	Joseph Pernet-Ducher
1935	Rochefort	apricot blend	hybrid tea	Charles Mallerin
	Texas Centennial	light red	hybrid tea	A. F. Watkins
	Eclipse	medium yellow	hybrid tea	Jean Henri Nicolas
	Karen Poulsen	medium red	floribunda	Svend Poulsen
1934	Luis Brinas	orange blend	hybrid tea	Pedro Dot
1933	Duquesa de Penaranda	orange blend	hybrid tea	Pedro Dot
1932	Mme Nicolas Aussel	salmon-carmine	hybrid tea	Joseph Pernet-Ducher
1929	Reveil Dijonnaise	red blend	climbing hybrid tea	Buatois
	Julien Potin	yellow	hybrid tea	Joseph Pernet-Ducher
1921	Mrs. George C. Thomas	salmon-pink	hybrid musk	Captain G. C. Thomas
	Imperial Potentate	medium pink	hybrid tea	Clarke Brothers
1920	Glenn Dale	white	climber	Walter Van Fleet
1919	Columbia	medium pink	hybrid tea	E. Gurney Hill
	Bloomfield Abundance	light pink	floribunda	Captain G. C. Thomas

PRAIRIE ROSE

See Rosa setigera.

PRESIDENTIAL ROSES

F ROM WASHINGTON ONWARD, ROSES HAVE been named for presidents. Among them are 'Calvin Coolidge' (glowing crimson, very hardy), 'Franklin D. Roosevelt' (velvet scarlet, fragrant), 'Herbert Hoover' (orange and gold, fragrant), 'President Lincoln' and 'Mister Lincoln', 'W. H. Taft', and 'John F. Kennedy'. The first ladies also have been widely honored with roses, including 'First Lady Nancy', 'Lady Bird Johnson', 'Pat Nixon', 'Rosalynn Carter', 'Jacqueline', and 'Barbara Bush'. □

PRINCE NURSERY

Robert Prince opened his Linnaean Gardens Nursery in Flushing, Long Island, around the 1740s.

T HE PRINCE NURSERY WAS ONE OF THE FIRST commercial nurseries in the United States dealing only in roses, initially listing only twelve varieties. Prince introduced into commerce many of the native roses that Thomas Jefferson purchased from him in an order dated July 6, 1791. The order covered fruit trees (such as apricot, apple, and peach), various other items, and roses, including a moss rose, white damask, musk rose, cinnamon rose, and *Rosa mundi.*

Imported roses offered by Prince at the time included *Rosa gallica* (main ancestor of the gar-den roses of Europe), *Rosa mundi* (pink, red, and blush striped variety), *Rosa centifolia* (moss rose first described in the 1600s in France), *Rosa cinnamomea* (deep lilac-pink flowers), white damask (possibly from Damascus or Syria), and 'Old Blush' (one of the most common and valuable of old roses; see entry). It was probably the business brought to Robert Prince by many important people that encouraged the growth of the nursery. A century later, the nursery was offering more than 1,600 varieties. □

'PRISTINE'

William Warriner produced another winner in this hybrid tea.

W HEN JACKSON & PERKINS (SEE ENTRY) introduced 'Pristine' in 1976, the rose immediately began winning prizes. Barbara Harding Oehlbeck, writing from near La Bella, Florida, praised 'Pristine' for its performance in the "warm, high-porosity soil and gentle climates of Florida."

'Pristine' was bred by William Warriner (see entry) for J&P from a cross between 'White Masterpiece' and 'First Prize'. A total of 2,386 seedlings were produced, of which only fourteen were selected for further evaluation. From that group, Warriner found one that he never rated less than XXXX—the highest possible marking. "Her coloration is unlike any other rose in commerce," he rhapsodized at the time on its ivory, shaded pink bloom. "The finest picotee effect is evident when she is half open. Rarely do you find an imperfect flower in any weather. Her form is outstanding, a great exhibition rose, symmetrical form all the way from bud to open flower." His praise was justified. 'Pristine' is still one of the finest hybrid tea roses in commerce. □

PROPAGATION OF ROSES

Gardeners have a variety of ways to produce roses.

THERE ARE SIX WAYS OF PROPAGATING ROSES: budding, grafting, layering, tissue culture, seed planting, and using cuttings. The simplest way for the ordinary gardener is to take cuttings, a method used to propagate miniatures, old garden roses, and some others. Here's how to do it.

Take a cutting from a plant that is in bloom. The cutting from a miniature should be three to four inches long. The cutting from a large-flowered type should be about nine inches long and have four to five good growth buds (eyes) below the flower. There should also be sets of five leaflets on the cutting. Once you have taken the cutting, cut off the base immediately below a set of leaves, then remove the flower and the bottom two sets of leaves. Dip the end of the cutting into rooting hormone powder. Plant the cutting, with one to one and a half inches of the stem under the soil. Cover the cutting with a plastic bag. Keep it misted and warm, and your rooting should be a success. Most roses sold in pots are produced this way.

Bareroot roses are budded by taking a growth bud (eye) from a plant and inserting it into a wild stock root. In about eighteen months, the bush is ready for sale. Budded roses make larger plants far quicker than those propagated by cuttings, but budding generally is not a procedure for an amateur. Neither is the more modern method of tissue culture, which requires almost laboratory conditions. For a discussion of seed planting, see the Hybridizing entry.

Layering is propagation by means of one of the canes on a growing plant. To layer a rose, bend a cane to ground level, being careful not to snap it. Make a small slit in the cane and hold it open with a pebble. Fix the cane in position with wire. Cover the cut with soil and leave it until it has rooted.

Grafting is the most difficult method and is best left to professionals.

Note that recently introduced roses are covered by plant patents, and it is illegal to reproduce them for resale. □

PRUNING

The goal of pruning, one of the simplest jobs in the rose garden, is to keep a plant young and healthy.

THE BETTER THE PRUNING, THE LONGER THE life of the rose. Pruning should make a plant grow the way you want it to grow and not the way nature is inclining it. Pruning should be done just before the plant breaks dormancy, and here is how to go about it.

Remove old canes that are gnarled, woody, diseased, or otherwise unhealthy, right to the bud union. Keep green canes from the previous season; just shorten them. Prune the bush to a height of about eighteen inches, but always below any blackened, yellowing, or bluish wood. In cutting, make a slanting cut about a quarter of an inch above an outward-pointing leaf bud (the little nipple inside the point where the leaves grow from the cane). Take away any spindly growth that is too weak to bear flowers.

Work on one bush at a time. Do the job thoroughly, including removal of weeds and spent wood. Immediately after pruning, gently scuffle the soil, and give a light fertilizer feeding to tell the bush that it's time to get on with growing again. □

'QUEEN ELIZABETH'

Its unusual characteristics made 'Queen Elizabeth' the first in a new class of roses—the grandiflora.

'QUEEN ELIZABETH', BRED BY WALTER E. Lammerts (see entry) and one of the finest roses ever to win the All-America Rose Selection award, was a new sort of rose. Its flowers were not quite big enough for a hybrid tea and not clustered enough for a floribunda; it was considered too tall for the floribunda class but not tall enough to be a climber. A new class of roses—the grandiflora—was created for it.

Other roses have since been classified as grandiflora, but 'Queen Elizabeth' remains the true measure of the class. The flower is pink, with good form. The plant has fine foliage and is quite free of disease. 'Queen Elizabeth' will grow anywhere: inland, on a high and windy hill, or facing the sea, on ground where other roses would be unhappy. It can be cut to ground level and still bring inspiring growth in a couple of years.

The rose, introduced in 1955, was named for Queen Elizabeth II at the beginning of her reign. There were hints of unhappiness among British growers that an American variety should be named for their queen, but it was soon seen as a fine compliment.

Although the rose was not entered in competition outside the United States, it was awarded the gold medal of the Royal National Rose Society in Britain to add to its American Rose Society Gold and the Gertrude M. Hubbard Gold Medal of the American Rose Society. It was later voted one of the world's favorite roses by the World Federation of Rose Societies.

In an interview in the January 1984 American Rose Society magazine, Lammerts recalled the background to the hybridizing of the rose. "I used 'Floradora'," he said, "because it was the first of the cinnebar red [terra cotta] colored roses. Its color intrigued me and I wanted to see if I could combine it with 'Charlotte Armstrong's' long bud form. I had no idea that 'Queen Elizabeth' would result." What he got was a rose out of character in color and with amazing vigor, a variety that is still regarded as one of the world's top roses. □

REAGAN, NANCY

THE FIRST ROSE NAMED TO HONOR NANCY Reagan was issued in 1967, when her husband, Ronald Reagan, was governor of California. 'Nancy Reagan', an orange-red hybrid tea, is practically out of commerce now. The team of Swim and Christensen brought out a rose called 'First Lady Nancy' in 1981, after her husband was elected president of the United States. It was a yellow hybrid tea with a tinge of light pink. But less than a decade later, it was unobtainable commercially in the United States. □

RED ROSE RENT DAY

A rose company continued a tradition that dates back to the Magna Carta.

SEVERAL OLD DEEDS IN AMERICAN HISTORY have the proviso that the rent be "one red rose yearly if the same be demanded." It is a custom that is believed to have come from England, where the common man could not own land and had to rent small pieces. After the Magna Carta was signed in 1215, substantial rents were often changed to merely token rents. William Penn and the Quakers brought the idea of the token rent with them to the New World.

The tradition of the red rose rent was continued in this century by the Conard-Pyle Company of West Grove, Pennsylvania. In the 1920s, the company acquired a farm in the rolling hills of southeastern Pennsylvania to use in growing roses. Robert Pyle, the head of the company, found a document that showed that the original deed had been granted in 1731 to John, Thomas, and Richard Penn. The 5,000 acres under this grant were subject to a rental fee of "one red rose yearly if the same be demanded." These terms were included in subsequent deeds.

In 1929, the first crop of roses bloomed on the new Conard-Pyle land. Robert Pyle decided to continue the old custom of the red rose rent. Thus, in June 1937, a red rose was given to the president of the local historical rose society. The following year, a ninth-generation descendant of William Penn, Philip Penn-Gaskell Hall, Jr., born only five miles from the rose fields, was the recipient. This time the fully paid-up rose rent was 205 blooms, one for every year since the deed was made minus the bloom given to the local historical rose society.

This was the start of Red Rose Rent Day, which became one of the great social rose events in the United States. World personalities were brought in to talk, and new roses were introduced. Unfortunately, economic factors brought an end to Red Rose Rent Day in 1984.

Also in Pennsylvania, there is a red rose rent attachment to Zion Lutheran Church at Manheim, the result of a deed in 1727 for land on which the church was built. A feast day of roses was inaugurated in 1892 as part of the commemoration. ◻

REJECTED ROSES

It is not often that a person or organization rejects the chance to be namesake of a new rose.

H YBRIDIZER RALPH MOORE (SEE ENTRY) once suggested that a then-unnamed yellow miniature rose should honor Olympic skating star Dorothy Hamill. Her agent's reply to the gracious offer was: "Miss Hamill is not endorsing any products at this time." The agent had no love of nature—and very little foresight—for the rose went on to become one of the top miniatures in the world under the name of 'Rise 'n' Shine'.

The most surprising rejection story of all concerns 'American Legion'. This cerise-red rose won medals in the 1920s from international rose shows in Portland and New York for its profuse bloom, strong fragrance, bright color, long stems, glossy foliage, disease resistance, lack of thorns, and great vigor. This is a recipe for the perfect rose, but the organization said, "No, we don't want a rose with our name." The rose is now lost. ◻

ROOSEVELT, THEODORE, AND FRANKLIN DELANO

These two American presidents had a love for the rose.

T HE ROOSEVELT INTEREST IN ROSES IS FA- mous. After all, the Roosevelt name does mean "field of roses."

Photographs of Theodore Roosevelt usually show him with a rose in his buttonhole. That rose was always the same—'Duchesse of Brabant' (1857), a pink tea rose of high quality that was able to stand cool weather. A painting of "Teddy" by John deCamp shows him with the rose in his buttonhole and a vase of roses on the table. In 1907, Roosevelt met with delegates to the American Rose Society Convention in the White House.

In 1946, on Franklin Delano Roosevelt's birthday, each member of the House of Representatives wore a white rose. He willed that he should be buried in his mother's rose garden in Hyde Park, New York. He wooed his cousin Eleanor there, and she now rests beside him among the roses. ◻

ROSA BRACTEATE

This is a beautiful rose with a wild reputation.

B RACTEATE IS KNOWN BY ALL SORTS OF names, from its official name of *Rosa bracteate* (in some places also *Rosa lucida*) to the farmer's disaster rose, the McCartney rose, the hedge rose, and the Chickasaw Rose. Some people call it the fried-egg rose because of its five pure-white, saucer-like petals surrounding a center of golden stamens. But it is best known as a troublemaker for farmers and ranchers.

Used by early settlers as windbreaks and fences, it spread everywhere with far more vigor than any other rose. Bracteate was propagated by seed blown for long distances, and just kept growing regardless of control measures. Spreading an impenetrable mass of bright-green shining foliage and white flowers over good pastureland, it could well be called a botanical barbed wire.

Bracteate spread across America and would

have been a worse ecological disaster had it been hardier. In parts of the South, especially Texas, it found its perfect home, with warmth and water to help it multiply. It brought beauty, but at a great price: the economic hardship faced by farmers and ranchers who lost pastureland to its spread. In places it still has not been eliminated, and its presence is so persistent that it could easily be regarded as native although it originated in China.

History tells many stories about bracteate. One is that it arrived in a package of roses ordered by Thomas Jefferson from the nurseries of William Prince at Flushing, Long Island, in the 1790s. No doubt many other gardeners ordered the bush, and it soon became naturalized. In its favor as an ornamental shrub was the fact that it flowered throughout the summer, which only about four species roses do. Despite its reputation in the southern United States as a weed, it became a parent of one of today's most beautiful climbing roses, 'Mermaid'. It passed along to 'Mermaid' its dislike of cold weather but not its ease of propagation. It gave the rose world a mightily attractive rose, however, with five huge, creamy-white petals brought strikingly alive with deep golden stamens. You could forgive a rose a lot for that. □

ROSA CALIFORNICA

The rose named after California doesn't always get the respect it deserves.

THE TINY *ROSA CALIFORNICA* IS OFTEN IG-nored in the rose history of the state, and it has been roughly treated by botanists, rose writers, gardeners, and farmers over hundreds

of years. Some suggest it is a nonentity and lacks distinctive characteristics. English author and rose breeder Jack Harkness, in his book *Roses* (1978), strongly disagreed: "I can scarcely believe my eyes when I see it dismissed as pink and uninteresting." He described the flowers, carried in great clusters, as "neat and small. . . . Their colour is lilac pink, light, with the lavender or lilac accentuated more definitely than in any wild rose, and yellow stamens to decorate it." There is nothing of a nonentity about a rose like that—but maybe it just needs the loving eyes of an expert to lead us toward its beauty. □

ROSA MINUTIFOLIA

Climatic adaptation helped this primitive rose survive.

THE HISTORICAL INFLUENCES OF *ROSA minutifolia* go deep into the past of America, with experts agreeing that it is one of the most primitive roses surviving in the world today. Yet this little pink-flowered species was discovered only in 1882, by botanists traveling in an area between Ensenada and El Rosario in Baja California. They were surprised that a rose could grow in land that was described by one traveler as "the most unfortunate, ungrateful, and miserable in the world." *Rosa minutifolia* had adapted to the conditions by blooming only in winter, setting seeds before the terrors of a hot, dry summer.

More than a century later, in 1985, a small colony of the rose was found in a barren area near San Diego, the only group known to be growing in the United States. Rosarian Lawrence Smith, with the help of Caroline

Stabile, took propagating material to the Quail Botanical Gardens in Encinitas, California. Their efforts were successful, and in their first batch they got four new plants of *minutifolia.* These have provided a basis for propagation of the rose that, it is hoped, will be established again locally and will go into botanical collections around the world. ▫

ROSA PALUSTRIS

The swamp rose is that rare rose that can withstand dampness and cold.

MY FIRST SIGHT OF THIS TRUE NATIVE, THE swamp rose, came as I traveled a Louisiana back road, close to swampland. The flowers, bright rose pink, were waving about on lax stems that grew to about six feet. The bush, growing uninhibited by man's pruning, sent its stems any way that nature decided before producing a tangled mass. Here was a rose growing in a swamp, which certainly dashed the belief that roses never do well with their feet in the muck. And what added to its interest was that this *Rosa palustris* was blooming out of season, much later than most other species roses.

The plant—with its reddish stems, hooked and broad-based prickles (few, but capable of holding their own), dark green foliage, and pink flowers about two inches across—stayed in my mind until one day, some years later, I came across *Rosa palustris* again—this time as a cultivated plant. Assessing the swamp rose, Texas nurseryman G. Michael Shoup called it "architecturally beautiful at all times," versatile in any landscape, either poorly drained soil or in a normal garden. It is said to be a native of southeast Canada and the northeastern United States, which is not surprising as it manages to survive dampness and the extremes of cold and heat, and is practically indestructible.

The swamp rose also has a place in European history. When the Empress Josephine allowed her love of the rose to fill the garden of Malmaison in Paris, she added the strange and lovely, but generally despised, swamp rose to her collection. And when Pierre-Joseph Redouté put together his great work "Les Roses," the swamp rose achieved another measure of fame by being among the roses painted by the world's greatest flower artist.

At home in the United States, the swamp rose was for many years a subject of confusion. Because of its wide dispersal, it was sometimes called *Rosa pennsylvanica, Rosa hudsoniana,* or *Rosa carolinana.* But botanically it is correctly *Rosa palustris,* though it's usually called by its popular name of swamp rose. ▫

ROSA SETIGERA

Prairie Rose is the popular name for this great American native.

ROSA SETIGERA, A WILD ROSE THAT SPREADS through North America, is the only native rose that is truly a climber. The almost thornless stems arch up to six feet high, making a marvelous sight when the deep pink flowers are in full bloom.

The long, slender growth of *Rosa setigera* takes over any support, tree, or bush near it and forms a wild, tangled mass unless controlled. To be truly a prairie plant, the rose had to be as durable and tenacious as the early American pioneers. *Rosa setigera* is tough, disease-resistant, and worthy of its high place among American native roses.

George Washington wrote about a wild rose hedge at Mount Vernon in 1785. The name of the rose is not given, but it probably was the Prairie Rose, which would have been growing abundantly in the region at that time. It was brought into cultivation early. The year 1810 is given as the time of its introduction into commerce. □

ROSA STELLATA

ROSA STELLATA, FOUND ORIGINALLY IN NEW Mexico in 1893, makes its home from West Texas to Arizona. It needs sun and well-drained soil, but for all that has been found to be very hardy. The bloom is large pink, with a hint of yellow at its heart. Gardeners might think the plant has a mildew problem, but not so. The impression comes from the hairy cover on the young stems, which look as if they had been dipped in flour. The hairy rose has a cousin, the Sacramento rose *(Rosa stellata mirifica),* that doesn't have the hairs. □

ROSA WICHURAIANA

When American rose breeders started using Rosa wichuraiana, *they opened the way to clambering, trailing beauty.*

NO ONE COULD HAVE GUESSED THAT *ROSA wichuraiana,* an almost prostrate Asian rose, would have the ability to pick up and carry on a greater range of color and flower shape than most other roses then being used in breeding new varieties. Among the fine roses that came from *wichuraiana* crosses were 'Dr. Van Fleet', 'Dorothy Perkins', 'Breeze Hill', 'Debutante', 'Evangeline', 'Excelsa', and 'Gardenia'. The effect of these varieties had a huge influence on the attitude in the United States toward roses. The new roses exhibited good characteristics of growth, color, and fragrance; they were easy to care for and were hardy.

Rosa wichuraiana itself got the name of the Memorial Rose because of its ability to grow everywhere and for every occasion. Not everyone loved it. One writer talked of its "strong canes beset with innumerable prickles which usurp the ground, making it a struggle for even grass to grow near it." But commercial rose growers, always looking for new varieties of ramblers, continued to use *Rosa wichuraiana.* Nothing has been produced to quite match the early American varieties bred from it, many of which are still available. Though these varieties have gone out of fashion, their rampant growth and flower production still have a place in gardens throughout the world. □

ROSE OF CASTILE

Early California missions made grateful use of the wild Rose of Castile.

JOHN PARKINSON WROTE IN HIS *PARADIUS* (1629) that the damask rose (later referred to widely as the Rose of Castile) "is of exceeding great use with us. . . . Besides the superexcellent sweet water it yieldeth, being distilled, or the perfume of its leaves, being dried, serving to fill sweet bags . . . [it] serveth to cause solubleness of the body, make into a syrupe, or preserved with sugar, moist or candied."

Many of these uses were important to traveling missionaries. Father Junipero Serra, writing from his mission house at the site of present-day San Diego, reported: "In the various arroyos along the road and in the place where we are now, besides the wild grape vines are Roses of Castile." He may well have made an identification mistake, for the rose he saw was probably *Rosa californica* (see entry). But later the Rose of Castile, a name given then to all sorts of damask roses, became an important part of mission gardens.

The Rose of Castile wasn't grown just for decoration. The petals could be used in the manufacture of oils and ointments. Victoria Padilla, in *Southern California Gardens* (1961), writes that old mission manuscripts "constantly refer to *aceite rosado,* the oil, and to *unguneto rosado,* the ointment made from flowers, and no mission dispensary was complete without a good supply of the dried flowers and hips."

The Rose of Castile, hardy and able to grow without much help from the missionaries, flourished during the years of Spanish rule as Father Serra set up mission houses at places such as Carmel, San Luis Obispo, and San Juan Capistrano. As newer varieties arrived on the garden scene, the old mission rose was passed over. It is seldom seen outside botanical collections today.

The Rose of Castile may well have been California's first immigrant rose. It may have been the variety written about by the Roman poet Virgil (70-19 B.C.) as the rose widely grown in Babylon. It may have been taken all over the world, first by the Crusaders and then by travelers. The notion that the rose was introduced to California by the Spanish, simply because the Franciscan fathers grew it in great numbers, is untrue. The French introduced it to California. Captain J. F. G. de la Perouse had this rose among a batch of plants when he traveled California in 1786. □

ROSE PLATES

Pictures of roses have made their way onto fine china.

In 1975, THE AMERICAN ROSE SOCIETY BEGAN a search for an artist to design a limited-edition rose plate. The artist would be asked to produce "the most beautiful rose ever painted." The society chose artist Luther Bookout of McAllen, Texas, a former Marine Corps officer who had grown up with roses. "My love of roses goes back to my mother," he said. "I can't remember when she didn't have roses planted everywhere."

Bookout's first plate for the American Rose Society was the yellow rose 'Oregold' and was an immediate hit. With each succeeding Bookout plate, the production run increased, but the value of these plates—with their creamy background on Gorham china, and 24-karat gold edging—remains high among collectors. One of the most spectacular of the plates shows 'Double Delight' (see entry), the raspberry and cream hybrid tea. □

ROSE RUSTLERS OF TEXAS

The modern rustlers of Texas have become famous as much for their name as for their activities. They rustle roses, in the most tenderhearted and modern way.

A CAVALCADE OF CARS DESCENDS ON A small Texas town. Out tumbles a collection of humans, dressed in sturdy clothes, boots, gloves, and hats. These are the rose rustlers. They don't carry guns. Instead they pack pruning shears and large scissors. Their aim is to save roses from extinction.

"It all began," says Joe M. Woodard, editor of *The Yellow Rose,* "in the fall of 1980 in Austin, when an announcement was made that Pam Puryear of Navasota had agreed to lead a tour of people interested in old garden roses." One visiting rosarian called them rustlers, and the name stuck.

Puryear says the story began for her when her mother came home one day after a ride in the country and said: "You ought to have come along; we saw the dearest pink rose blooming along a fence on the road to the city dump." That was the day her "life of crime" began. She visited the rose found by her mother and looked at it in awe. Here was a rose that had lived "for years beyond counting and yet it prospers here where only God waters it." She was struck by the realization that "there are other roses in the world besides hybrid teas!"

From then on, there was no stopping her in the search for old roses. "I cased the county for the most likely places, such as cemeteries of early date, and the homes of black women. . . . The latter are gold mines for the seeker after old garden roses. For unlike their white counterparts, black women in rural areas are less likely to succumb to the latest ARS ratings. They know what grows well, they share favored roses among themselves, and they invariably have green fingers. And they are proud to share cuttings with their neighbors."

Puryear described how she secures old roses.

> My technique in approaching the homeowner who boasts an old rose bush is to saunter to their door, adopting a nonchalant attitude, and trying to project honesty and goodwill. I then compliment the lady of the house on her skill and taste and offer to purchase cuttings. I usually offer to exchange some rooted plants from among the extras I have collected.
>
> When I have gleaned cuttings I take them home to what used to be the vegetable garden. I carefully dip the ends in rooting hormone. . . . Many years have to pass before the rooted cuttings can be moved to their permanent places and before they bloom. However I feel about them as the Audubon Society feels about golden eagles: If they are lost, we aren't going to get any more.

Puryear's advice to anyone who loves old roses is to keep on "rustling." That is advice that has been taken up by people in Texas and other parts of the country (see the entries on Lost-and-Found Roses and Cemeteries). You can read about the rustlers in publications like *Old Texas Rose* and *The Yellow Rose,* where you will find the writings of people like Margaret Sharpe, William Welch, Joe Woodard, and Pam Puryear.

Joe Woodard reported on a "rose rustle" in which about a hundred people took part. "One stop was at a very grand old house with columns, terraces, bays, and towers in Fayetteville, near Austin, Texas, where an old lady of ninety-two invited all one hundred people to tour her home, which was filled with antiques. And outside she had many mature old roses, which they were welcomed to take cuttings from." They scouted several other homes, farms, cemeteries, abandoned houses, and other likely growing places. By the end of the day, they had collected thirty-three different roses. Among them was only one that was unknown, a white tea rose.

Rose rustlers seldom take a full rose bush. They know the roses they find need protection and may not grow anywhere else. So they take cuttings and propagate them, and often return to give some care to the old bush. Bushes are sometimes dug up if bulldozers are waiting to get to the site. Then the bush is taken and saved. But so many have been lost to the insatiable appetite of progress that you can understand why Texas rosarians like to say: "Rustle a rose a day." □

ROSE STAMPS

THE U.S. POSTAL SERVICE HAS ISSUED SEVeral stamps with rose connections. Among them was a three-cent stamp in 1967 honoring nineteenth-century horticulturalist and historian Francis Parkman (see entry). A fifteen-cent stamp in 1978 featured two roses in a stylized design by Mary Faulconer, depicting two roses by William Warriner (see entry), 'Medallion' and 'Red Masterpiece'. □

THE RUN FOR THE ROSES

The Kentucky Derby has been called "the run for the roses" since 1925.

THE KENTUCKY DERBY, FASHIONED AFTER the English Derby, is the oldest classical horse race in the United States. It earned its nickname from the fact that the winning horse is garlanded with a wreath of roses.

The first information on the role of roses at the Kentucky Derby dates from 1883, when E. Berry Hill, a New York socialite and gambler, sent a rose to each lady attending a Derby party in Louisville. An 1896 newspaper article said the winner of the race that year, Ben Brush, was draped with a collar of white and pink roses tied with white and magenta ribbons. A few years later, a garland of evergreens and red and white roses was used. In 1902, roses were usurped by carnations. In 1904, 'American Beauty' roses got into the act, and from then on it seems that roses held their place. In 1925, the Derby was dubbed "the run for the roses" by New York sports columnist Bill Corum, who later became president of Churchill Downs, the Kentucky Derby track, in Louisville.

From 1931 to 1985, Mrs. Kingsley-Walker (of the Kingsley-Walker Nursery in Louisville) designed and made the winner's garland. After her death, the honor passed to her daughter, Betty Korfhage of Korfhage Nursery. In 1989,

Kroger and Company, a Midwest grocery chain, was given responsibility for making the garland and continues to handle the assignment. Kroger asked Indiana hybridizer Von C. Weddle (see entry), who is a member of the Louisville Rose Society, to produce a red rose to be used for future Derby garlands. The rose, called 'Rose of the Garland', is now undergoing tests and will, Weddle hopes, be available in 1994. The 1990 and 1991 garlands used a rose called 'Kentucky Royalty'. About 600 blooms are used in making each Derby garland, the most prestigious bunch of roses in American sports. □

SAVILLE, HARMON
(BORN 1924)

A hobby grew into a major commercial operation.

In 1965, HARMON SAVILLE, HIS WIFE, CHIP, and their family were settled in a neat little waterside cottage in Gloucester, Massachusetts. He was an executive with a company that manufactured dehydrated foods. He was also a fisherman, hunter, camper, and canoeist. The picket fence around the house needed a rose. They bought one—and so began an amazing rise to fame in the rose world.

Saville had found a new hobby. In 1971, he decided to turn the hobby into the business of selling and hybridizing miniature roses. He moved to Rowley, Massachusetts, and development of the Nor'East Roses began. The business has since expanded to include a California base. He now sells about a million miniature rose bushes every year.

The list of miniatures raised by Saville includes 'Acey Duecy', 'Baby Katie', 'Center Gold', 'Good Morning America', 'Little Jackie', 'Mark One', 'Minnie Pearl', 'Party Girl', 'Rainbow's End', 'Single's Best', and 'Winsome'. More recently he has added 'Whoopi' (for movie star Whoopi Goldberg) and an All-America Rose Selection winner for 1993, 'Child's Play'.

Saville has become a leader in the world of roses. Today he has the biggest privately owned rose operation in the United States, producing roses he has bred himself as well as introducing top varieties from amateur breeders. □

SCHOENER, FATHER
GEORGE M. A.
(1864–1941)

The Padre of the Roses was a pioneer in breeding giant American roses.

Born in Steinach, Germany, Father George M. A. Schoener trained for the priesthood. He loved to be known as the Padre of the Roses, usually signing his articles The Padre. He began his work in Brooks, Oregon, where his hybridizing was done outdoors in his small country churchyard. He served the spiritual needs of Indians in a sparsely settled part of Oregon as he pursued his interest in roses.

In a letter written in 1914 he said that his experimental work took up every minute of his spare time. He said he had hybridized about 3,000 roses that year and gathered more than 2,000 rose slips in working toward his goal of "adapting the rose to every soil and climate. I took *Rosa acicularis* from the far north and *Rosa gigantica* from sunny and warm India, as well as *Rosa moyesii* of Turkestan and *Rosa valkana* of Oregon." His work was perhaps of more interest to the geneticist than the normal gardener, but his research was invaluable.

Poor health led him to move in 1917 to Santa Barbara, where his hybrid perpetual 'Arrillaga'—a large, glowing pink rose that was a heavy summer bloomer but had few fall flowers—was introduced by Bobbink and Atkins in 1929. But it was his rampant shrub, 'Schoener's Nutkana', that brought him lasting fame as a hybridizer.

'Schoener's Nutkana' was a cross between the giant Oregon species, *Rosa nutkana,* and 'Paul Neyron', the largest-flowered hybrid perpetual. The resulting seedling grew into a sprawling shrub with rose-pink blooms. It became an important parent used by many famous breeders. Jean Henri Nicolas (see entry) produced 'Shenandoah', a fragrant climbing crimson, using 'Schoener's Nutkana'. Ralph Moore (see entry), father of the miniature rose, worked with it, too.

Father Schoener also used the massive *Rosa gigantea,* the strongest known climber, which can reach 100 feet. His persistence in breeding from this rose was almost fanatical. Among the roses he bred from *Rosa gigantea* were 'Santa Barbara Queen', 'Golden West', 'Calpurnea', and 'The Padre's Triumph'.

In Santa Barbara, Father Schoener found conditions that did not favor the germination of rose seeds. On one occasion he got no seedlings whatsoever from 60,000 seeds. He asked for help from William Crocker, a famous plant life specialist at the Boyce Thompson Institute in Yonkers, New York. Crocker took Father Schoener's next crop of 49,000 seeds and, by using stratification methods, produced almost 16,000 seedlings.

Father Schoener was a prolific writer, and one of the little gems of rose publishing still to be found today is his catalog of roses and dahlias, which he called *The World's Best Roses.* This twenty-page booklet carried a plea for a national garden of genetically important roses, one of his great passions.

Father Schoener's dream was that Santa Barbara would have a great botanic garden and become a city of roses. His most impressive project was the planting of 111 hybrids of *Rosa gigantea* along a Santa Barbara thoroughfare, which he hoped would be known as Avenida de las Rosas. He could often be seen, in his clerical black suit and hat, pruning and tying. "After twenty years of ceaseless trials," he wrote, he had succeeded in planting "111 giant rose trees, up to twenty feet high and ten feet spread, in thirteen distinct varieties from white to cream, pink, orange, yellow and red, some colors even excelling the high, flashy colors of the much admired Spanish roses." His aim, he said, was "to demonstrate that the rose can well be used for street planting, not only as the greatest flowering object but even as a shade tree." Some years later the great avenue of rose trees was damaged, and eventually they were removed.

He had one other dream—that his hometown in Germany would become a rose city, too. Now the director of the local high school, Peter Schwoerer, aims to make Steinach a city of roses, using as many of Father Schoener's roses as he can find. □

SCHWARTZ, ERNEST W. (1904–1977)

Schwartz was a prolific amateur hybridizer who made his biggest mark in miniature roses.

ERNEST SCHWARTZ WAS A PARTNER IN AN automotive servicing business, and the roses in the garden of his Baltimore home

Massachusetts. The miniatures included such top performers as 'Cuddles', 'Donna Faye', 'Fairlane', 'Humdinger', 'Little Sir Echo', 'Pacesetter', 'Puppy Love', 'Zinger', 'Littlest Angel', and 'Little Linda'. A garden to his memory has been established at the American Rose Society garden in Shreveport, Louisiana. □

SHAKERS

The beauty of the rose was not its attraction to the Shakers.

A SMALL GROUP OF SHAKERS, SEARCHING FOR religious freedom and a more devout communal way of life, left England in 1774 and settled near Albany, New York. The rose was important to them—but only as a practical plant, not a decorative one. This attitude was explained in a 1906 article by a Shaker sister in *Good Housekeeping* magazine:

> The rose bushes were planted along the sides of the road which ran through our village and were greatly admired by the passers-by, but it was strongly impressed on us that the rose was useful, not ornamental. It was not intended to please us by its color or its odor. Its mission was to be made into [medicinal] rose water and if we thought of it in any other way we were making an idol of it and thereby imperilling our souls. In order that we might not be tempted to fasten a rose upon our dress or to put it into water to keep, the rule was that the flower

were his relaxation and his pastime. He eventually took to hybridizing, and he registered twenty-four roses in commerce.

Schwartz was the epitomy of the amateur rose grower who becomes so well known that people think he is a full-time professional. Even before he retired from the automotive business, a number of his varieties—floribundas, hybrid teas, and grandifloras—had been accepted by companies like Conard-Pyle and Melvin Wyant. These roses included 'Flaming Arrow', 'Grand Opera', 'Magic Moon', 'Masked Ball', and 'Sea Foam'.

When Schwartz moved into miniatures, his roses began tumbling out with awards of excellence from Nor'East Miniatures in Rowley, should be picked with no stems at all. We had only crimson roses as they were supposed to make stronger rose water than the paler varieties. . . . In those days no sick person was allowed to have a fresh flower to cheer him; he was welcome to a liberal supply of rose water to bathe his aching head. □

SHAKESPEARE

THE WORDS ENGRAVED ON A LARGE STONE in the International Rose Garden in Portland, Oregon (see entry), along with a portrait of Shakespeare, are worthy of the Bard:

> Of all flowers
> methinks a rose is best.

But Shakespeare didn't write these words. Fred Edmunds, Jr. (see entry), said that his father, Fred Sr., when having the stone engraved, reckoned that the quotation was good enough for Shakespeare—and so attributed it to him. But the quotation really should be credited to John Fletcher (1579–1625). □

SHELDON, ERNEST (BORN 1919)

This rose grower's specialty is giving roses away.

ERNEST SHELDON, A MEMBER OF THE DALLAS Rose Group, gives away tens of thousands of miniature roses each year. He goes out to his garden every morning, cuts his roses, and then heads out to give them away. "A rose brings love," is his dictum.

Sheldon said that his garden contains "about 150 varieties, 514 bushes, growing in 335 seven-gallon plastic containers." The blooms he cuts daily make their way to weddings, receptions, anniversaries, churches, nursing and retirement homes, gift shops, restaurants, offices, dinners, banquets, and just about any function you can mention. They go to people who have something to celebrate, and to people in sorrow. I was included on his gift list in October 1991, when I was speaking about miniatures at the American Rose Society convention in Norfolk, Virginia. Sheldon sent me a bouquet of forty-nine roses in fifteen different varieties.

How many blooms does he take from the garden? In one 215-day season, he reported, he gave away 70,755 blooms. □

SHEPHERD, ROY E. (DIED 1962)

Roy Shepherd made two important impacts on American rose history: a valuable book and a fine shrub.

ROY SHEPHERD'S BOOK *THE HISTORY OF THE Rose* is fundamental reading for anyone with an interest in the American rose scene up to the book's publication in 1954. It relates rose history in a very readable manner. Shepherd, from Medina, Ohio, said in his introduction that the book was the result of "forty years study of rose literature, considerable correspondence with rose growers around the world, and the personal observations of the author, who has, during the past twenty-five years, collected and grown all the obtainable species and old roses and many of the modern ones."

As a hybridizer Shepherd achieved a lasting place in rose growing with 'Golden Wings', a remontant—repeat—flowering tall shrub. The blooms are always attractive, with wide, creamy-yellow flowers of five petals and interesting deeper-colored stamens. The rose was introduced in 1956, two years after publication of the book. □

SHIPWRECK ROSE

LEGEND THAT SAYS THE CRIMSON-PURPLE China rose 'Louis Philippe' found its way to America when it was washed up on a sand bar off Long Island in April 1842 from the wreck of the ship of the same name. It may well have happened—but according to Mike Shoup at the Antique Rose Emporium in Texas, the rose was actually planted in 1836 at the home of the Texan-born minister to France, Lorenzo de Zavala, who brought the rose home with him from the court of St. Cloud. So if you ever have to talk about the rose, you can have the legend—or the truth. □

SHOWING ROSES

The art of exhibiting brings together all the techniques of the garden: the growing, the careful tending, and the sharing of roses.

THERE ARE NO SECRETS TO WINNING CONSIStently at shows as long as you follow good, normal cultivation methods. For a weekend show, begin cutting blooms as early as Wednesday. Choose early morning or late evening for cutting. Cut all blooms a little longer than you think will be necessary. By cutting the stem long, you will be able to later cut it under water, which will avoid blooms going limp.

Place the stems into tepid water immediately after cutting (don't wet the blooms). Ordinary water with a few drops of lemon or other citrus juice will be good enough for their development. A mixture of one part carbonated water (7-Up, Mountain Dew, Sprite, or any bubbly drink) to two parts tap water also seems to be effective. If blooms go limp, hold the stem in very hot water for a few seconds, and they will begin to perk up like magic.

Place blooms in containers covered with a plastic bag, which helps retain moisture in the bloom. Store the blooms in a refrigerator. Clean the foliage after cutting, with a small damp piece of cloth, and remove any bugs or pieces of dirt. Place a name tag to each flower as it is cut. Remember that blooms will go on growing after they are cut. Blooms left in direct sunlight or in warm rooms will deteriorate far quicker than those stored in cooler temperatures. If, on the night before the show, some flowers you have cut still seem too tight, take them from the refrigerator and leave them at normal room temperature.

Give yourself plenty of time at the show site. Read the schedule thoroughly. Select your best-looking blooms. Clean and groom them so that they look vibrant and eager to catch the judges' eyes. In a tight finish for the best bloom, it often comes down to what might seem minor points. This is where the arrangement of the blooms (especially in multistem classes) comes into play. Blooms should be evenly matched for size and form, and colors should be combined so they don't scream at you.

Here is a list of things to avoid when you show roses:

• A bloom that has gone beyond the halfway-open stage (except in appropriate classes).
• A bloom that has lost its vibrancy in color.
• A bloom that includes any foreign bodies (a small piece of paper, foam, cotton wool, or an aphid).
• Crooked stems.
• Any side buds in classes for individual blooms. (In classes for sprays, however, all buds should be left intact.)
• Wrong variety names.
• Stem on stem; the main bloom stem should not have part of another stem attached.
• Stems that are too long and have too much foliage.

Finally, let me share a funny rose-show story. A first-time exhibitor arrived at a show, unsure of the identification of the three flowers he brought along. Three eminent exhibitors studied the roses and agreed on the identification, which they wrote out for the beginner as he hurried away to enter his roses. The new exhibitor won three awards. As he viewed his winning entries, a puzzled look on his face, one of the experts who had identified the roses for him asked if something was wrong. "Yes," he replied, "these roses of mine were given three different names, but I cut them all from the same bush." ◻

SORORITY ROSES

THIRTEEN NATIONALLY RECOGNIZED SORORIties at American colleges and universities have the rose as their official flower. At the installation ceremony for Iota Alpha Pi, a red rose is given to each new member. ◻

SPENCER, ANNE (1882–1975)

Her garden was a source of inspiration for poet Anne Spencer.

HARLEM RENAISSANCE POET ANNE SPENCER loved her Lynchburg, Virginia, garden. A poet of international renown, she was school librarian in the town for twenty-four years. Her garden inspired many of her poems. She established a traditional small garden around the cottage where she wrote. The garden grew as her fame grew, and she received such notable visitors as Martin Luther King, Jr., James Weldon Johnson, George Washington Carver, and Marian Anderson.

After Spencer died in 1975, a group of local historians and garden lovers led by Jane Baber White brought the overrun garden back to life. "Many old roses were found in poor condition, gnarled roots with ten-foot stems protruding," White wrote. With the help of heritage rose expert Carl P. Cato, the roses were rescued, replanted, and named. The restored Spencer home is now on the National Register of Historic Places and is a Virginia Historic Landmark.

The last word comes from Anne Spencer herself:

> This small garden is half my
> world
> I am nothing to it—when all is
> said,
> I plant the thorn and kiss the
> rose,
> but they will grow when I am
> dead. □

STATE FLOWERS

THE ROSE IS THE OFFICIAL FLOWER OF GEORgia, Iowa, North Dakota, the District of Columbia, the Canadian province of Alberta, and of the United States of America. In addition, a number of roses have been named for states. Roses that bear state names and are still in commerce are the following:

'Alabama': pink-blend hybrid tea.
'Alaska': white hybrid tea (available in France).
'Arizona': orange-blend grandiflora.
'Arkansas': orange-red hybrid tea.
'California': *Rosa californica,* very light pink shrub.
'Carolina': *Rosa carolina,* medium pink shrub.
'Colorado': red-blend hybrid tea (available in France).
'Georgia': apricot-blend hybrid tea.
'Hawaii': orange-red hybrid tea.
'Indiana': medium-red hybrid tea.
'Louisiana': white hybrid tea.
'Montana': orange-red floribunda (available in Canada; also known as 'Royal Occasion').
'Nevada': white hybrid *moyessii.*
'Ohio': medium-red shrub.
'Oklahoma': dark red hybrid tea.
'Tennessee': orange-blend miniature.
'Texas': yellow miniature.
'Virginia': *Rosa virginiana,* medium-pink species.

Other states that have had roses registered in their names include Illinois, Pennsylvania, Mississippi, and New Mexico, but these are no longer available commercially. □

STEMLER, DOROTHY (1914–1987)

Dorothy Stemler's love of old roses led her to write two books and a highly prized catalog.

WHENEVER OLD ROSES OF AMERICA ARE discussed, the conversation slips around to this lady whose annual catalog, *Roses of Yesterday and Today,* was so erudite and beautiful that it became a collector's item. She ran Tillotson's Roses in Watsonville, California, after the death of her husband, Will Tillotson, in 1957. She operated a garden that carried extensive quantities of old roses, produced the catalog, and wrote two fine books: the *Book of Old Roses* (1966), with her own illustrations, and *Roses of Yesterday* (1967), with watercolors by Nanae Ito.

Stemler described old roses as "living works of art. They should be in every garden, whether large or small, for their value in landscaping. All their beauty is not in their flowers alone. There are shrubs with delicately patterned foliage, colorful foliage, heavy foliage; ones that produce great masses of spring blooms, followed by bright colored hips, and ones that bloom repeatedly. There are forms, colors, and fragrances unknown in today's roses."

Her favorite rose was 'La Reine Victoria', which she described as being a "tall, slender shrub growing to five or six feet. The clear pink, delightfully perfumed flowers are cupped with petals precisely placed like feathers on a bird's breast. They never open to a loose, full-blown flower, but hold their cupped form to the last."

With descriptions as accurate and appealing as this, it is little wonder that her catalog printing every year totaled about 18,000 copies. □

SWAMP ROSE

See Rosa palustris.

SWIM, HERBERT C. (1907–1989)

Top hybridizer Herb Swim was associated with twenty-five All-America Rose Selection awards, twelve of which were his own productions.

THE ACCOLADE FROM THE AMERICAN ROSE Society accurately describes Herb Swim as "one of the greatest of all American hybridizers." Praise was echoed in honors from colleagues, universities, and international rose groups during a lifetime in which he produced many of America's greatest roses: 'First Love', 'Montezuma', 'Pink Parfait', 'Angel Face', 'Circus', 'Sutter's Gold', 'Mojave', 'Oklahoma', 'Mister Lincoln' (see entry), 'Royal Highness', 'Summer Sunshine', 'Double Delight' (see entry), 'Brandy', and many more.

Swim recorded in his book, *Roses—from Dreams to Reality* (1988), that the first roses in his memory were in the front yard of his parents' farm in Stillwater, Oklahoma. "There was only one yellow rose in that garden, and it was a shrub just outside my bedroom window. During the flowering season I would look outside each morning to see if any new flowers had appeared on that yellow during the night." He surmised that the variety was 'Harison's Yellow' (see entry), of which "it was the custom to obtain 'slips' from friends, neighbors and/or relatives. Every housewife knew how to root them."

It seemed to him from an early age that "a livelihood in some sort of agriculture would be pleasant," and he enrolled in the School of Agriculture at what was then Oklahoma A&M College (now Oklahoma State University). As an undergraduate he studied pomol-

member of the first group to sit down and plan the All-America Rose Selections (see entry). Armstrong was among the first winners of the award in 1940 with a rose bred by Walter E. Lammerts (see entry), whose job Swim took over in October 1940.

He took his first All-America Rose Selection awards in 1948 with 'Pinkie', a floribunda with polyantha breeding, and a dark red hybrid tea, 'Nocturne'. He went on to win twelve All-America Rose Selection awards on his own but was associated with twenty-five winners, which he shared with such hybridizers as Jack Christensen, Arnie Ellis, O. L. Weeks, and David L. Armstrong.

At age forty-eight he began working with O. L. Weeks (see entry) in a company they called Swim and Weeks. This was another extraordinary partnership, and their roses were soon among the AARS winners with such great varieties as 'Mister Lincoln', 'Royal Highness', and 'Angel Face'. An accumulation of health problems brought on his retirement, and the partnership was dissolved in 1967—but within a year he was back at Armstrong Nurseries, in the research department. He took final retirement in 1973.

Just before his death in 1989 he completed his book *Roses—from Dreams to Reality,* which is a handbook, as well as a history, for anyone wanting to begin rose hybridizing. Looking back on his life, he wrote: "It appears as though I was guided quite directly to a vocation that led to as much fulfillment as I can imagine." □

ogy and did his graduate work in landscape architecture. He found that plant genetics interested him most. At Armstrong Nurseries (see entry), where he went to work in 1934, his job was breeding not just roses but also peaches, nectarines, apricots, plums, berries, and camellias. Among his list of successes were the peaches Junegold and Saturn, the apricot Gold Nugget, Panamint nectarine, Bonanza Red raspberry, and the camellia Brigadoon.

But his inherent love was the rose. He was a

THE TEXAS RESEARCH FOUNDATION

ESTABLISHED IN 1946 BY A GROUP OF Texas commercial rose growers, with Eldon W. Lyle (see entry) as its director, the aim of the Texas Research Foundation is to carry out studies into all aspects of rose growing. The foundation is credited with improving rose understocks, bringing about the change from dusting crops to spraying them to control diseases, showing how to store budwood over winter so that work can be carried out early in spring, and continuing the search for new varieties of the rose. □

THAXTER, CELIA (1835–1894)

WRITER CELIA THAXTER WAS RHAPSODIC about flowers. In *An Island Garden* (1894), she wrote about her small garden at Shoals Island, Maine. Her description of flower arranging brings to life the beauty of her roses. She arranged them starting with "the palest rose tints . . . and slightly mingling a few with the last few white ones—a rose tint delicate as a baby's hand; then the next with a faint suffusion of a blush and go on to the next shade, still very delicate, not deeper than the soft hue on the lips of the great whelk shells in southern seas; then the damask rose color and all tints of tender pink, then the deeper tones to clear, rich cherry and on to glowing crimson, through a mass of this to burning maroon." Her words are evocative enough to send any gardener in search of roses to match her descriptions. □

THOMAS, CAPTAIN GEORGE C., JR. (1873–1932)

Thomas is best remembered today for producing the great understock rose 'Dr. Huey'.

CAPTAIN GEORGE C. THOMAS, JR., WAS A Renaissance man, successful as a rose hybridizer, rose writer, deep-sea fisherman, swimmer, golf course designer (many of California's finest courses), and aviator (he earned his military title as a World War I pilot). He also wrote *The Practical Book of Outdoor Rose Growing* (1914). Thomas, from a socially prominent Pennsylvania family, grew roses from all over the world at his Chestnut Hill home. J. Horace McFarland (see entry) called Thomas "nearly as rose crazy as any man could be."

After World War I, Thomas made his home in California, in what is now Hollywood, where he built two famous gardens. He scoured the countryside for old specimens of rare tropical and semitropical fruit, moving them from as far as sixty miles away. His gar-

"fences bowered with clustering roses practically every month of the year. . . . Pergolas and verandahs sweet and fragrant with large flowered climbers." Thomas wanted to break away from the single and semidouble climbers that were being produced by the top breeders and bring in roses with more delicate blossoms and style—but still with hardiness. He believed that the more "tender" varieties of climbers, such as Noisettes and climbing teas, were of great value. He did not achieve his ideal, but came close to it.

Thomas gave the name Bloomfield to most of his roses. In *Climbing Roses,* G. A. Stevens names more than forty, from 'Bloomfield Acrobat' to 'Bloomfield Volcano'. 'Bloomfield Abundance' is still highly prized in rose gardens. He also named other varieties, among them 'Ednah Thomas', for his wife, and 'Sophie Thomas', for his daughter. Stevens said that the problem with the Thomas roses was that they did not "climb much or bloom freely after their summer display." Nevertheless they are still remembered today, and, if they can be found, make good pillar-growing varieties.

Thomas is best-remembered today for producing 'Dr. Huey' (see entry), a *wichuraiana* climber with fairly large maroon-red flowers. 'Dr. Huey' assumed a far different role in life than what Thomas expected. The rose became famous as the life-saver of commercial growers who used it as understock, especially for millions of roses grown in California. It can often be found in gardens and cemeteries where the rose budded to the 'Dr. Huey' stock has died, but the root has stayed alive and developed into huge mounds that have gone wild. □

den landscape designer, Charles G. Adams, wrote: "One prize was a bearing date palm which, with its box of earth, weighed over twenty-five tons and required a string of three great trucks for its forty-mile journey." Adams also recalled bringing in "ancient climbing roses, with trunks like trees, of such romantic varieties as 'Gloire de Dijon', 'Duchesse d'Auerstaedt', 'Pink Cherokee', 'Rose of Castile', and 'Lamarque'."

Mrs. Helen W. King—president of the California Rose Society—said Thomas had a vision of California rose gardens as being

THOMASVILLE, GEORGIA CITY OF ROSES

THE REPUTATION OF THOMASVILLE, GEORGIA, as the City of Roses started almost a century ago when Danish immigrant Peter Hjort (pronounced "yort") set up a nursery there in 1898. The Hjort nursery garden is now an All-America Rose Selections trial garden and Thomasville holds a rose festival and show that is one of the nicest annual rose events in the United States. □

THORNLESS ROSES

A California rose breeder is marketing ouchless roses.

BOTANISTS REFER TO THE THORNS ON A ROSE bush stem as prickles. They vary greatly in size and shape, but most are short and sharp. They have no known purpose—except perhaps to make you take care as you walk among the roses. Buddhist philosopher Pilnay said: "There is no picking the rose without being pricked by thorns." He should know. He was a gymnosophist, a naked philosopher. I know exactly what he means. For me, a rose without a thorn is a misnomer. I subscribe to the words of poet Christina Rosetti:

> A lady of all beauty
> Is a rose upon a thorn.

I am not enamored with thornlessness. The regular tiffs I have with my thorny roses just make me realize how beautiful they are.

Harvey Davidson, a rose breeder in Orinda, California, apparently disagrees with me. Sometime in the 1960s, as he was trying to breed disease-free roses, he discovered that he had unintentionally bred a rose with almost no thorns. He called it 'Smooth Sailing', and it became the first in a series of roses that has achieved success throughout the world. From this one rose, Davidson bred a succession of varieties that he says are 95 to 100 percent thorn-free. They include 'Smooth Angel', 'Smooth Lady', 'Smooth Velvet', 'Smooth Melody', 'Smooth Prince', and 'Smooth Perfume'.

Some roses in the past have been described as thornless. 'Zephirine Drouhin', 'Kathleen Harrop', and the single-flowering *banksia* roses are the most notable. But growers have never shown any real interest in doing anything with them. In 1986 the first of the Davidson roses, trademarked as Smooth Touch Roses, went on sale throughout the United States and immediately gained favor with the public. Commercial rose growers were not all that enthused. Leading British grower Jack Harkness wrote that with "a lifetime of hearing customers grumble at thorns, we can be sure that thornless roses would be an important commercial asset within our trade." But when he talked to other growers, the response was lukewarm. Harkness said that for himself, he likes thorns.

Harvey Davidson continues to believe in his roses. A rose that is simply thornless is not good enough for him; they have to be good plants, too. He has found that the credit for repressing thorns belongs to a floribunda, 'Little Darling', that has been widely used in American breeding and has been responsible for keeping down the number of thorns on miniature roses. His 'Smooth Sailing' was a cross of 'Little Darling' with 'Pink Favorite' (that also carries fewer thorns than most). Davidson now sells about 50,000 ouchless rose bushes a year, and he is continuing the search for more thornless varieties. □

'TOUCH OF CLASS'

The enthusiasm of two American hybridizers led to one of the major rose success stories of the 1980s.

It was love at first sight. Jack Christensen and Tom Carruth (see entries), hybridizers with Armstrong Nurseries, were in France in 1979 to seek out rose seedlings for their company. Agent Rene Royon took them to various rose fields. "During one of these jaunts," Carruth recalls, "we drove along the side of a small plot, and suddenly a half row of a pretty coral pink seedling stood up and shouted *me*, as certain seedlings have a tendency to do."

Both hybridizers were stunned by the beauty of the rose. But Royon told them the rose had already been taken away for testing by another American firm, Jackson & Perkins. All that the two American hybridizers could do was to ask if they could grow some plants of the rose just in case J&P decided against exercising its right to buy it for marketing in the United States.

Christensen and Carruth didn't see much hope. As 'Touch of Class' (then known by its French name 'Marechal le Clerc') grew for them in California, it became more and more beautiful in their eyes. They kept pressing for a decision, but J&P delayed. Finally, to the

amazement of Christensen and Carruth, J&P turned it down. It didn't quite live up to their standards, said J&P.

Christensen and Carruth were thrilled and immediately bought rights to grow and sell it in the United States. If they had not seen the rose on that glorious day in France, it might have become just an also-ran, another among the thousands of seedlings each year that don't make it. Instead, 'Touch of Class' survived and prospered, and this pink hybrid tea became the rage of U.S. rose fanciers in the 1980s. □

TOURNAMENT OF ROSES PASADENA, CALIFORNIA

One of the most spectacular parades of roses in the world, the Pasadena Tournament of Roses began with grateful people who realized how lucky they were to live where the sun shone and the roses grew.

Professor Charles F. Holder moved to the area of what is now Pasadena in 1886 and, a couple of years later, formed a hunting club. He was also an enthusiastic gardener who wanted to let people elsewhere know that while they were having typical winter weather, the California sun was shining. So the Hunt Club organized a floral display, amusements, and a celebration of the ripening of the orange. The date was set: January 1, 1890.

The message went out: "Ladies and gentlemen are requested to bring with them to the Park, all roses possible, so that strangers and tourists may have the full benefit of our floral display." There was no parade on that first occasion, but the park was packed with people and animals and roses. The horses had garlands of roses around their necks. Oranges were given away, and celebrants competed in events like foot races, bicycle races, tug of war, and sack races. Prizes included gold medals, silver watches, and a full set of the works of Dickens. The Pasadena Daily Evening Star called it "the greatest event of similar nature ever held in the country."

Who could have foreseen that eventually New Year's Day would not be the same for the people of the United States without the Pasadena Tournament of Roses, with its floats and millions of flowers, followed by the year's biggest college football game, the Rose Bowl. Famous people began serving as parade marshal. In 1939, it was Shirley Temple; in 1964, former President Dwight D. Eisenhower. Other grand marshals included Arnold Palmer, Walt Disney, Bob Hope, and Billy Graham.

Supplies of roses are now refrigerated for months before they are needed, ensuring plenty of blooms for making floats. In 1991, although there was said to be a shortage of rose blooms, one float was decorated with 100,000 roses. More than 300 million viewers worldwide watched the parade on television. □

TWOMEY, JERRY (BORN 1915)

Jerry Twomey took up rose breeding after his retirement and won the coveted All-America Rose Selections award twice.

JERRY TWOMEY, BORN IN CAMROSE, ALBERTA, Canada, was the eldest of nine children. He produced gladioli bulbs to help pay his school fees. Encouraged by his parents and grandparents, who were devoted to horticulture and agriculture, he went further and in the early 1930s bred a gladioli, 'Margaret Beaton', named for his grandmother. It was chosen as the world's most beautiful gladioli at the 1939 World's Fair in New York. "It made me about $10,000 in the depths of the Depression," he said. "You can't imagine the luck in that."

Twomey studied genetics at the University of Manitoba and then studied at the University of Minnesota. He went to work for Harris McFayden Seed Company, a Canada-based firm, earned a great reputation for mass production of seed, and eventually took over management of the firm. The Canadian government asked his help with seed production during World War II. Working with others, he shortened vegetable seed production time from two years to one, thus doubling production. He also developed wheat strains that could withstand very low temperatures. In 1945, he began his own company, T&T Seeds in Manitoba.

Then, after retirement, he turned to the rose. In 1981, he met Lawrence Smith, a noted California rosarian, and Smith's knowledge of varieties and parentage sparked Twomey's enthusiasm. For a decade, Twomey, living in San Diego at the time, worked on theories and experimentation. "I was in the greenhouse at 7 a.m. until noon," he said. "Then I'd come home and have the dining room table laid out with seedlings and pollen. I'd study them and take notes. At night I'd read." The challenge he set for himself was to develop hardy, low-maintenance garden roses that wouldn't need "poisons to keep them good."

Twomey won an All-America Rose Selection award in 1991 with 'Sheer Elegance', a rose that is being tipped as the greatest hybrid tea for showing since 'Touch of Class'—and as a very good garden variety. "This is a rose everyone will like," wrote columnist Dick Streeper in the *San Diego Union*. The next winner, 'All That Jazz', in 1992 marked an unheard-of achievement: a rose amateur with back-to-back AARS winners. The new rose exemplified all that Jerry Twomey had been seeking. It is a shrub rose that not only is disease resistant but is also practically pest resistant. "I have never seen any rose more disease resistant," said Daryl Johnson, curator of the

Portland, Oregon, Rose Gardens. Clair Martin of the Huntington Botanical Gardens in Southern California says the rose is impervious to disease. Tom Carruth of Weeks Roses describes 'All That Jazz' as a rose that will "take the heat or the cold and just keeps on jammin.'"

Twomey's red hedge rose 'Freedom' (not to be confused with the yellow rose 'Freedom') is a great step for those wanting freedom from disease in a strong-growing plant. His grandiflora 'Audrey Hepburn' is a beautiful pink bloom that has entranced international rose growers. Among his other successes are 'Winning Colors', 'Endless Dream', 'Proud Mary', and a miniature, 'Apache Princess'. Success like Twomey's can bring big financial rewards, but he obviously believes that money isn't everything. "The only record you leave behind you here," he said, "is that you have contributed a little—in this case some beauty to the world." □

TYLER, TEXAS

Tyler is a city of roses, the flowering heart of Texas.

COMMERCIAL ROSE PRODUCTION AROUND Tyler, near Waco, began in the 1870s. Farms in the area had been growing cotton, but with the arrival of mechanical harvesting, the small units found cotton to be too expensive a business. Farmers turned to roses. Within half a century, Tyler became almost a center for rose production.

Today, in a thirty-five-mile radius of the city, half of the roses used in the United States are produced by about 120 nurseries formed into cooperatives, of which Co-Operative

Rose Growers and Consolidated Rose Growers are the biggest. Only the large scale of commercial growing in California seems to rob the Tyler area of the title of Rose Capital of the World.

The rose blooms in Texas with magnificence beginning in late spring, and the season culminates with the Tyler Rose Festival, held every October for the past sixty years. Tyler also has an important rose garden, with 20,000 plants (slimmed down from 35,000 at one time). The twenty-two-acre rose garden began life as an eroded hillside of red clay gullies and was transformed into a parkland, with roses planted there for the first time in 1952. □

'UNCLE JOE'

Mystery continues to shroud the origins of this top-rated show rose.

ONE OF THE MYSTERIES OF THE ROSE world is where 'Uncle Joe' came from and whether a rose called 'Toro' is actually the same rose. The great exhibition hybrid tea began its life with a mix-up. The deep red French-bred rose 'Papa Meilland' had just arrived on the American market, and Joe Kern received budwood of it from exhibitor Harold Weaver. But the budwood turned out not to be 'Papa Meilland' at all, but a deep red rose distinct in many ways.

When Kern discovered that he wasn't selling 'Papa Meilland', he replaced all the roses he had sold under that name. He was going to destroy the unknown rose, but his brother, John, convinced him that it could be a top show rose. They named it 'Uncle Joe'. They had only a small number of bushes, so to increase the stock they sent wood to another Ohio grower—where the rose ran into new difficulties.

Joe Kern supposedly picked up his 'Uncle Joe' plants from the grower and later sold some. Among the purchasers was commercial grower Melvin Wyant, who discovered a rose in the batch that was, in his opinion, quite unlike the rest of the 'Uncle Joe' plants. Joe Kern registered his rose as 'Uncle Joe'. Melvin Wyant registered his intruder rose as 'Toro'.

A new mix-up was building. Exhibitors were showing both roses, and at times judges argued that they were misnamed. They could see 'Toro' as 'Uncle Joe' and vice versa. Some exhibitors found their roses being disqualified for being wrongly named, in some judges' opinions. The American Rose Society finally decided that the roses were one and the same. 'Toro' would be eliminated, and 'Uncle Joe' would stand.

But mystery still remains. First of all, where did Harold Weaver, famous for his rose imports, get the original plant? He does not seem to have made any comment about the mix-up. Secondly, was there really another strange rose in the package that Melvin Wyant purchased, or was it just a case of one 'Uncle Joe' bush being slightly different, possibly because of varied soil conditions or even a trick of the light?

The mystery is unresolved and probably will remain so because the principals involved are now dead. As for 'Uncle Joe', it continues to win top awards. □

UNKNOWN SOLDIER

SGT. EDWARD F. YOUNGER HAD THE SAD TASK at the end of World War I of picking the American unknown soldier. Four bodies of unidentified American soldiers were sent to Chamons-sur-Marne from French graveyards. The sergeant signified his choice by placing a bouquet of red roses on one casket. □

VAN FLEET, DR. WALTER
(1857–1922)

*Walter Van Fleet was a modest man who let his
historic accomplishments in rose breeding speak for
themselves.*

WALTER VAN FLEET WAS GENIAL, COMPAN-
ionable, and hospitable, yet the shyest
of men when anyone began to say a compli-
mentary word about his accomplishments.
"He summed up all of America's best in roses,"
said rose writer J. Horace McFarland (see
entry).

Van Fleet was from New York, and was a
medical doctor who gave up medicine to turn
his attention to horticulture, working with
berries, corn, tomatoes, dahlias, and gladioli.
He developed a blight-resistant strain of chest-
nuts. His real fame came through roses. For
many years he worked in relative obscurity for
the Department of Agriculture at a farm,
Glenn Dale, between Baltimore and Washington, D.C. McFarland called him "a born
scientist."

Van Fleet's ideal was to breed roses that
would bloom all season long and take care of
themselves so that, in his words, "there might
be beauty every growing day." He developed
the ideal of dooryard roses (see entry), carrying beautiful flowers, luxuriant foliage, disease
resistance, and hardiness.

Because Van Fleet worked for a federal
agency, the roses he was producing were not
being released to the public. This annoyed

many rose people, especially McFarland, who
recounted in *Memoirs of a Rose Man* that he once
visited Glenn Dale in Van Fleet's absence and
found a "gorgeous rose blooming at its beautiful best, row upon row." McFarland wanted
the Department of Agriculture to permit public introductions of the roses it developed. He
and fellow roseman Robert Pyle (see entry for
Conard-Pyle Company) took an armful of the
new rose to Secretary of Agriculture Henry
Wallace to plead their case for the beautiful
flower.

The result was that the rose was shown at
Portland, Oregon—and was named for Wallace's daughter. Thus 'Mary Wallace' became
the first of the dooryard roses to get into production. It was a rose that climbs and sprawls
but always grows and blooms. Another milestone was achieved when the department allowed a contract for distribution with the
American Rose Society.

Greater roses were still to come from Van
Fleet. One that has left its mark forever on
rose growing was initially named 'Daybreak'
by Van Fleet and his wife. The Henderson firm
of New York bought all plants except one,
which stayed with the Van Fleets. Trying to
rush the propagation, Henderson lost all the
plants. They could renew their stock only
through the one Van Fleet had retained. Henderson then decided the rose should not be
called 'Daybreak', but should carry the name
of the hybridizer himself. It was named 'Dr.
Van Fleet'. In his book *Climbing Roses,* G. A.

Stevens explained the importance of the rose. "I approach this rose with awe and humility, although I have never liked it very much. Its color is a wishy-washy pink, characterless and flat, but its influence has been stupendous. Its introduction broke the garden's thralldom to innumerable fussy little cluster-flowered ramblers which bore us to distraction with their infantile prettiness and indistinguishable differences. Here was an heroic rose, of noble size and perfect form, borned on a rampant plant, first of a new race of climbers. Its value and importance to rose growers in cold climates can hardly be estimated." It can still be purchased from rose growers throughout the world.

Other great roses followed, ones that, according to Stevens, "would furnish all the climbing roses needed in a comprehensive garden": 'American Pillar' (see entry); 'Sarah Van Fleet' (for his wife); 'Breeze Hill' (see entry); 'Birdie Blye'; 'Glenn Dale'; 'Heart of Gold'; roses for the Lovett sisters Alida, Bess, and Mary; and 'Silver Moon', a rose of tremendous vigor that brought together the blood of the *wichuraiana* and the Cherokee Rose (see entry).

On the very day he was buried, after his sudden death in 1922, Van Fleet was to have been presented with the Gold Medal of the city of Portland, Oregon, by the Secretary of Agriculture. On his death, the farm periodical *Rural New-Yorker* praised Van Fleet as "a great man. He has left to the world enduring gifts of beauty and increasing usefulness." □

WALSH, MICHAEL H. (1848–1922)

Prolific hybridizer Michael Walsh produced most of the top climbing roses of his day.

THERE ARE ROSES STILL GROWING IN THE finest gardens of the world that were hybridized by Michael H. Walsh. Names like 'Excelsa', 'Hiawatha', 'Minnehaha', 'Lady Gay', and many others keep alive the memory of the man who came to America from Bangor, North Wales, at the age of eleven.

Walsh took to gardening early in his life. He eventually moved to Woods Hole, Cape Cod, Massachusetts, where he took charge of the Joseph S. Hay estate and began his intensive work in producing better climbing roses. He became one of the country's most prolific hybridizers, with his roses winning top awards—especially 'Excelsa', which was being called the perfect replacement for the over-planted 'Crimson Rambler'.

Not everyone agreed. G. A. Stevens, in *Climbing Roses* (1933), claimed that 'Excelsa' is so easy a prey to mildew that it is a "pest." But rosarian J. Horace McFarland found the Walsh roses "enduring, living, blooming, glowing monuments" to the hybridizer. McFarland said that 'Excelsa' had brightness as well as beauty; Stevens, on the other hand, felt it had a "disreputable, faded look."

McFarland wrote of the "indescribably pleasing form" of Walsh's 'Evangeline', a tremendous producer of lasting, single, rosy-white flowers. Stevens, not quite as enthusiastic, called 'Evangeline' "a good representative of pale pink cluster flowering *wichuraiana*," but he said that any similar variety could be substituted. He gave 'Evangeline' top marks for its "peculiar fragrance and enormous vigor." Walsh regarded his own 'Lady Gay' as an improvement on 'Dorothy Perkins', but the two varieties were so alike that often one was sold under the other's name.

Staying within the *wichuraiana* range, Walsh produced the bulk of the top roses of his time.

'Hiawatha' still produces an abundance of deep carmine blooms, but 'Minnehaha' did not last quite so long as her Indian lover, being generally out of commerce now. An extensive collection of Walsh roses are still carried by nurseries. The Woods Hole Historical Collection in Cape Cod maintains a garden of Walsh roses. In France, there is an extensive collection at the beautiful garden of Roseraie de l'Hay outside Paris. A stone was erected in Walsh's memory on a piece of land opposite Little Harbor, east of the library in Woods Hole. Its inscription reads,

> Near this place lived
> Michael H. Walsh
> who made
> The Rambler Rose
> World Famous □

WARRINER, WILLIAM (1922–1991)

A trio of fine roses made William Warriner the only hybridizer to win three All-America Rose Selection awards in one year.

THE 1960s AND 1970s WERE A GOOD TIME for the Jackson & Perkins rose empire, thanks to the work of their mild-mannered hybridizer, William Warriner. He produced winner after winner for J&P, plus a string of gold medals from around the world. He once told me, with far too much modesty, that many of the fine roses he produced were the result of "hunches and accidents." He agreed that many people looked on rose breeding as an art, but said that as far as he was concerned, it was a job.

Of course Warriner wasn't merely a worker as he poured his efforts into producing roses like 'Pristine', 'Shining Hour', 'Pleasure', 'Class Act', and a string of All-America Rose Selection winners that stretched from 1973, with 'Medallion', through 'America', 'Color Magic', 'French Lace', and that astonishing threesome of 1980, when he became the only hybridizer ever to have three AARS winners in one year, 'Love', 'Honor', and 'Cherish'. His last winners before his death were two awards for the mini, 'Pride 'n' Joy', and a hybrid tea, 'Brigadoon'. Since then, Warriner's hybrid tea 'Rio Samba' won a 1993 AARS award.

Warriner's roses prove the truth of his

words: "The flower is still the reason for growing roses, and its form and color are what we get excited about." In the mid-1970s, I was with him in the fields of California, and he showed me a coffee-colored climber that I agreed was something that would catch the public imagination. But the J&P directors didn't agree; they didn't like the color. It was some fifteen years before 'Butterscotch' was introduced to the market. But Warriner stuck with it because it was a flower that should be seen by the public. It was just another step in the progression of the rose, which he believed would always go on and on producing breakthroughs and new types. □

WASHINGTON, GEORGE (1732–1799)

Those who wish to believe a bit of romantic fiction can take to heart the frequent comment that George Washington was the first rose hybridizer in the United States.

IT WOULD INDEED BE ROMANTIC TO THINK OF the father of the country out in his cabin yard hybridizing roses. I hate to disappoint you. There is no proof that George Washington ever had anything to do with roses, other than to buy some.

It is often said that Washington produced the rose 'Mary Washington', a double, white-tinged pink, fragrant Noisette hybrid musk, vigorous and quite hardy. The fact is that no one really knows where the rose came from. It achieved wide distribution when, in 1890, plants were propagated at Mount Vernon and sold as souvenirs. And the legend built. But 'Mary Washington' could not have been

around in Washington's time; it is a Noisette, a class that didn't come into being until much later. The rose almost disappeared from the catalogs in the 1920s, but a number of nurseries in the United States now promote it. They no longer suggest it was hybridized by George Washington—but neither do they offer anything more than a question mark for its beginnings.

The storytellers also credited George Washington with being responsible for 'Martha Washington', a name given to all sorts of roses sold in the United States. The name seems to have disappeared from most catalogs about 1920. Undocumented tradition also includes the 'Nellie Custis' rose, said to have been planted by Washington and named for a family granddaughter. In *Old Fashioned Gardening* (1913), Grace Tabor described it as a "fragrant white, velvet textured flower of romance." That romance, she wrote, it acquired from witnessing "the love making and betrothal of ardent Lawrence Lewis, the General's favorite nephew, and black-eyed Nellie Custis, his wife's granddaughter." The spell of this rose could "stimulate indifferent or procrastinating suitors. . . . Hence these rich white buds and blossoms have ever been much sought by maids of high and low degree, whose affections are set on the unsuspecting and unresponsive; for to present 'him' with either flower or bud, so tradition avows, or lead him to inhale its fragrance, quickens the coldest masculine heart—such was the rare quality of these old lovers' love, clinging to, intoxicating and saturating for all time the sympathetic rose, even as the rose breathed its fragrance, over and around them, to heighten their delight."

The question of Washington's interest in roses was raised during debate in 1985 on the resolution to make the rose the National Floral Emblem (see entry). Among the correspondence was a letter from Kent Brinkley, landscape architect at Colonial Williamsburg Foundation, to the effect that while it was known that Washington made rose water and used rose hips for medicinal purposes, there is nothing to be found about him actually breeding a rose. Brinkley's letter to Donald F. X. Finn, executive director of the United States Constitution Bicentennial, said that Washington did not have a formal rose garden at Mount Vernon and placed his roses randomly between flowers and vegetables.

Brinkley said that he found documentation that among the varieties grown by Washington were the Celsiana Damask Rose, 'Old Blush', Scotch Rose, and Rosemundi Rose. "All of these were listed varieties even in Washington's day," Brinkley wrote, "and I found no reference whatsoever to any roses which Washington developed and/or named as a breeder of roses."

Brinkley wrote that Washington's "primary interest in roses as ornamentals seems focused upon two 'wild' varieties which are commonly found in hedgerows: Sweetbriar Rose (*Rosa egalanteria*), planted in a circle at the edge of his lawn near the gate as noted in an entry made in his diary in 1786, and also the Wild Pennsylvania or Swamp Rose (*Rosa palustris*), which Washington ordered from Bartram's Nurseries in 1792. . . . Another revealing entry in his diary notes that there are so many roses in his garden that it 'takes Old Sal two days to pick them all.' Old Sal was Sally, a personal house servant of Mrs. Washington's staff." □

WEDDLE, VON C. (BORN 1912)

A late bloomer, Von Weddle bred some good hybrid tea roses and invented a device to protect show roses.

Indiana amateur hybridizer Von Weddle took early retirement in 1960 from the field of coin-operated amusement machines and decided to take rose growing seriously. He began rose breeding in 1975 with the encouragement of long-time friend Charles P. Dawson (see entry). He produced a number of good hybrid teas, such as 'Elizabeth Taylor', 'Maid of Honour', 'Big Duke', 'Sophia', and 'Louisville Lady'. He demonstrated the problems that an amateur hybridizer has in getting his roses on the market when he told me that one company had kept one of his roses in its test garden for six years without making a decision on it.

Weddle withdrew the rose from this company and sent it to a Canadian grower, who immediately put it on the market. That rose was the dual pink 'Elizabeth Taylor', which has become a staple variety for U.S. exhibitors. He has also produced 'Rose of the Garland' specifically to garland the winner of the Kentucky Derby (see Run for the Roses).

An inventor, Weddle achieved national success with his patented Rose Keepers, plastic tubes that hold long-stemmed blooms fresh and undamaged on the way to shows. Rose Keepers are now part of every exhibitor's equipment and are marketed through the Texas rose firm of Kimbrew Walters. □

WEEKS, O. L.
(BORN 1911)

For nearly fifty years, Ollie Weeks produced high-quality roses at his California nursery.

INTERNATIONAL ROSE BREEDER SAM MCGREDY, asked who grew the best roses in the world, said Ollie Weeks. The Weeks reputation for fine roses goes back to 1937, when Weeks and his wife, Verona, began their business in Ontario, California.

An independent, even ornery plantsman, Weeks and Verona kept overheads low, produced only what they knew could sell, and kept the quality high. A citation from the All-America Rose Selections said of him: "A wonderfully imaginative man who has asked no one for anything and yet gives so much of himself in so many ways. He possesses a vision to see what he wants to achieve and works tenaciously toward that goal."

His wife, Verona, told me that her husband "clearly attached himself to roses and loved the soil and working the soil and looking at a beautifully manicured field of anything growing. . . . I think the secret of Ollie's success was that he loved what he was doing and he worked at it. He was and continues to be a 'dirt man.'"

Weeks introduced many fine roses. When 'Paradise' was launched, lavender roses were out of fashion. But here was a different rose, "one of the most distinctive and novel hybrid tea roses ever produced," said the All-America Selections citation. It was an immediate eye-catcher, with lavender petals tipped with a ruby-red rim. It was bred from 'Swarthmore' crossed by an unnamed lavender seedling that had fewer petals and without the classic form of 'Paradise'. The blooms were big and spiraled, high-pointed, and oblivious to weather. Add to that a good fragrance, and all that was needed was a good bush. That was something most of the lavender-shaded hybrid teas had not been blessed with. But 'Paradise' grew into a vigorous plant, deserving the words of Verona Weeks in their 1978–79 catalog, citing the rose's "novel color combination of lavender and ruby, with all the bonus assets of excellent bud and open bloom, plant growth, habit, foliage, floriferousness, and fragrance."

'Sweet Surrender' is another special rose from Weeks, a soft, almost silvery-pink hybrid tea that may not be the most vigorous rose in the garden but is blessed with an intense fragrance. Other first-class roses from Weeks are 'Arizona', 'Alabama', 'Arkansas', 'Georgia', 'Louisiana', and 'Autumn Gold'. There were All-America Rose Selection winners such as 'Perfume Delight', 'Sweet Surrender', 'Gypsy', and 'Bing Crosby'. Weeks introduced a line of thornless roses beginning with 'Old Smoothie' in 1970. Another success was the neat, decorative series he called 'The Talk' roses, such as 'Baby Talk' and 'Town Talk'. Weeks sold his rose-growing business in 1985 after nearly fifty years of operation. □

WESTCOTT, CYNTHIA (1899–1983)

Rose writer Cynthia Westcott was known for a wry sense of humor and an ability to get right to the heart of a matter.

CYNTHIA WESTCOTT WAS AN OUTSTANDING rosarian who became famous for her book *The Plant Doctor*, published in 1937. She also wrote books on plant diseases and bugs, but when she wrote *Anyone Can Grow Roses*, no publisher wanted it. She finally took a chance and gave it to a publisher without receiving a financial advance, just for the chance to have in print what she felt in her heart. The book was a runaway success, going through five hardback editions and then paperback.

Westcott once worked for the U.S. Department of Agriculture, looking into the problem of azalea petal blight. "They didn't really expect me to get anywhere," she once confided. "It was a special assignment during the war years [World War II] and all they wanted me to

do was to sit there and keep the seat warm for the men to return. But I fooled them. I solved the mystery." When the American Rose Society honored her at a New Jersey banquet in 1975, President Gerald Ford sent his congratulations. So did top rosarians everywhere, and the rose 'Cynthia' was named for her.

Westcott was down to earth, with a wry sense of humor and an ability to get right to the heart of the matter. When someone at the American Rose Society meeting mentioned azalea blight, she told them, "Forget it. This is a rose meeting!" Her books are still very much a part of the literature of plants today. □

WHITE HOUSE ROSE GARDEN

This famous garden, a witness to history, deserves better care.

CRAB APPLE TREES ARE TAKING OVER THE most-photographed rose garden in history, overshadowing the roses in every way. Roses like full light, and they don't get it anymore at the White House Rose Garden. The garden is only fifty by one hundred feet, so putting it in shape shouldn't break the national budget.

Situated only a few steps from the French doors of the Oval Office, the garden has witnessed events great and small, such as the visit of Queen Elizabeth II, the wedding of Tricia Nixon, John F. Kennedy's walk with Martin Luther King to warn him the FBI had him under surveillance, Jimmy Carter's dinner for NATO heads of state — and the introduction of Millie's puppies to the press. For most Rose Garden events, potted roses are brought in to cover up the poor performance of the garden roses.

The garden was originally installed by the first wife of Woodrow Wilson, Ellen Louise Axson, and was updated by John F. Kennedy. Rachel Lambert Mellon, a renowned private garden designer, was asked to replant the garden in 1961–1962. Mellon relates a startling incident from that replanting. Writing in a White House Historical Association article, Mellon recalled,

> One day, while we were removing the old soil and replacing it with new, we cut into a mysterious cable buried in a corner of the garden. It turned out to be the hot line that set off the nation's military alert. The scene was suddenly alive with security guards. To the alarm of everyone, we learned that the cable had been hastily installed in World War II by the Navy. Records of its location were inaccurate, hence our innocent intrusion. This startling experience was handled with calmness. Not even the President reprimanded me for deep digging.

During the redesign, Mellon also planted a large spring-flowering section with snowdrops, primroses, violets, tulips, and grape hyacinths. And the roses bloomed on until the crab apples grew and shaded them. Among the varieties that have been planted and grown in pots sunk in the ground (an inadequate method of growing roses over the long term)

are 'First Lady Nancy', 'Pat Nixon', and 'White Lightnin'. □

WILD ROSE OF BUTTE COUNTY

'Mrs. Mina Lindell'

THE ROSE REGISTERED AS 'MRS. MINA LINdell' was found by Mina Lindell in Butte County, South Dakota, and recognized by rosarian J. Horace McFarland (see entry) as a distinct variety of its own. Like many romantic "found" roses, 'Mrs. Mina Lindell' is no longer available commercially.

Mina Lindell, in writing about her find, said: "These roses grow on the west side of a hill and I have noticed that there was a clump of single roses and then a clump of double roses over near them. The roses grew about a mile from Butte at a place called Castle Rock."

McFarland, who recognized the rose in 1924 and named it for Lindell, said that finding a double wild rose on the prairie of South Dakota was noteworthy. "The plant sprouts freely so it will not be necessary to bud, graft, or grow from cuttings," McFarland wrote. "It is dwarf, light pink, and ruggedly hardy." □

WILLIAMS, J. BENJAMIN (BORN 1912)

Hybridizer J. Benjamin Williams produced a new type of rose, which he called the Mini-Flora.

BACK IN 1973, J. BENJAMIN WILLIAMS OF Silver Spring, Maryland, began to produce what he considered a new race of roses. They were sturdy, small, and perfect for gardens. They were too large for miniatures and too small for floribundas, so he decided to call them Mini-Floras. He suggested the name to the American Rose Society, which turned it down with the remark that there were too many classifications already. So Williams trademarked the name. It is still his, and no one has come up with a better one for the rose that is now being produced internationally, though people have tried. Among other names used in referring to Mini-Floras are patios, sweethearts, cushion roses, and macromini.

Williams won an All-America Rose Selection award with 'Rose Parade' in 1975, and many other roses followed. These include 'Hotel Hershey', 'Patio Patty', 'Elizabeth Scholtz', 'Slava', 'Red Fountain', 'Astra', 'Amber Flash', 'Stardance', 'Gabriela Sabatini', 'Peggy Rockefeller', 'Orange Velvet', and many others.

In the years since 1965, Williams and associates have established, at their own cost, three major rose gardens in cooperation with All-America Rose Selections: the Abbey Alrich Rockefeller Museum Rose Garden at Colonial Williamsburg, Virginia; American Horticultural Society River Farms Rose Garden (this was George Washington's second farm in Mount Vernon overlooking the Potomac River); and Brookside Gardens Park and Botanical Gardens, established and maintained by the Maryland Park and Planning Commission in Silver Spring, Maryland. In addition to hybridizing, Williams serves as horticultural consultant to government and industry. Under the administration of President Lyndon Johnson, he was charged with inspection and evaluation of the Federal Beautification Program. □

WINCHEL, JOSEPH (BORN 1910)

One of Joseph Winchel's roses went on to acclaim despite a mix-up in identification.

JOE WINCHEL, BORN IN MISSOURI AND RAISED in Kansas, was a model-maker for General Motors in Michigan when he fell in love with a woman named Agnes and with roses at about the same time. He said that if she married him, his life would be a bed of roses. He couldn't have guessed then the truth of these words.

Winchel began hybridizing roses and soon was producing winners, among them 'Flaming Beauty' and 'Dolly Parton'. After retirement from General Motors, he moved to Shreveport, Louisiana, and later to Harbor City, California. Despite the problems of amateurs getting their roses on the market, his offerings have won high acclaim, including such fine hybrid teas as 'Dallas Gold', 'Double Perfection', 'Dorothy Anne', 'American Dream', 'Temptations', 'Imagination', and 'Agnes Winchel.'

With roses there are often elements of luck and romance, and it was no different in the story of Joseph Winchel. In 1989, he asked Thomas Cairns, a writer, editor, and exhibitor, to test his new rose 'Agnes Winchel'. Cairns picked up the roses in Wasco, California. He sent some off to top exhibitors, who began to acclaim the rose—but said it wasn't 'Agnes Winchel'. Cairns investigated and discovered the error. Winchel had actually dug up a seedling from a row adjacent to 'Agnes Winchel'.

Cairns then pleaded the case of the strange rose, and in 1991 Agnes and Joe Winchel decided that it would be named 'Editor Tommy Cairns'. This was a well-deserved naming, honoring a man who helped spearhead the editorial process at the American Rose Society during difficult years. The new rose got rave reviews. □

WINTER CARE

Cold weather means special care for roses.

IF YOU EXPECT LENGTHY PERIODS WITH TEM-peratures under twenty degrees Fahrenheit (minus seven degrees Celsius), rose plants in the ground should be covered and those in pots should be moved to shelter. The main dangers come from heavy frosts, freezing conditions, and cold winds, especially if these occur after new growth has started.

Before roses are "put to bed" for winter, they should have a good watering to maintain moisture in the canes. A little fertilizing can be done with this winter care. Lay a light covering of leaves around the bush and scatter over it some bonemeal, which is slow acting and will help the bush return to life in spring.

Protecting the bush is your most important responsibility, and the measures you need to take depend on the severity of the weather where you live. Styrofoam boxes provide effective protection from the extremes of North American weather. These boxes, made from two-inch-thick sheets, can be put in place in preparation for bad weather. Before the weather hits, the tops can be put on. The boxes are held in place by stakes.

Most areas don't require the stringent step of using Styrofoam boxes. Instead, at the first threat of freezing conditions or cold winds, cover plants with organic material—leaves, hay, or straw, topped with soil from another part of the garden. (The organic covering can be held in place with chicken or netting wire, with fir branches that keep their foliage, or with the fiberglass mesh material widely advertised in rose magazines.) The organic material provides moisture and protection and can be left on until the danger passes.

Gardeners should be aware of the potential problems in covering their bushes with organic material. Its weight might break some stems. If the weather doesn't get cold enough, plants can rot beneath the covering. And the cleanup process isn't as easy as it is often made out to be (straw is particularly hard to clean away in the spring). You can avoid damage from the leaves, hay, or straw by first putting a plastic covering over the bush, then putting the organic material over it, and then covering it all with the mesh material. For small plants, a one-gallon plastic milk container might serve as the initial plastic covering.

When you make a cozy winter home for a rose plant, you are often just as likely to provide better conditions for rodents. Not only will they take advantage of the home, but they will also eat the plant. You may have to put out some poison bait. And at last, when it appears the good weather has returned to stay, just take out the garden hose on a warm day and wash the organic covering away. You will probably be surprised at the amount of growth that has begun underneath.

There is another thing you might keep in mind in fall before the bad weather sets in. If you are caught unaware by cold, drying winds or freezing conditions, an old blanket can be staked into the ground, over the bushes, as a temporary emergency cover. The same goes for an upturned bucket or barrel weighted down with a brick to keep it from blowing away. Like so many things in gardening, ingenuity is well rewarded.

Tree and standard roses are far more susceptible than rose bushes to freezing because they stand so high. If conditions warrant, tree roses should be dug up and buried horizontally in the ground. There are upright Styrofoam coffinlike covers made to cover these trees. You also can use the old-fashioned method of covering the whole tree with straw and then tying it on with sacking or blanket material. It's important that the crown of the tree be well-covered with material that will keep it both moist and safe from freezing. The simplest way to handle tree and standard roses in a cold part of the world is to plant them in large pots. In winter, move them to an unheated shed, cellar, or garage. □

WORLD'S FAVORITE ROSE

THE WORLD FEDERATION OF ROSE SOCIETIES selects a favorite variety at international conferences every few years. Two American-bred roses have so far won this award—'Queen Elizabeth' (see entry) in South Africa in 1979, and 'Double Delight' (see entries) in Canada in 1985. Other winners were 'Peace' (see entry)—the first to take the award (England, 1976); 'Fragrant Cloud' (Israel, 1981); 'Iceberg' (Ger-

many, 1983); 'Papa Meilland' (Australia, 1988); and 'Pascali' (Belfast, 1991). The breeder of the winning rose receives a specially commissioned painting of the variety. □

WRIGHT, PERCY (1898–1989)

Hybridizer Percy Wright of Saskatchewan produced hardy shrub roses in the 1930s and 1940s, many of which are still used today.

THE HYBRIDIZING WORK OF PERCY WRIGHT, using many species roses, is still the basis for modern experiments into hardiness. Stanley Zubrowski of Prairie River, Saskatchewan, is now working to bring together a collection of the successful breeding lines used by Wright.

Wright was also a writer of considerable ability, and his work appeared regularly in editions of the *Canadian Rose Annual.*

Wright once wrote of going out "into the bush" and attempting to identify a patch of wild roses before using them as mother parents for future crosses. "I was vexed with myself when I could not be sure they were either *macounii* or *acicularis* (species roses). They seemed to have the characters of each." He pollinated some of the roses, and to his amazement found that one of them was completely fertile, a chance hybrid between the two species roses. Little wonder he had trouble identifying it. He then used this "found" rose for breeding. □

YELLOW ROSE OF TEXAS

THE YELLOW ROSE OF TEXAS WASN'T A ROSE at all. The famous song by that name is said to recall the story of Emily Morgan, who sent word to General Sam Houston of a forthcoming attack while she kept Mexican General Santa Anna occupied with love rather than war. Her message got through and helped Texan forces win the battle of San Jacinto and their freedom from Mexican rule. Surely she deserves a rose for herself, a bright yellow one. But Texas has never designated an official rose nor has anyone named a rose for Emily Morgan.

'Texas' is a yellow miniature produced by Poulsens of Denmark; a much older rose, 'Texas Centennial', is prized by growers of older varieties. Texans wanting to keep in touch with the world of the rose can read the quarterly magazine *The Yellow Rose*, edited by Joe Woodard and published by the Dallas Area Historical Rose Group. ☐

ZARY, KEITH (BORN 1948)

The director of research for Jackson & Perkins looks at the world of the rose through the eyes of a geneticist and sees startling changes ahead.

KEITH ZARY, BORN IN SASKATOON, SASkatchewan, Canada, received his doctorate in plant genetics in 1980 from Texas A&M.

He worked in Minnesota as a vegetable breeder for five years before joining William Warriner (see entry) at Jackson & Perkins. When Warriner retired, Zary became director of research.

Zary found that working with Warriner taught him a great deal about the special United States' requirements for new roses. He was encouraged to visit other breeders to learn their market requirements. His current rose breeding program is primarily directed in garden roses to hybrid teas, with miniatures and shrubs being seen as the only real areas of growth. His hope for the immediate future is the elimination of black spot. He expects it to be a slow process that will ultimately be successful.

Zary sees major changes in the future as knowledge of genetics starts bringing more practical results. Here are some of his predictions:

• In a couple of generations, rose breeders as we know them will be extinct. Instead, they will be partners with genetic engineers. Together they will manipulate the genes of roses in ways beyond our imagining.

• Roses will become much more commonly seen. Their value as plants will be enhanced as they become increasingly disease- and insect-resistant, more fragrant, and available in all forms, colors, and habits. There will be roses suitable for all climates and locations, making them extremely important plants in the landscape.

• Roses will begin to lose their mystery.

Throughout their glorious history, roses have been held special. By exploiting the genetic potential of roses, the special will become commonplace, and we will lose some of the romantic glow that roses have always imparted to us. □

INDEX